Catholic Education Globally: Challenges and Opportunities

Volume 1

Series Editors

Leonardo Franchi, School of Education, University of Glasgow, Glasgow, UK

Sean Whittle, Visiting Research Fellow, St Mary's University Twickenham, London, UK

Quentin Wodon, World Bank, McLean, VA, USA
  Loyola University New Orleans, New Orleans, LA, USA

This book series will share high quality analytical work on Catholic schools and universities globally, as well as works on other education systems that can be useful to Catholic education. A particular emphasis will be placed on contemporary issues faced by Catholic education, including assessing the sustainability of Catholic educational institutions, maintaining their vibrancy in different contexts, and ensuring that their services reach the poor and vulnerable. The series will include monographs and edited volumes. It will provide a unique contribution to scholarship on Catholic education with an emphasis on learning from the experiences of different countries. The series will welcome full length books that are international in nature, discussing challenges and opportunities in such a way that learning across countries may take place. Regional and global perspectives will be sought both in terms of the scope of the analysis and in terms of the scholars contributing to the series. The intent is to also include perspectives about Catholic education that may be critically constructive. The series should be of interest not only to researchers and school administrators, but also to teachers and even parents, whether they are interested in Catholic education or more broadly in discussions about what the aims of education could or should be.

Please contact Grace Ma (e-mail: grace.ma@springer.com) for submitting book proposals for this series.

Leonardo Franchi · Richard Rymarz
Editors

Formation of Teachers for Catholic Schools

Challenges and Opportunities in a New Era

Editors
Leonardo Franchi
School of Education
University of Glasgow
Glasgow, UK

Richard Rymarz
Broken Bay Institute-TAITE
Sydney, NSW, Australia

ISSN 2731-8001 ISSN 2731-801X (electronic)
Catholic Education Globally: Challenges and Opportunities
ISBN 978-981-19-4726-1 ISBN 978-981-19-4727-8 (eBook)
https://doi.org/10.1007/978-981-19-4727-8

© The Editor(s) (if applicable) and The Author(s), under exclusive license to Springer Nature Singapore Pte Ltd. 2022
This work is subject to copyright. All rights are solely and exclusively licensed by the Publisher, whether the whole or part of the material is concerned, specifically the rights of translation, reprinting, reuse of illustrations, recitation, broadcasting, reproduction on microfilms or in any other physical way, and transmission or information storage and retrieval, electronic adaptation, computer software, or by similar or dissimilar methodology now known or hereafter developed.
The use of general descriptive names, registered names, trademarks, service marks, etc. in this publication does not imply, even in the absence of a specific statement, that such names are exempt from the relevant protective laws and regulations and therefore free for general use.
The publisher, the authors, and the editors are safe to assume that the advice and information in this book are believed to be true and accurate at the date of publication. Neither the publisher nor the authors or the editors give a warranty, expressed or implied, with respect to the material contained herein or for any errors or omissions that may have been made. The publisher remains neutral with regard to jurisdictional claims in published maps and institutional affiliations.

This Springer imprint is published by the registered company Springer Nature Singapore Pte Ltd.
The registered company address is: 152 Beach Road, #21-01/04 Gateway East, Singapore 189721, Singapore

Acknowledgements

The editors are grateful to all the chapter contributors (below) for their diligence and patience during the writing process. Their insights have surpassed our expectations. A short biography of each contributor is found at the end of each chapter.

The New Era: Why It Matters for Catholic Teacher Formation

The front matter will frame some of the key issues that this edited volume seeks to address.

The choice of Catholic Teacher Formation as the frame of the present volume offers a wide canvas. Other terms such as Catholic Teacher Education, Catholic Teacher Training and Catholic Teacher preparation are also possible. "Formation" is the preferred term as it includes (a) both the educational and training paradigms of how teachers are prepared for service and (b) the possibility of seeing this process as lifelong, not just for the short number of years in which academic and professional qualifications are gained. The essays in Part I focus on the initial period of pre-service formation while acknowledging the wider issues which are pertinent to the jurisdiction in question. Part II's "Current Topics" are examples of more general challenges which need addressing in all teacher formation programmes. It is not intended to be an exhaustive list but simply a set of contemporary themes which invite meaningful contributions for all with an interest in successful education systems.

The term "New Era" is a reference to Pope Francis' comment that we are living through not just a period of change but a more profound change of era. This New Era directly applies to Catholic schools which, in the English-speaking world, are configured in different ways because of historical precedent and localized societal factors. There are, however, some significant common elements that arise from consideration of and response to powerful cultural forces.

An important aspect of the New Era is the contested place of religion in the wider culture. This is manifested in several ways. The chains of memory that tie groups to religious beliefs, metaphors and behaviours are becoming more fragile (Hervieu Leger, 2002). Assumptions about socialization and affiliation of those in Catholic school communities are not easily made. The socialization pathways that for previous generations ensured a level of connection between young people and religious communities are now far more tenuous. Socialization is a key aspect of core identity formation, and if any institution, certainly religious institutions, lose a ready means of socializing younger generations, then embedding young people in religious communities becomes increasingly problematic (Smith et al., 2014). In addition, the disassociation of religion and spiritualty, alongside the rise of individualization, gives many people the clear option of finding meaning and direction outside of conventional religious categories (Flanagan & Jupp, 2007).

These changes to the place of religion in the wider culture certainly impact on teachers in Catholic schools as they are socially well integrated. Teachers in Catholic schools often manifest a sense of personal identity that has much in common with their peers in the wider culture (Rymarz, 2020). Three features of this identity will be highlighted here. First, many Catholic teachers see religious belief and practice as one part of a broader identity that is referenced to wider cultural trends. One way of describing this more diffuse sense of being part of a religious community is to see affiliation in terms of interpretive autonomy (Dillon, 2018). This highlights the importance of personal choices and the negotiation that individuals undertake in relation to religious affiliation. This is especially pertinent for teachers working in Catholic schools, as for many of them entering a religious institution on a professional basis invites them to reconsider their religious links and assumptions.

Second, a major trend in the wider community is to see personal identity in terms of values as opposed to identification with a set of fixed, abiding principles. Religious affiliation is also impacted by this cultural shift, and, for many, religion is seen increasingly as a moral system to which one aspires. Two well-known iterations of these overarching moral systems are the concepts of Moralistic Therapeutic Deism (MTD) and Individual-Choice norms. The concept of MTD was first developed by Smith and Denton and described the worldview of teenagers as being marked by three key descriptors (Smith & Denton, 2005). This worldview sees religion as a moral system which at its best generates behaviours that benefit the individual and are directed to community expectations and standards. MTD is highly personal and positivistic with the notion of God relegated to a kind of impersonal, distant force that is part of the universe but not in an involved or decisive way. So the focus for beliefs and behaviour shifts to the individual; but an individual who is heavily influenced by the dominant social norms of the day (Bouma, 2007).[1] In many ways, MTD is a type of default position to which most without strong counter views can easily subscribe. The concept of MTD has been further developed. Denton and Flory, writing in 2021, note that in what they call MTD 2.0, the importance of moralism as the defining feature of young adult worldviews is even more enhanced today at the expense of other descriptors (Denton & Flory, 2020).

Inglehart extends this notion of the importance of values in defining personal worldview. He notes that a critical descriptor of modern culture is the alignment of an increasing number of people across the Western world to values he calls Individual-Choice norms. This is now a dominant trend, and its influence can easily be seen in a variety of religious communities (Inglehart, 2021). These norms place a priority on individual autonomy and are directed towards the self-actualization of the individual as opposed to more communal expressions of values. The primacy of personal choice can work counter to the aims and aspiration of all institutions—and certainly Catholic schools—as they depend on broad agreement on the goals and ethos. These goals

---

[1] For a less sanguine discussion of likely cultural trajectories see, Zygmunt Bauman, *Wasted lives: Modernity and its outcasts,* Cambridge: Polity Press, 2004.

are often expressed in communal language where the emphasis is on collective and collaborative processes that underline the stated aspirations of the institution. For teachers who are influenced by the norms of the wider culture, this requirement of communal identification and support can bring with it a range of challenges, many of which will be addressed in later chapters of this volume.

The resilience of Catholic schools in relation to traditional Church structures such as parishes, in many instances, positions Catholic schools as the public face of the Church and the interface between Church and people. Catholic schools often appear to be vigorous and continue to attract enrolments. Stoltz and his colleagues note that even where the place of religious institutions in the wider culture is increasingly contested Catholic schools continue to attract enrolments (Stoltz et al., 2015). They argue that rather than seeing secularization as a static, unidirectional phenomenon, a better way to consider it as a hallmark of the new era is to see secularization as a dynamic multifaceted process that sits alongside religion as a factor in shaping the wider culture. This is nowhere more evident than in enrolments in Catholic schools. Parents may be increasingly secular, at least in the classical sense of religion playing a less and less significant part in daily life (Dobbleare, 2002): parents are prepared, however, to countenance enrolling their children in faith-based schools. Even in detraditionalized cultures, religious institutions such as schools can have a place if they can be seen to be offering something that cannot be replicated in other ways in the public sphere (Heelas, 1996). Stoltz and his colleagues use the metaphor of secular religious competition to describe a dynamic that can be seen in how parents choose schools for their children. It can also be used when we consider the choices that teachers make to work in Catholic schools. They too may not be actively associated with religious communities but can see the attraction of working in a faith-based school. There could be a wide variety of reasons behind this willingness or even enthusiasm to work in a Catholic school. If secular religious competition theory is followed, it is important to see this choice as part of a dynamic process that may draw people into religious institutions that are not conventional parish structures.

Catholic schools do, however, seek to maintain a high level of association with the broader Church, and this is manifested in official documents, governance practices and in the demands placed on teachers recruited to work in schools. The tension between the expectations on teachers to identify with the goals and aspirations of the school and wider cultural changes make this association more problematic. This highlights the need for an ongoing discussion on teacher formation. For instance, Pope Francis in an address to the Congregation for Catholic Education wrote:

> I would like to limit myself to recalling the features of an educator and his or her specific duty. To educate is an act of love, it is to give life. And love is demanding, it calls for the best resources, for a reawakening of the passion to begin this path patiently with young people. The educator in Catholic schools must be, first and foremost, competent and qualified but, at the same time, someone who is rich in humanity and capable of being with young people in a style of pedagogy that helps promote their human and spiritual growth. Youth are in need of quality teaching along with values that are not only articulated but witnessed to. Consistency is an indispensable factor in the education of young people! Consistency! We cannot grow and we cannot educate without consistency: consistency and witness! For this, an educator is himself in need of permanent formation (Pope Francis, 2014).

A key question that arises, in the context of Catholic education, is what is the best way to understand teacher formation, or to use Pope Francis' term, permanent formation, and how is it best carried out?

Catholic schools do not, and should not, operate in isolated bubbles. Like the wider Church, the Catholic school and, by extension, any educational body associated with the Church, must live in the middle of the world, taking full account of its joys and sorrows. This is not to fall victim to the "spirit of the age", whatever that might be, but, rather, to act in the light of the Incarnation: we are not spectators at the drama of life.[2]

To address the current tension between (a) the expectations on teachers to identify and align with the goals and aspirations of the Catholic school and (b) the wider cultural changes that make this association more problematic requires some fresh thinking on how to find meaningful points of contact between the Church's traditions (and Tradition) and current educational–cultural mores. If Catholic educational institutions are places where such traditions are explicated and lived, this only highlights the need for an ongoing, open-ended discussion on the aims and ends of Catholic teacher formation

As we have seen, there are, and always have been, areas of tension between a culture which seems to disregard the importance of religion and the life of the Church. The profound challenges offered by the New Era are the latest articulation of this phenomenon. What does this mean for the health and continued existence of the Catholic school?

Data shows diminishing levels of religious practice in what we call the West (the territory designated as ripe for the New Evangelisation).[3] In his important book, *Mass Exodus: Catholic Disaffiliation in Britain and America since Vatican II,* Stephen Bullivant noted that the broad pattern of disaffiliation in young Catholics is typically a gradual process, and one marked by both ambivalence and ambiguity. This necessary level of nuance reminds us that we are rarely dealing with one-off "conversions" to other or no forms of religious belief but a slow slippage away from religious commitment in general and to Catholic practice in particular.[4]

Within this picture of overall diminution of religious identity, the figures for young people are especially concerning. To interpret this data with the level of seriousness it deserves would require another book but suffice it to say that local circumstances often come into play and it would be unwise, and bordering on superficial, to attempt

---

[2] If the Catholic educational tradition is not presented as a cultural phenomenon—understood as a process which seeks to reform the culture of families and wider society—, it too easily becomes a specialized enclave of society wherein esoteric notions of spirituality echo off the walls of its enclosed spaces.

[3] Some interesting data on the views of Catholics in the United States of America is available here: https://www.pewforum.org/religious-landscape-study/religious-tradition/catholic/.

[4] On this theme, Tim O'Malley suggests that 'disaffiliation and affiliation alike must be understood not exclusively as concerned with individual events in the life of a person, rather, we must contemplate the social reality in which we abide.' A New Model for Understanding the Dynamics of Catholic Disaffiliation, *Church Life Journal*, 31 May 2021: https://churchlifejournal.nd.edu/articles/what-drives-catholic-religious-disaffiliation/.

here or elsewhere a universal diagnosis. What is clear, however, are the serious implications of this phenomenon on the numbers of young people considering a teaching career in Catholic schools. To put it simply, Catholic teachers normally require some form of Church approval as a sign of religious commitment in order to teach in a Catholic school (not to mention the appropriate academic qualifications). If fewer young people are part of the group we can describe as "practising Catholics", then it follows that the pool of prospective Catholic teachers becomes ever smaller.

The *Instrumentum laboris* (working document) for the 2015 conference commemorating 50 years of *Gravissimum educationis* (Vatican II's *Declaration on Christian Education*) does not shy away from the challenges the Church's educational mission faces:

> A growing number of young people are drifting away from the institutional Church. Religious ignorance or illiteracy are rising. Catholic education is an unglamorous mission. How can students be educated to exercise their freedom of conscience and take a stance in the immense domain of values and beliefs in a globalized society? (Congregation for Catholic Education, 2014, III, 1, g.).

The document continues by offering an initial diagnosis (albeit without hard data):

> In many countries, Catholic schools do not receive adequate pastoral guidance in the multireligious context they are supposed to evangelize.
>
> As far as educators are concerned, "deculturation" is limiting their knowledge of cultural heritage. Easy access to information, which nowadays is broadly available, when it is not selected with critical awareness, ultimately favours widespread superficiality among both students and teachers, not only impoverishing reason, but also imagination and creative thinking.
>
> The number of educators and teachers who are *believers* is shrinking, hence making Christian testimony more rare. How can a bond with Jesus Christ be established in this new educational context? (Congregation for Catholic Education, 2014, III, 1. g).

Taken as a whole, the insights from the working document indicate that the chain of memory which connects each generation to previous generations in matters of religious faith has become progressively weaker. Common bonds of knowledge and morality seem to have atrophied, leading to fractures in the life of the Church and wider society. In a *Letter to the Diocese of Rome* in 2008, Pope Benedict had this to say:

> Educating has never been easy and today it seems to become more and more difficult. Parents, teachers, priests and all those who have a direct responsibility to educate know this well. One speaks, thus, of a great "emergency in education," confirmed by the many failures that too often result from our efforts to form solid persons, capable of working with others and of giving meaning to their life. It is not unusual, then, that the new generations are faulted, as if the children that are born today are different from those that were born in the past. One speaks, moreover, of the "generation gap" that certainly exists and is a burden, but is the effect, rather than the cause, of the lack of transmission of certainties and values (Pope Benedict XVI, 2008).

The diagnosis of a breakdown in relationships is a heavy charge to pose. Of course this might not be the case in many of the countries of the Global South but is surely a significant factor, at least in the culture of the countries of the Global North.[5]

Pope Francis, in agreeing with the broad description of the educational challenge as diagnosed by Pope Benedict, has sought to sketch out a suitable global response. His thinking has emerged in the *Global Compact on Education*, presented in 2020 (Pope Francis, 2020). Instead of a direct focus on the so-called catechetical outcomes of Catholic education—understood as the explicit commitment to foster the Catholic faith of young people in schools—the *Global Compact* directs its focus on seven big issues of contemporary society.[6] It asks the (Catholic) school to make the realization of these objectives a priority in its planning and mission. Crucially, it reminds the readers that this response, despite the use of language which is essentially non-religious, is driven by Christian Humanism.

In the video message to mark the launch of the *Global Compact*, Pope Francis could not be clearer about its inspiration and source:

> Finally, dear brothers and sisters, we want to commit ourselves courageously to developing an educational plan within our respective countries, investing our best energies and introducing creative and transformative processes in cooperation with civil society. In this, our point of reference should be the social doctrine that, inspired by the revealed word of God and Christian humanism, provides a solid basis and a vital resource for discerning the paths to follow in the present emergency (Pope Francis, 2020).

The attachment to *Christian Humanism* is perhaps an example of the "generation gap" identified by Pope Benedict. Yet to what extent are the nuances of the term Christian Humanism intelligible to the current generation of Catholic educators and those responsible for policy formation in Catholic schools? Furthermore, is the use of apparently secular language in the aims of the *Global Compact* a helpful bridge between the Catholic and secular visions of education or is it a sign of an accommodation too far?

Responding to such questions allows us to begin to reclaim the tenets of Christian Humanism for the present age although it is the term itself, not just its intellectual and pastoral principles which needs rediscovering.[7] To be clear, Christian Humanism is

---

[5] For more on this and for a summary of some recent data, see Franchi, L. and Rymarz, R. The education and formation of teachers for Catholic schools: Responding to changed cultural contexts, *International studies in Catholic education*, Vol. 9, Issue 1, 2017.

[6] These are summarized as follows: (1) to make human persons the centre of every educational programme; (2) listen to the voices of children and young people; (3) to encourage the full participation of girls and young women in education; (4) to see in the family the first and essential place of education; (5) to educate and be educated on the need for acceptance and in particular openness to the most vulnerable and marginalized; (6) to be committed to finding new ways of understanding the economy, politics, growth and progress that can truly stand at the service of the human person and the entire human family, within the context of an integral ecology and (7) to safeguard and cultivate our common home.

[7] For a summary of Christian Humanism and related understandings of Humanism, see the Introduction in A. MacDonald, Z. von Martels and J. Veenstra (Eds.), *Christian humanism: Essays in honour of Arjo Vanderjagt* (ix-xix). Leiden/Boston: Brill, 2009.

the key which unlocks the potential for contemporary Catholic Higher Education—the locus of Catholic teacher formation—to speak to multiple audiences, not least those with a disregard for the place of religion in society:

A renewed Christian Humanism has the potential to integrate learning, imagination and the virtues with a compassionate, humble yet confident spirituality, nurtured by the Church and in dialogue with all people of goodwill. It will be illuminated by scripture. It will tell a story about humanity's place in the universe, the complexity and paradoxes of human existence, gifts and vulnerabilities and how to be present to the world with all its challenges, opportunities and needs (Sullivan, 2021).

As Catholic Teacher Formation is (or should be) embedded in Catholic Universities (or similar institutions), it follows that some alignment between Christian Humanism and Catholic Higher Education is a necessary goal. Essentially, Christian Humanism is a way to unite the transcendental claims of Christianity with the promotion of human flourishing. The Incarnation is, for Christians, a sign that religious belief is much more than a form of esoteric, unworldly spirituality but has definite claims on how we act and live in the middle of the world. What happens to the body and material things matters!

The Incarnation—the root of Christian anthropology—made possible the correlation of faith and reason that gave birth to the universities and, more generally, to an openness towards all sources of truth. From early on, many Christian theologians believed in a universal divine pedagogy, whereby God works through human cultures permitting their highest achievements to become the genuine expression of divine truth (Zimmerman, 2016). The linking of Incarnation, Christian Anthropology, faith/reason and universities is one response to the challenges of New Era as it affects all institutions of Catholic education, not just the Higher Education networks. We can begin to discern therein the seeds of a renewal of Catholic Teacher Formation. With the *Global Compact* setting the context for a fresh agenda for Catholic Education, our task is to integrate these principles into the wider processes of Catholic Teacher Formation. In so doing, we will be forming a corps of teachers who are rooted in tradition but with the necessary acumen to shape their mission in a way suitable to their local situation.

Our attention turns now to practicalities. How can Christian Humanism inform, support and shape and, ultimately, *refresh the processes of* Catholic Teacher Formation? Such a reform would allow the various formation processes for pre-service and in-service teachers to be rooted in the history of ideas and authentic cultural dialogue. The New Era, with all the challenges found in so-called Moralistic Therapeutic Deism, demands no less than a sincere re-examination of how we present our ideas in the public square in a way that is both respectful and robust.[8]

To sum up this section, Catholic Teacher Formation must be embedded in the Catholic University (or associated body). It offers a space for a dialogue between the

---

[8] For more on Moralistic-Therapeutic Deism and what it means for education, see Franchi, L. and Rymarz, R. (2007). The Education and Formation of Teachers for Catholic Schools: Responding to Changed Cultural Contexts, *International studies in Catholic education*, 9 (1), 2–16.

Catholic intellectual traditions and the specific need of the teaching profession; this dialogue is, in turn, an expression of Christian Humanism:

> Catholic teacher education, to be clear, is the union of two highly contested terms: Catholic education and teacher education. Each is host to a multitude of literature, ideas and policies on its ideal conceptual shape. It should come as no surprise to us that there is still much debate on what this should be (Franchi & Rymarz, 2017, p. 7).

Given this context, which is, in fact, an opportunity to rethink the conceptual framework of Catholic Teacher Formation along Christian humanistic lines, programmes of study can, within some flexible parameters, explore the wider definitions of humanism as a term in intellectual history and thereby show how it can be applied to, the Catholic educational vision.

The Catholic University is not solely as a dispensary of knowledge but a common space wherein understanding and meaning are sought collegially.[9] A key local arrangement, therefore, is the construction of channels of communication between Catholic Universities and Catholic schools. Obviously how this works will vary depending on a number of factors, not least the geography of particular jurisdictions. The pandemic-induced discovery of the opportunities offered by forms of remote-learning might offer new possibilities for cross-border initiatives in higher degrees and professional development. Furthermore, the development of good working relationships with professional educational associations and NGO-type bodies is an opportunity to present the tenets of Christian Humanism not as a solution for the Catholic educational sector only but as a meaningful and heartfelt contribution to wider debates on educational ideas and values. In so doing, the Catholic community is offering its voices as partners in dialogue with a view to building school communities which offer the opportunity of human flourishing to all.

Overview of the Book

This volume is designed to widen the conversation around Catholic Teacher Formation in Anglophone jurisdictions. It will offer a range of perspectives on how prospective teachers for Catholic schools are prepared both academically and pastorally for their professional role.

The volume develops a field of study—Catholic Teacher Formation—which the editors have explored in two recent publications: The Education and Formation of Teachers for Catholic Schools: Responding to Changed Cultural Contexts, *International Studies in Catholic Education*. 2017. 9 (1) 2–16 and *Catholic Teacher Preparation: Historical and Contemporary Perspectives on Preparing for Mission*. Bingley: Emerald Publishing Ltd, (2019). Both works opened up for further discussion issues which had been hitherto largely dormant and in need of research. The present volume

---

[9] For more on this see Franchi, L. (2021). Catholic Teacher Education. *Global Catholic Education Knowledge Notes*, Retrieved from: https://e09c9478-419d-4177-930b-8abd3c6e96ac.filesusr.com/ugd/b9597a_0d6db86c59714789ae9ec3d5718441d7.pdf.

offers a fresh angle on this important field by bringing together observations from selected local contexts on what Catholic teacher formation looks like as a set of organized processes and structures.

Given (a) the importance of teacher formation to the success of schools and (b) the substantial footprint of Catholic schools worldwide, any study which unites teacher formation and Catholic education has the potential to make a successful impact on policy and practice. The international overview offered in Part I reminds readers that Catholic Teacher Formation is shaped and formed by a host of local circumstances. Whether such localized approaches are always for good or ill is not the focus of the chapters in Part I, but they manifest a reality which is often more nuanced and multi-layered than some would admit. Part II brings some of the big issues affecting education and wider society into the heart of debates on Catholic Teacher Formation. A Church truly open to dialogue with wider ideas cannot but engage creatively with new challenges to its established ways of working. In an Epilogue, Quentin Woden broadens the debate beyond Anglophone jurisdictions by offering some very important data and insights on the global picture.

Readers of the book will benefit from exposure to concise explanations of the nature of Catholic Teacher Formation processes. The thematic essays offer a platform for recognized scholars to engage critically with themes which are having, and will continue to have, a profound impact on how teacher formation in general and Catholic Teacher Formation in particular, can be shaped in the New Era which is highlighted in the title.

References

Bauman, Z. (2004). Wasted lives: Modernity and its outcasts. Polity Press.
Bouma, G. (2007). Australian soul: Religion and spirituality in the 21st century. Cambridge University Press.
Congregation for Catholic Education. (2004). Educating today and tomorrow: A renewing passion. Instrumentum Laboris. Retrieved from https://www.vatican.va/roman_curia/congregations/cca theduc/documents/rc_con_ccatheduc_doc_20140407_educare-oggi-e-domani_en.html
Denton, M. L., & Flory, R. (2002). Back-pocket god: Religion and spirituality in the lives of emerging adults. Oxford University Press.
Dillon, M. (2018). Post secular Catholicism: Relevance and renewal. Oxford University Press.
Dobbelaere, K. (2002). Secularization: An analysis at three levels. Peter Lang.
Flanagan, K., & Jupp, P. (Eds.). (2007). A sociology of spirituality. Ashgate.
Franchi, L. (2021). Catholic teacher education. Global catholic education knowledge notes. Retrieved from https://e09c9478-419d-4177-930b-8abd3c6e96ac.filesusr.com/ugd/b95 97a_0d6db86c59714789ae9ec3d5718441d7.pdf
Franchi, L., & Rymarz, R. (2017). The education and formation of teachers for catholic schools: Responding to changed cultural contexts. International Studies in Catholic Education, 9(1), 2–16.
Heelas, P. (1996). Detraditionalization and its rivals. In P. Heelas, S. Lash, & P. Morris (Eds.), Detradtionalization (pp. 1–21). Blackwell.
Hervieu Leger, D. (2002). Religion as a chain of memory. Rutgers University Press.
Inglehart, R. (2021). Religion's sudden decline: What is causing it, and what comes next. Oxford University Press.
MacDonald, A., von Martels, Z., & Veenstra (Eds.). (2009). Christian humanism: Essays in honour of Arjo Vanderjagt. Brill.

O'Malley, T. (2021). A new model for understanding the dynamics of Catholic disaffiliation. Church Life Journal. Retrieved from https://churchlifejournal.nd.edu/articles/what-drives-catholic-religious-disaffiliation/

Pope Benedict XVI. (2008). Letter of his holiness Pope Benedict XVI to the faithful of the diocese and city of Rome on the urgent task of educating young people. Retrieved from https://www.vatican.va/content/benedict-xvi/en/letters/2008/documents/hf_ben-xvi_let_20080121_educazione.html

Pope Francis. (2014). Address to plenary session of the congregation for Catholic Education. Retrieved from http://www.vatican.va/content/francesco/en/speeches/2014/february/documents/papa-francesco_20140213_congregazione-educazione-cattolica.html

Pope Francis. (2020). Video message for the launch of the global compact on education. Retrieved from https://www.vatican.va/content/francesco/en/messages/pont-messages/2020/documents/papa-francesco_20201015_videomessaggio-global-compact.html

Rymarz, R. (2020). "I like the practical side." Early career teachers in Catholic schools, interpretative autonomy and negotiating secular and religious boundaries. A preliminary study. Pedagogia Cristiana, 14, 127–143.

Smith, C., & Denton, M. (2005). Soul searching: The religious and spiritual lives of American teenagers. Oxford University Press.

Smith, C., Longest, K., Hill, J., & Christoffersen, K. (2014). Young Catholic America: Emerging adults in, out of, and gone from the Church. Oxford University Press.

Stoltz, J., Purdie, M., Englberger, T., Konemann, J., & Kruggeler, M. (2015). (Un)Believing in modern society: Religion, spirituality, and religious-secular competition. Ashgate.

Sullivan, J. (2021). Catholics, culture and the renewal of Christian humanism. Religions, 12(5). Retrieved from https://www.mdpi.com/2077-1444/12/5/325

Zimmerman, J. (2016). Introduction. In J. Zimmerman (Ed.), Re-envisioning Christian humanism: Education and the restoration of humanity. Oxford University Press.

Contents

Part I Essays Exploring the Challenges and Opportunities Facing Catholic Teacher Formation in Particular National Contexts

1. **Catholic Teacher Formation in the Land Down Under** 3
   Michael T. Buchanan

2. **Catholic Teacher Formation in Northern Ireland** 15
   Niall Coll

3. **Catholic Teacher Formation in Scotland** 27
   Roisín Coll and Stephen Reilly

4. **Catholic Teacher Formation in America** 43
   Max T. Engel

5. **Catholic Teacher Formation in the Republic of Ireland** 55
   John-Paul Sheridan

6. **Catholic Teacher Formation in England and Wales** 67
   Sean Whittle

Part II Catholic Teacher Formation: Engaging with Current Topics

7. **Formation for Leadership in Catholic Schools** 81
   Ken Avenell

8. **Reflections on the Vocation of the Teacher: Formation, Agency and Meditation** 93
   Julie Harvie and Kathleen Kerrigan

9. **Teacher Formation: An Augustinian Study in Learning Truth and Beauty** 105
   Renée Köhler-Ryan

10	Teacher Formation in a Digital Age .... Mary E. Hess	117
11	Bridges into Mystical Wisdom: Using Carmelite Spirituality in Teacher Formation .... Michelle Jones	129
12	Valuing and Cultivating Dialogue Amongst Learner–Educators: Ongoing Challenges for Post-Primary Religious Education Teachers in Catholic Schools .... Bernadette Sweetman	139

Epilogue: Teacher Training and Policies in the Global South: Approaches and Tools from the World Bank 151

End Matter: Catholic Teacher Formation: Why It Matters 167

About the Editors

Leonardo Franchi specializes in Religious Education at the University of Glasgow where he was Director of Catholic Teacher Education from 2012 to 2016. He is Member of the Executive of the *Association for Catholic Colleges and Institutes of Education* (ACISE) and Director of the Mater Christ Academt Trust in Cumbria, England. His principal research interests and areas of publication are the nature of religious education and initial teacher formation. e-mail: Leonardo.franchi@glasgow.ac.uk

Richard Rymarz is Head of Religious Education and Director of Research at the Broken Bay Institute—TAITE. Prior to this, he held the Peter and Doris Kule Chair in Catholic Religious Education, St. Joseph's College, University of Alberta. He has had wide experience in educational research and teaching, especially work on Catholic schools, teacher formation and moral and religious education. His most recent books examine moving from theory to practice in religious education and the history and future directions of teacher formation. e-mail: richard.rymarz@bbi.catholic.edu.au

Part I
Essays Exploring the Challenges and Opportunities Facing Catholic Teacher Formation in Particular National Contexts

Chapter 1
Catholic Teacher Formation in the Land Down Under

Michael T. Buchanan

Abstract Within Catholic education, it is commonly understood that teaching is regarded as a vocation and the extent to which a Catholic school achieves its mission depends primarily on the teachers dedicated to this apostolate. Catholic schools throughout Australia have a long history of supporting teachers who are committed both formally and informally to their own formation for mission. In recent times, concerns within Catholic education have emphasised the need for ongoing systematic formation opportunities that are meaningful and accessible to *all* teachers in Catholic schools. This chapter envisions that accessibility to ongoing spiritual direction for all teachers in Catholic schools is vital when historical circumstances within and beyond Australia are considered along with current insights pertaining to the make-up of teachers populating Catholic schools.

Keywords Lay teachers · Faith formation · Identity · Religious education

1.1 Historical Background

To appreciate teacher formation in the contemporary context, it is first necessary to understand the emergence of Catholic education in Victoria, Australia. In the Port Phillip District, Catholic schools began during the colonial period, and the first Catholic school, St Mary's School, Williamstown was led by Mr. John Wilson in 1842 and prior to that in 1839, a Franciscan friar, Fr Geoghan, appointed Mrs Catherine Coffey to teach religious education in Melbourne (Rogan, 2000). The continuation of lay appointments to Catholic schools by the clergy accelerated under the leadership of Bishop Goold in 1848, until the passing of the Education Act (Vic) in 1872 (Synan, 2003). From the onset, the appointment of lay teachers for Catholic schools in Victoria was influenced by a British post-Napoleonic mindset which held that education could create moral and obedient citizens based on Christian religious principles (Stone, 1969). Key to this, according to the Society of the Propagation

M. T. Buchanan (✉)
Australian Catholic University, Level 6 Room 460.6.17, 250 Victoria Parade, East Melbourne, VIC 3002, Australia
e-mail: Michael.Buchanan@acu.edu.au

© The Author(s), under exclusive license to Springer Nature Singapore Pte Ltd. 2022
L. Franchi and R. Rymarz (eds.), *Formation of Teachers for Catholic Schools*, Catholic Education Globally: Challenges and Opportunities 1,
https://doi.org/10.1007/978-981-19-4727-8_1

of Christian Knowledge, was the formation of teachers. A well-formed teacher was deemed to be a person who "understood the principles of Christianity, attend church frequently, behaved in a humble and meek manner and kept an orderly family. Additional requirements included having an ability to teach, write in 'a good hand' and understand arithmetic" (O'Donoghue & Moore, 2019, p. 17). The selection and appointment of lay teachers for Catholic schools in Victoria by the clergy established the foundations of a close link between education and parish life. To educate the colony's future generations, the clergy aimed to choose lay people formed in Christianity, committed to Christian living and Church attendance. The lay teachers' connection with parish provided the nexus for the clergy to support ongoing Christian formation for teachers. The elements of family life, parish and school were foundational to the formation of lay teachers in Catholic schools during the early colonial period. However, the events of 1872 led to the demise of many Christian denominational schools and the unemployment of many lay teachers. While Victoria was the first parliament to legislate for compulsory education that was free and secular, the other parliaments within colonial Australia followed suit and the impact on Catholic education in Victoria was similar to that of other jurisdictions across the Australian landscape.

In 1872, James Wilberforce Stephen introduced a Bill into the parliament of Victoria which succeeded in establishing state-based education that was compulsory, free and secular. The passing of the Education Act (1872) by the Parliament of Victoria also brought an end to government funding for denominational schools throughout the colony. This caused many Church schools of various denominations to close due to a lack of funds needed to pay the wages of lay teachers and to administer the schools. For the Catholic community, the representation of Catholic schooling throughout the colony of Victoria was important for various reasons. It was regarded as an institutional force against liberalism and secularism, which had universally challenged the Catholic faith as an integral dimension of education. Catholic education contributed to the formation, education and potential social elevation of many Catholic children who were from poor backgrounds (Cloud, 2017). It was also regarded as vital in ensuring the survival of Catholic schooling in Victoria, which was "seen by the Church as one of its instruments for holding on to, and re-establishing its control over, the faithful" (O'Donoghue, 2004, p. 79).

The importance of Catholic schooling in Victoria provided the impetus for Archbishop Goold to encourage priests and religious to write to religious congregations in Europe and invite them to come to Victoria to teach and run Catholic schools. The replacement of lay teachers with ordained and professed religious would reduce the costs of running Catholic schools and enable them to survive. The generous response was outstanding and ensured the survival of Catholic schools to continue to shape young Catholics in a manner that aimed to serve the Church's mission for approximately one hundred years without any state funding. The focus on lay teacher formation during this time took a turn for the worst.

The staffing of Catholic schools with religiously professed men and women from various religious congregations around the world ensured that children could continue to be educated in Catholic schools. Due to the lack of funds available to pay the wages of lay teachers, very few held teaching positions in Catholic schools in the latter part of the nineteenth and early part of the twentieth centuries. The spiritual formation needs of the lay teachers in Catholic schools were not a priority and were shrouded within a mindset, which at the time suggested that members of religious congregations were regarded as spiritually superior to lay people, including lay teachers (Cloud, 2017). In fact, the establishment of a Catholic teacher training college at the commencement of the twentieth century was initially geared principally towards the training of the religiously professed who would staff Catholic schools. O'Donoghue (2018) has argued that the virtual absence of lay teachers in Catholic schools up to the 1970s fuelled a perception that members of Catholic religious orders were superior to all lay people in the eyes of God and the Church and that the relative anonymity of the laity in Catholic teacher training colleges until sometime after the Second Vatican Council (1962–1965) did little to alter this mindset.

Against this backdrop of an implied lay inferiority, lay teachers tended to be employed in Catholic schools only in situations where there were no professed religious available to teach (O'Donoghue & Burley, 2008). Lay teachers holding these positions were excluded from leadership roles and were not allowed to contribute to policy development because they were deemed to be living a lesser form of faithfulness in their daily lives (Cloud, 2017). The professional and religious formation of the lay teacher was virtually neglected as the religious status of a lay person was perceived to be inferior (Cloud, 2017). To maintain a superior religious status and to remain faithful to their religious vows, members of religious orders were encouraged to have very little social contact with the laity (O'Donoghue, 2018). Thus, the rules and regulations governing several religious congregations were oriented towards setting themselves apart from the laity, who were perceived as inferior (O'Donoghue, 2004). Some rules were quite detailed and specific in limiting the degree of communication allowed between religious and lay people (including their own family members) because it was generally believed "that if the religious came into regular contact with lay people, this could easily lead to a loosening of the reins of their own desires, thus threatening their commitment to the religious life and their vowed status" (O'Donoghue, 2004, p. 80). This line of thinking was reflected in the limited involvement lay teachers would initially have if employed in a Catholic school. Consequently, consideration for the formation of lay teachers during this time was virtually non-existent and overshadowed by the rules in place to protect the spiritual lives of the professed members of religious congregations who dedicated themselves to the apostolate of Catholic education.

During the latter part of the twentieth century, the dominance of professed religious teachers in Catholic schools began to diminish due to key changes in the Church and society in general. The aftermath of the rulings of the Second Vatican Council (1962–1965) marked the decline in the number of religiously professed dedicated to the apostolate of Catholic education.

There were various reasons for this decline in addition to the growing impact of secularism and the consequent waning of numbers entering religious life (Beyers, 2014). Some religious had expanded into other ministries associated with the founding charism of their own religious congregations, and this ultimately led to a decline or withdrawal of their involvement in Catholic education. Some existing members of religious congregations chose to leave religious life because the rulings of the Second Vatican Council (1962–1965) contrasted with their reasons for joining in the first place. In 1966, Australia had 19,413 religious (sisters, brothers and clerics), and by the commencement of the second decade of the twenty-first century, the number has declined to 8422 (Dixon et al., 2011). The decline in the number of professed religious in schools paved the way for a rapid growth in the employment of lay teachers in Catholic schools.

The period following the Second Vatican Council (1962–1965) was marked by an increased orientation of many religious congregations towards other ministries and a decline in their involvement in the apostolate of Catholic education. It also marked a significant growth period in the building of new Catholic schools by the various Catholic dioceses across Australia to meet the ever-increasing growth in student population accelerated by post-war immigration (Buchanan, 2021). The growth in Catholic schools and student populations together with the decline in religiously professed sisters and brothers marked a resurgence in the employment of lay teachers and leaders in Catholic schools. Although the Congregation for Catholic Education (formerly the Sacred Congregation for Catholic Education) repeatedly emphasised the role and formation of the teacher as integral to aid the potential of a Catholic school to achieve its purpose, there was uncertainty around the formation needs of lay teachers dedicated to the apostolate of Catholic education (CCE, 1997; SCCE, 1977). As it was in the early colonial period, a lay teachers' connection to parish appeared as a key foundation for employment in Catholic schools and/or acceptance in Catholic teacher training colleges.

For approximately three decades after the Second Vatican Council (1962–1965), the various Catholic teacher training colleges and institutes across Australia had selection processes that generally required an applicant to have, in addition to appropriate academic grades and certificates, a reference from their parish priest, a character reference that could possibly attest to their commitment to Christian living, and a personal statement outlining their interest in Catholic education. Those shortlisted from these applications were generally invited to attend an interview before a panel of Catholic education leaders which generally consisted of a principal of a Catholic school, a leader in a diocesan Catholic education office and an academic staff member from the Catholic teacher training college/institute. This level of consideration reflected a way of determining whether an applicant was not only suitable for teaching but suitable to be formed as a teacher for Catholic education. Key to this was the applicant's connection to parish life and Christian living. As in the early colonial period, teacher formation and suitability for teaching in a Catholic school centred around whether a person understood the principles of Christianity, attended church and could read or write. The formation of Catholic educators was regarded an ecclesial endeavour, where lay teachers could be assured of the commitment and dedication of the parish, priests and wider ecclesial community as pivotal to their formation as lay teachers for Catholic education (Sacred Congregation for Catholic Education, 1982). Therefore, a lay teacher's commitment to parish life and Christian living remained key to their potential for formation.

By the end of the twentieth century, the teaching and leadership of Catholic schools devolved almost exclusively to the laity. Despite the fundamental importance attributed to the role of a teacher in a Catholic school, there was little evidence of an encompassing systematic approach to the formation of all lay teachers for Catholic education across Victoria, which is responsible for the education of approximately one quarter of the student population (in other Australian states and territories, the respective dioceses educated approximately one-fifth of the student population within their respective jurisdiction). The Catholic Education Office in the Melbourne Catholic Archdiocese, which is the third largest in the world with around 400 schools, has over many years like other dioceses in Victoria, supported the formation of teachers to participate in accredited pastoral, religious and theological courses through sponsorship programmes. This was a common practice amongst many dioceses throughout Australia (Graham, 2011). Sponsorship has enabled some lay teachers to fulfil accreditation requirements and to also acquire theological and religious education qualifications, but the National Catholic Education Commission (NCEC) has suggested that more needs to be done and has emphasised "the need for greater strategic focus on formation ..." (NCEC, 2017, p. 5). The Australian Bishops Commission for Catholic Education established the NCEC as the peak body for Catholic education in Australia and is responsible for the coordination and representation of Catholic schools and school authorities. It liaises with Australian Federal and State Governments who have legislative authority over all schooling systems within their respective jurisdictions and in consultation with State and Territory Catholic Education Commissions works towards national policy consensus and resourcing that represents and serves the needs and interests of Catholic school communities.

Given the decline in member of religious congregations teaching in Catholic schools and the rapid growth in the employment of lay teachers, the NCEC's (2017) call for an organised intentional approach to the faith formation of lay teachers has emerged as a key priority in need of systematic development that is accessible to all teachers in Catholic school throughout Australia. The *ongoing* formation opportunities for professed religious dedicated to the apostolate of Catholic education were generally along these lines; however, the formation opportunities generally encountered by lay teachers have tended to be *one-off* experiences (Hughes, 2008). Individual schools over the years with the support of their diocese have encouraged various creative and worthwhile formation opportunities for lay teachers such as a day in the annual school calendar devoted to staff formation, as well as options for retreats, immersion experiences, pilgrimages and many other opportunities. While this approach aligns with the perception that every aspect of Catholic schooling can harbour a formative dimension, more consideration needs to be given to establishment of a formation that is systematic, ongoing and accessible to all teacher in all Catholic schools (NCEC, 2017).

In summing up the background of teacher formation in the land down under, it is plausible to argue that from the early colonial period to 1872 lay teachers populated and headed Catholic schools. They were generally appointed by parish priests, and the nexus for their formation was their commitment to parish life or Church attendance and their willingness to live Christian lives (O'Donoghue & Moore, 2019). From the

1870s to the 1970s, social and legislative changes led to the massive decline in lay teachers in Catholic schools and the rapid uptake of professed religious who taught and built more Catholic schools. The spiritual life of a professed religious person was regarded as superior to that of a lay person. Lay teachers during this time were seldom employed in Catholic schools and generally only in situations where a professed religious person was not able to fill a teaching post. Lay teachers in these positions were not able to hold school leadership positions or contribute to school policy as they were perceived as inferior spiritual beings (Cloud, 2017). The aftermath of the Second Vatican Council (1962–1965), together with the growing impact of secularisation and post-war migration, saw the growth in Catholic school populations and the decline in professed religious available to teach in Catholic schools. During this period, the employment of lay teachers in Catholic schools escalated and, opportunities for formation for mission were on the agenda (Sacred Congregation for Catholic Education, 1982). However, these formation experiences tended to be one-off and offered by schools and Catholic educations offices overseeing Catholic education in a diocese (Graham, 2011). It was commonly presumed that lay teachers were living Christian lives that were enriched by a strong connection to parish life. The twenty-first century began to reveal cracks in this perception that could no longer be ignored if meaningful faith formation opportunities for lay teachers are to be offered.

1.2 Formation for Mission Today: Challenges and Responses

Catholic schools can employ teachers who have initial teacher training qualifications and who are eligible for professional registration as a teacher in their geographical jurisdiction. Ideally, Catholic schools would want to employ a critical mass of teachers who have studied Catholic religious education and theology as part of their initial teacher training qualification. However, the excessive demand for such teachers outweighs the supply. Consequently, many Catholic dioceses across Australia try to offer sponsorship to teachers in their schools who wish to undertake postgraduate qualifications in religious education and theology. While those who undertake studies in religious education and theology have commented on its impact on their own formation, higher education learning has been traditionally based around lectures and research underpinned by curricula and syllabi that are conducive to knowledge transfer that is measured by the achievement of cognitive learning outcomes (Buchanan, 2020).

The characteristics of teachers in Catholic schools suggest that ongoing faith formation of teachers requires more systematic attention that focuses on the teachers themselves as key resources in their own formation (NCEC, 2017). Therefore, to meet the formation needs of lay teachers in the twenty-first century, an account of who makes up the teaching population in Catholic schools is necessary. Recent statistics indicate that across Australia, eighty per cent of the primary school teachers and sixty-one per cent of secondary school teachers identify as Catholic and only about twenty-five per cent of these teachers who identify as Catholic engage regularly in a Catholic worshipping community outside of their school experience. A significant percentage of teachers in Catholic schools have little, if any, familiarity with Catholic beliefs and values. In Catholic secondary schools, thirty-nine per cent of the teachers do not identify as Catholic, and in Catholic primary schools, twenty per cent of the teachers do not identify as Catholic. This equates to approximately one-third of the teacher population in Catholic schools not identifying as Catholic (NCEC, 2017). These statistics set the current landscape and compromise the potential for parish communities to be key contributors in the formation of most lay teachers in Catholic schools. It has been suggested that a national systematic approach to lay teacher formation for mission be developed and adopted (Graham, 2011; NCEC, 2017). What should this look like and what are the challenges?

The make-up of teachers populating Catholic school in Victoria and across Australia should influence decisions about approaches to teacher formation. There needs to be a major rethink about the potential of the parish and wider ecclesial community in supporting the formation of teachers for mission in Catholic schools, and further consideration should be given to other possibilities that will be accessible to the diverse teacher population in Catholic schools. After all, only some sixteen per cent of lay teachers have a connection to a Catholic faith sharing community other than the Catholic school in which they work. For this reason, it is unreasonable to expect that the local parishes and wider ecclesial community carry the load of the direct formation of the entire population of lay teachers in Catholic schools. The National Catholic Education Commission acknowledges the concerns of bishops, diocesan education offices, religious institutes and public juridic persons for systematic, developmental and well-resourced formation programmes but has emphasised that in the twenty-first century, the responsibility for formation rests with the principals, leadership teams and the governance bodies of Catholic schools (NCEC, 2017). Emphasising the responsibility for formation towards the leadership of the Catholic school, rather than within the context of the parish and wider Catholic community, communicates an insightful understanding of the importance of meeting people where they are at. Richard Rymarz's (2018) ground-breaking insights into understanding ways forward for teacher formation in Catholic schools indicated that in general teachers are very happy to work in Catholic schools and become involved in contributing to the religious dimension of the Catholic school, but their religious connection does not tend to extend to their lives outside the school. Viewed in a positive light, Rymarz's insight suggests that religion can play a prominent part in the professional life of teachers who work in Catholic schools. Therefore, formation of teachers should take place in the context of the faith community to which the teachers are associated with and in most cases that is the Catholic school.

A major challenge for a systematic Catholic school-centred teacher formation approach is that the school needs to be set up to provide expert ongoing formation for all lay Catholic educators and avoid offering a suite of one-off experiences which tend to be ineffective in the long term (Graham, 2011). For approximately eighty-four per cent of lay teachers, the Catholic school is the only place where they actively support and participate in a religious mission (see also NCEC, 2017; Rymarz, 2018). Therefore, faith formation for lay Catholic educators needs to take place in the Catholic school where their encounter with religious orientations is likely to be most salient. Their formation needs to be an "intentional, ongoing and a reflective process that focuses on the growth of individuals and communities from their lived experiences, in spiritual awareness, theological understanding, vocational motivation and capabilities for mission and service in the Church and the world" (NCEC, 2017). Drawing on insights from *A Framework for Formation for Mission in Catholic Education* (NCEC, 2017), the potential for a Catholic school to support lay teachers in the systematic spiritual and religious formation in the apostolate of Catholic education needs to be within the context of certain understandings.

Lay teachers need to understand that the mission of the Catholic school is Christ centred. The leadership within a Catholic school has a responsibility to enable all members of the school community to experience the school as a sign and instrument of Christ's presence in the world (Sultmann & Brown, 2016). A Christ-centred school community allows lay teachers who have no other connection to the Catholic tradition, the opportunity to come to know, love and imitate Christ in their professional and personal lives (Graham, 2011). Lay teachers need to experience within the school context, a Christological understanding that enables them to grasp his humanity and divinity through scripturally rich and ecclesially grounded encounters (O'Collins, 2013). Catholic educators constantly wrestle institutionally and personally with many complexities posed by competing theological positions expressed by the magisterium and professional theologians. Lay teachers need to be connected to their school, a faith community that invites them into theological understandings, that enables them to develop a healthy insight into the crucial hermeneutical questions that continue to reside at the heart of Catholicism (Torevell, 2013).

Lay teachers who freely accept a position in a Catholic school have a responsibility to understand the identity and mission of a Catholic school and the role they play in helping the school to achieve its mission. According to Graham (2011), the school has a responsibility to engage staff in formation experiences that enable them to encounter and participate in the building of a Catholic school community that enables them, as matter of conscience to make personal and professional choices about their participation in the identity and mission of the Catholic school. Lay teachers in Catholic schools need to understand how to differentiate between individual and school community needs and to recognise when it is appropriate to focus energies on building a communal Catholic religious identity and culture within the school. This is an understanding that individuals must come to terms with as there is no homogeneous Catholic school identity applicable to all schools (McDonough, 2019).

Lay teachers are people who have a part to play in living out their vocation, which is oriented towards reaching out to young people with a view to making a significant contribution to saving the world through the apostolate of Catholic education (Doyle, 2017). A teacher in a Catholic school needs to understand that the cultivation of a teacher's vocation in the context of Catholic education is one that is oriented towards doing the will of God (Jacobs, 2005). A vocation expressed through teaching in a Catholic school enables teachers to forge a connection with the Catholic tradition and to be responsive to enabling the Catholic school to achieve its mission (NCEC, 2017). Formation for mission in Catholic education is not a collective endeavour. It is a personal journey experienced by many teachers dedicated to the apostolate of Catholic education, and each person's faith journey is a personal one shared and encountered within the context of the Catholic school which finds expression as a faith sharing community. School communities are key to the formation of the teacher's heart because they are the places where teachers are invested in carrying out the religious mission of Catholic education in situations where their own personal story and everyday reality are invested (NCEC, 2017).

The insights from *A Framework for Formation for Mission in Catholic Education* (NCEC, 2017) considered in this chapter are not presented as understandings that one would expect a teacher to be imbued with from the onset of their commitment to Catholic education. Formation for mission is an ongoing encounter and a lifelong endeavour, where the spiritual journey of each teacher is individual and diverse and is best placed to occur within the context of the school as a faith sharing community that the teacher is connected to. It is unrealistic to place the burden of lay teacher formation solely on the parish communities and the wider ecclesial community when the evidence suggests that for most teachers in Catholic schools, these locations are beyond their immediate reality (NCEC, 2017). Catholic schools need to rethink how they support the lifelong formation of teachers because without such commitment, Catholic education will be challenged in its ability to achieve its goals (Miller, 2007).

One approach gaining momentum in diverse settings, including Catholic schools in Australia, is spiritual direction (Ault, 2013; Buchanan, 2019; Crawley, 2016; Grizzle, 2018). Catholic education authorities and the wider ecclesial community acknowledge the pivotal importance of teacher formation in terms of enhancing a Catholic school's potential to achieve its goals, but ultimately the key resource to formation is the teachers themselves (NCEC, 2017). The life stories, experiences and encounters of each individual teacher are unique and, within the context of a Catholic school as a faith community, worthy of opportunities for deep reflection. Spiritual direction can be core to the formation and growth process of a teacher at any stage in their spiritual and professional journey. It is a process that, through co-authored conversations between the director and directee, teachers can make meaning of their own lives and contributions to the religious dimension of the school (Crawley, 2016). It can help an individual teacher make sense of who they are as a person dedicated to the vocation of a teacher in a Catholic school. Spiritual direction can offer deep formation for the individual which can also lead to enriching the school as a faith community (Grizzle, 2018).

1.3 Concluding Remarks

Teacher formation for Catholic education in the land down under has traditionally been supported by a teacher's commitment and involvement in parish life and Christian living and the support that flows from Catholic leaders, parish, priest and the wider ecclesial community. While this perception of how formation may be encountered still rings true for some, the factors which have impeded the evolution of teacher formation in this way include the decline in lay teachers in Catholic schools between the 1870s and 1970s and a devaluing of the role of lay teachers during this period in terms of role status within the school including their perceived spiritual and religious integrity (Cloud, 2017). The aftermath of the Second Vatican Council together with growth in secularisation and an immigration boom resulted in a rapid growth in Catholic schools and the employment of lay teachers. While Catholic education leaders, parishes and the wider ecclesial community saw it as their role to support the formation of lay teachers, the reach of these support structures has been highly compromised in the twenty-first century because the only connection to a Catholic faith community for eighty-four per cent of teachers is the Catholic school. Formation for each individual teacher needs to take place within the context of a supportive Catholic school community, and it needs to be personal and ongoing. Each school needs to provide access to high-quality spiritual direction in an organised ongoing basis to all teachers. Their formation will be enhanced by the opportunity to reflect on their individual vocation as a teacher which is central to their own diverse spiritual journeys and their unique contribution to Catholic education.

References

Ault, N. (2013). Theological reflection and spiritual direction. *The Australasian Catholic Record, 90*(1), 81–91.

Beyers, J. (2014). The church and the secular: The effect of the post-secular on Christianity. *Hervormde Teologiese Studies, 70*(1), 1–12. https://doi.org/10.4102/hts.v70i1.2605

Buchanan, M. T. (2019). The transmission of religion: Reconceptualising the religious education leader. In M. T. Buchanan & A. M. Gellel (Eds.), *Global perspectives on Catholic religious education in schools volume II: Learning and leading in a pluralist world* (pp. 139–150). Springer.

Buchanan, M. T. (2020). Teacher education: What Australian Christian schools need and what higher education delivers. *International Journal of Christianity & Education, 24*(1), 96–107. https://doi.org/10.1177/2056997119892642

Buchanan, M. T. (2021). Identity formation and Australian Catholic schools: Examining the role of the religious education teacher. In R. Wills, M. de Souza, M. A. Bakkar, J. M. McMahon, & C. Roux (Eds.), *The Bloomsbury handbook of culture and identity from early childhood to early adulthood.* Bloomsbury.

Cloud, N. (2017). Teaching in Catholic schools from the perspectives of lay teachers, 1940–1980. *Education, Research and Perspectives, 44*, 70–97.

Congregation for Catholic Education. (1997). *The Catholic school on the threshold of the third millennium.* St Paul's.

Crawley, D. (2016). Authority in spiritual direction conversations: Dialogic perspectives. *Journal for the Study of Spirituality, 6*(1), 6–19. https://doi.org/10.1080/20440243.2016.1158452

Dixon, R., Reid, S., & Connolly, N. (2011). See I am doing a new thing: The 2009 survey of Catholic religious institutes in Australia. *Australasian Catholic Record, 88*(3), 271–283.

Doyle, J. (2017). *Tools and fuels: How Catholic teachers can become saints, beat burnout and save the world*. Choicez Media.

Graham, J. D. (2011). Daring to engage: Religious and spiritual formation of lay Catholic educators in Australia. *International Studies in Catholic Education, 3*(1), 25–39. https://doi.org/10.1080/19422539.2011.540138

Grizzle, A. F. (2018). Group spiritual direction: offering spiritual depth and community building in diverse settings. *Journal of Spiritual Formation and Soul Care, 11*(2), 218–227. https://doi.org/10.1177/1939790918798830

Hughes, G. (2008). *The spirituality of teachers in Catholic schools*. John Garrett Publishing.

Jacobs, R. (2005). *Building spiritual leadership density in Catholic schools*. National Catholic Education Association.

McDonough, G. P. (2019). Pluralizing Catholic Identity. *Religious Education, 114*(2), 168–180. https://doi.org/10.1080/00344087.2018.1560744

Miller, J. (2007). Challenges facing Catholic school: A view from Rome. In G. Grace & J. O'Keefe (Eds.), *International handbook of Catholic education: Challenges for school systems in the 21st century* (pp. 449–480). Springer.

National Catholic Education Commission. (2017). *A framework for formation for mission in Catholic education*. National Catholic Education Commission.

O'Collins, G. (2013). Developments in christology: The last fifty years. *Australasian Catholic Record, 90*(2), 161–171.

O'Donoghue, T. A. (2004). Rescuing lay teachers in Catholic schools from anonymity for the period 1870–1970. *Education, Research and Perspectives, 31*(2), 78–93.

O'Donoghue, T. A., & Burley, S. (2008). God's antipodean teaching force: An historical exposition on Catholic teaching religious in Australia. *Teaching and Teacher Education, 24*(1), 180–189.

O'Donoghue, T. (2018). The experience of being a lay teacher in Catholic schools: An approach for investigating the history of an under-researched field. *Espacio, Tiempo y Educación, 5*(2), 163–178. https://doi.org/10.14516/ete.182

O'Donoghue, T., & Moore, K. (2019). *Teacher preparation in Australia: History, policy and future directions*. Emerald Publishing Limited.

Rogan, F. (2000). *A short history of Catholic education: Archdiocese of Melbourne 1839–1980*. Catholic Education Office.

Rymarz, R. (2018). 'We need to keep the door open': A framework for better understanding the formation of younger teachers in catholic schools. In R. Stuart- & J. Shortt (Eds.), *Christian faith, formation and education* (pp. 197–210). Springer.

Sacred Congregation for Catholic Education. (1977). *The Catholic school*. St Paul's.

Sacred Congregation for Catholic Education. (1982). *Lay Catholics in schools: Witnesses to faith*. St Paul's.

Stone, L. (1969). Literacy and education in England 1640–1900. *Past and Present, 42*(1), 91.

Sultmann, W. F., & Brown, R. (2016). Leadership and identity in the Catholic school: An Australian perspective. *International Studies in Catholic Education, 8*(1), 73–89. https://doi.org/10.1080/19422539.2016.1140419

Synan, T. (2003). *A journey in faith: A history of Catholic education in Gippsland 1850–1981*. David Lovell Publishing.

Torevell, D. (2013). Liberation, Catholic education and the nature of theology: An essay to assist Catholic teachers with problems in this field. *International Studies in Catholic Education, 5*(2), 218–232. https://doi.org/10.1080/19422539.2013.821348

Michael T. Buchanan Ph.D. is the Deputy Head of School—Theology and an Associate Professor of Religious Education in the Faculty of Theology and Philosophy at Australian Catholic University. He lectures in faith-based leadership and religious education curriculum, leadership and formation. He has published widely in international scholarly journals, and his book publications include *Global Perspectives on Catholic Religious Education in Schools, Leadership and Religious Schools: International Perspectives and Challenges.* Michael is the immediate past editor of *Religious Education Journal of Australia.* He is an Honorary Professor at Bishop Grosseteste University, UK, and an Affiliate Associate Professor at the University of Malta, Malta. Michael.Buchanan@acu.edu.au

Chapter 2
Catholic Teacher Formation in Northern Ireland

Niall Coll

Abstract Acknowledging Northern Ireland's long history of sectarian strife between Catholics and Protestants and its "consociational" model of power-sharing government today, the essay introduces the region's distinctive educational landscape with its extensive network of Catholic schools and state-funded Catholic teacher education university college (St Mary's). It also touches both on claims that the very existence of Catholic schools perpetuates sectarian division and, *au contraire*, Catholic education's defence of its positive contribution to education and life. Looking to the future, in the face of both the strong currents of secularization and Northern Ireland government policy which encourages a technocratic and bureaucratic approach to education, the essay recognizes the characteristic attitudes, often unsympathetic to religion, of typical student teachers today. Catholic teacher formation in Northern Ireland, it is argued, needs, if it is to be fit for purpose, to speak to these concerns and explore ways to offer student teachers a better intellectual and personal experience of the Catholic vision of education.

Keywords Sectarianism · Ethno-political · Secularization · Managerialism · Generation Z/iGens

2.1 Context

Any worthwhile reflection on the future of Catholic teacher formation in Northern Ireland must begin with an acknowledgement of the peculiar history and character of the region. While increasingly marked over recent decades by the currents of both secularization and the beginnings of multiculturalism so characteristic of the West, it is still a place where religious affiliation—overwhelmingly either Protestant or Catholic—plays a significant factor in shaping people's sense of their own personal and political identity. The roots of this stance are deep and complex, reaching back over eight centuries to the beginnings of English conquest of Ireland and the later

---

N. Coll (✉)
Parochial House, Donegal Town F94 D8X0, Ireland
e-mail: niallcoll30@gmail.com

© The Author(s), under exclusive license to Springer Nature Singapore Pte Ltd. 2022
L. Franchi and R. Rymarz (eds.), *Formation of Teachers for Catholic Schools*, Catholic Education Globally: Challenges and Opportunities 1,
https://doi.org/10.1007/978-981-19-4727-8_2

settlement in the north of the island of Protestants (mostly Scottish Presbyterians) in the seventeenth century, sowing the seeds of bitter divisions in ethnic, political, economic and religious matters. Ireland was partitioned in 1921: the overwhelmingly Catholic south (later the Republic of Ireland) left the UK to become an independent state, while the then two-thirds Protestant north became Northern Ireland and remained in the UK under British rule.

From its foundation, the new Northern Ireland state's Protestant Unionist government exercised power unfairly over the Catholic nationalist minority, leading to the emergence in the 1960s of the Civil Rights Association to protest against injustices. The distinguished Catholic ecumenist, Michael Hurley SJ, has sympathetically acknowledged that "Behind this discrimination lay a deep-seated fear of Rome" (2002, p. 262). Irish Protestants have a long history of fearing and attempting to subjugate the native Catholic population and their faith. Their outlook—often rather bluntly summarized in more recent times as a policy of "No Surrender"—meant that Catholic grievances were never taken seriously following the establishment of the northern state. The Provisional IRA emerged in December 1969 and by 1971 had acquired an offensive capacity. Simultaneously, different forms of Unionism and Loyalism coalesced in the Ulster Defence Association, formed in December 1971. The gun had reappeared with a vengeance in Irish politics and the world looked on in disbelief and horror. By the time of the 1994 ceasefire, over 3600 people had lost their lives in an ethno-sectarian conflict known colloquially as "The Troubles" (Jackson, 2010). The Good Friday Agreement of 1998 brought an end to violence and established what is termed a "consociational" model of power-sharing government involving the main political parties, unionist and nationalist, to help achieve "conflict regulation" (O'Leary, 2019, p. 1–2). Almost a quarter of a century later, Northern Ireland remains a hotly contested political terrain, geographically part of the island of Ireland but politically part of the UK. Its internal divisions and divided loyalties have returned to international attention in recent times due to protracted and ongoing tensions between the European Union and the UK over the region's special status inside the EU single market and customs union following Brexit (Cochrane, 2020).

2.2 The Educational Landscape

Having set the larger historical and political context, it is now helpful both to examine briefly the general shape of schooling and identify some key educational themes which typically animate debate in Northern Ireland as a prelude to a brief discussion of the future of Catholic teacher formation there. One important fact that needs acknowledgement right away is that the emergence of an almost wholly denominational education system in nineteenth-century (pre-partition) Ireland is largely accounted for by the legacy of the strong animosities and fear of proselytism which were such a feature of the time. Following partition, the main Protestant denominations in the fledgling Northern Ireland state were soon able to transfer their schools into a state-controlled system (Controlled schools), confident that their de facto Protestant ethos and character were assured. Meanwhile, the Catholic bishops were determined to secure and defend Catholic interests, especially in relation to the church's role in education (McGrath, 2000). This means, a century later, that across Northern Ireland, there are today 489 Catholic schools (Maintained schools), primary and secondary, serving the needs of 45.5% of the school population (Catholic Trustee Service, 2021). Between them, the controlled and maintained sectors account for over 90% of all children at school in Northern Ireland (Gracie, 2021; Richardson, 2019). In one way or another, it is clear that the ethno-politico divisions in society are reflected in the parallel systems for the Protestant and Catholic communities, in addition to a small religiously integrated sector of schools and a number of Irish medium schools (Duffy & Gallagher, 2017; The Economist, 2021).

The integrated schools sector began as a parent-led initiative seeking to establish religiously mixed schools where children from both Catholic and Protestant backgrounds would be educated together. Social attitudes and opinion poll data has consistently reported high levels of parental support for integrated schools, but, intriguingly, this has failed to ignite school enrolments take-up for these schools which languish at around 7% of pupils (Hansson & Roulston, 2020). Meanwhile, the Irish medium school sector—mostly *Gaelscoileanna*—attracts 2% of pupils (Gracie, 2021). Under the 1989 Education Reform (Northern Ireland) Order, the Department of Education Northern Ireland (DENI) has a statutory duty "to encourage and facilitate the development of integrated education that is to say the education together of Protestant and Roman Catholic pupils" (DENI, 1989). While this policy is strongly supported by the cross-community Alliance Party (Hagan & Eaton, 2020), the two main political parties in the power-sharing government, the Democratic Unionists and Sinn Féin (unionist and nationalist, respectively) are lukewarm in their approach to it (Hansson & Roulston, 2020). In one way or another, it is clear that Northern Ireland polarization means "'integrated' schools for all children are not a realistic option" at the moment (Hughes, 2011, 847). That being so, the most striking educational initiative of the last decade is the emergence of what is known as shared education. This government policy accepts the reality of a dual system but works to increase cooperation between schools. Schools maintain their distinct and separate structures and identities while committing to collaborative partnerships which bring pupils and students together on a regular basis for joint, curriculum-based classes (Hansson & Roulston, 2020). Significantly, this halfway house tests the patience of those who are anxious to press on with the introduction of a fully integrated system (Emerson, 2021).

2.3 Criticism of Catholic Education

Having introduced the historical context and structure of schooling in Northern Ireland, a flavour of the particular debate concerning Catholic education there is appropriate. To begin, it can be acknowledged that there is general consensus that, in a society emerging from violence, schools play a key role in the task of peace building for the future (Gracie, 2021). Catholic education in Northern Ireland is keenly aware of this role and very resistant to any suggestion that it might in any way sympathize with or assist in the promotion of sectarian attitudes (The Catholic Bishops of Northern Ireland, 2001; Catholic Schools Trustee Service, 2021). In the light of the region's peculiar history, it is to be expected that the role of education should be closely scrutinized and monitored to gauge how effective schools are in promoting tolerance, mutual understanding and the common good (Donaldson, 2007). There is a long history of assertion in media, academy and politics that if Northern Ireland is to become a pluralist, accommodating and tolerant society at peace with itself, then it must insist on integrated schooling: "The (not always) unspoken corollary is that faith-based schools—specifically Catholic schools in the context of Northern Ireland—are in some way inferior, backward, and even dangerous in so far as they … contribute to division and the continuation of sectarian attitudes" (Donaldson, 2007, p. 231; Gallagher, 2005). One of the small band of notable protagonists for Catholic education locally, Bishop Donal McKeown, has repeatedly been to the fore arguing, *au contraire*, that access to faith-based education is a key characteristic of modern pluralist society that Catholic schools thrive in the most modern and advanced societies and that they tend to provide good value for the public money that they receive. He goes on to argue that the real sign of maturity in Northern Ireland will not be when everyone goes to a secular school, but, rather, "when diversity of provision is seen as an enrichment for society and not as a threat to its stability" (McKeown, 2011). Not dissimilar sentiments are expressed by Philip Barnes, who, writing from a Northern Ireland Protestant faith perspective, and as one who is also well acquainted with religious education in schools in England and Wales, affirms the contribution of faith schools to the realization of legitimate and progressive educational values including the cultivation of tolerance, moral integrity and civic virtue (Barnes, 2005). Elsewhere Bishop McKeown has strikingly asserted that Catholic schools "are not creating bigots" and gone on to observe that they are larger (in number and pupil numbers) than the controlled state sector schools and, significantly, more mixed racially and religiously, and in social class composition, educating more of the new immigrants (many of whom belong to other world faiths) (Quoted in O'Leary, 2019, p. 286).

In its important long-term policy document, *A Shared Future* (2006), the Northern Ireland government acknowledges that "The exercise of parental choice is central and both integrated and denominational schools have important roles to play in preparing children for their role as adults in a shared society". But it goes on to add the qualification that "There is a balance to be struck, however, between the exercise of this choice and the significant additional costs …". In the years since, it has been clear that successive power-sharing executives in Northern Ireland respect the rights of parents to express a preference for schools that reflect a religious or integrated ethos. It is clear, however, that whatever the grudging willingness to tolerate Catholic schools in practice, a strong opposition to their very existence lurks just below the surface in the Democratic Unionist Party and was memorably expressed by a former First Minister, Peter Robinson (2010), when he accused them of representing "a benign form of apartheid" and called for an end to government funding of Catholic schools as part of a push towards an integrated education system.

In the face of common assumptions internationally that the Northern Ireland conflict is predominantly, even completely, a religiously motivated one, it needs to be acknowledged again to an international readership here that the conflict is more ethno-political in character and that religious voices have been well represented among those to the fore in promoting peace and reconciliation. In the wake of the Second Vatican Council (1962–65), considerable ecumenical progress was made at an unofficial level (Coll, 2013). The outbreak of violence in the 1960s "spurred or shamed" the Catholic Church and the Protestant denominations into making official contact for the first time. Against the background of escalating violence, the leaders of the four main churches in Ireland, Catholic, Presbyterian, Church of Ireland and Methodist, formed a working group to calm fears and promote peace, and this grouping has been a staple of Northern Ireland life since. Truth be told, it is clear that at the moments of greatest challenges, "Churches were more ready than the political parties to stretch out hands of friendship" (Gallagher & Worrall, 1982). Indeed, one of the most important church initiatives during the troubles was the work of the Redemptorist Peace Ministry among republicans, especially associated with Fr Alex Reid, which was so important to ending violence and creating the conditions that made the Good Friday Agreement possible (McKeever, 2017; Scull, 2019).

2.4 Teacher Formation in Northern Ireland

Teacher education in Northern Ireland is an all-graduate profession, and there are five main providers of teacher education: three universities (Queen's University Belfast, University of Ulster and the Open University) and two university colleges (St Mary's University College and Stranmillis University College (both of which are affiliated to QUB) (Moran, 2012). St Mary's offers a range of avenues for those who wish to teach. At undergraduate level, it offers a B.Ed. (Hons) in either primary or post-primary education and a PGCE route with a special focus on Irish medium schools. The Certificate in Religious Education is offered to students on all teacher education programmes: possession of this award is required before obtaining a post in a Catholic primary school and very useful for appointments to post-primary schools too. During the period of study, the Certificate in Religious Education enables students who so wish (the great majority) to gain knowledge and understanding in areas such as biblical theology, Scripture, theology, church history and catechetics alongside practical curricular guidance for teaching placements in schools (St Mary's, 2021). In an interesting recent concession, students at St Mary's sister university college, Stranmillis University College (historically closely aligned with the Controlled, de facto Protestant sector), are now offered the possibility of also undertaking the Catholic RE Certificate in a manner which is validated through St Mary's (Meredith, 2019).

The number of initial teacher education places is specified by the government, the two university colleges each accounts for 40% of the places available, while Queen's

University and Ulster University have 10% each (Hagan & Eaton, 2020). Traditionally, entry into the teaching profession is highly competitive, resulting in the selection of more academically able students (Moran, 2012, p. 143). In line with the "consociational" pattern of society, the state-funded St Mary's University College is the main provider of initial teacher education for those who wish to teach in Catholic schools in the region (Hagan, 2016). It was founded in 1900 by the Dominican Sisters for the education of Catholic women teachers and has included males since 1985. Using Benne's typology of Christian institutions, it seems fair to argue that, at least hitherto, St Mary's falls under the category of a "critical-mass" college in which "the critical mass … [is] strong enough to define, shape and maintain the public identity and mission of the college consonant with the sponsoring tradition" (Quoted in Hagan, 2016, p. 107). Following the establishment of the Northern Ireland state in 1921, nationalist (Catholic) politicians were sympathetic to church control of the schools which served their children. This is undoubtedly explained by the fact that their people were largely devout Catholics, among whom the clergy retained influence. A further attraction was their well-grounded assumption that Catholic schools were more likely to promote an Irish or Gaelic ethos in contrast to a state-controlled school system whose loyalties would almost definitely be orientated towards the union with Great Britain and the crown (McGrath, 2000; Hansson & Roulston, 2020). In this context, the Catholic bishops were "determined to maintain control of teacher training" and the choice of teachers for the Catholic school system (McGrath, 2000, p. 243).

Today, however, a century later, a rapidly changing landscape of religions and belief in Northern Ireland means that it is a more religiously diverse and secular society where many of the students being recruited are less in tune with Catholic practice (Francis et al., 2020; Kieran et al., 2022). In common with trends in the West so clearly identified by the philosopher, Charles Taylor (2007), theirs in general is a culture of authenticity which emphasizes the importance of each individual finding and living out his or her own way of being human (Trueman, 2020). In one way or another, the influence of all the Christian churches and particularly that of the Catholic Church on culture is in rapid decline (Gribben, 2021). Clearly, then, the close embrace between northern Catholicism and nationalism that arose in the nineteenth century has weakened (Foster, 2008, p. 58). Indeed, it has been apparent since the 1980s that the political parties which represent Catholic voters in Northern Ireland display deference to "nationalist" rather than Catholic values (McGrath, 2000).

2.5 Looking to the Future of Catholic Teacher Formation in Northern Ireland

The decline in the traditional religious paradigm in Northern Ireland, as elsewhere in the West (Franchi & Rymarz, 2017), underlines the need for a deep discernment about new models of formation and training for Catholic teachers. This in a society where there are already many raised voices calling for the abolition of state-funded Catholic teacher education on the grounds that it perpetuates sectarian divisions (Transforming Education, 2021). These challenges accentuate the need for both a clear theological and pedagogical vision and commitment to the distinctive work of Catholic education in an increasingly secular society. In what follows, two brief observations will be made: one regarding the attitudes of typical Catholic student teachers today and the other concerning the political and economic climate in which (state-funded) Catholic schools in Northern Ireland have to operate.

1. Student teachers today: As we look to the future, Catholic teacher formation in Northern Ireland needs a clearer grasp of the general outlook of its student teachers today in terms of how they typically approach questions about life and meaning. Because of the massive influence of popular Anglo-American culture on young people throughout the West, not least in Northern Ireland with its strong cultural and linguistic links with the USA, some awareness of US experience and literature may be enlightening (Smith et al., 2014; Twenge, 2017). There, the so-called Generation Z or iGens, that is young people who have reached puberty since around 2011, the age cohort overwhelmingly represented in the ranks of those in teacher training today, have been the subject of various studies. Successor to the Millennial Generation, people typically born between 1981 and 1996 (Bauman et al., 2014), Generation Z are the first generation to have grown up with access to the Internet and portable digital technology from a young age, greatly shaping their typical approaches to life. Like the Millennials, they are often noted for their self-absorption, dependence on technology, detachment from traditional institutional networks, interest in personal development and tendency to understand themselves as spiritual rather than religious (Bauman et al., 2014). Generation Z, however, it is argued, are also distinct from the Millennials and previous generations on account of the intensity of their disdain for inequality based on gender, race or sexual orientation (Twenge, 2017). These preferences, especially in terms of attitudes towards gender and sexuality—such hot-button issues in the West today—mean that they are a generation largely at odds, and in a very open way, with many official Catholic teachings. In a nutshell, many, though by no means not all of them, seem to be part of a move away from religion that is not haphazard, small or uncertain. (And this trend is not restricted to Catholics but also involves members of other Christian traditions.) It seems that many of them, in particular, distrust religion for what their age cohort interprets as its tendency to promote what they interpret as anti-gay attitudes and its general opposition to abortion (Trueman, 2020; Twenge, 2017). In addition, Generation Z seem to be less interested in socializing in person and interacting with peers face to face (Twenge, 2017)—a tendency no doubt exacerbated by the ongoing COVID-19 pandemic and the restrictions on socialization that have ensued. These characteristic attitudes need to be taken seriously and addressed directly in the particular programmes designed to shape and form Catholic teachers in Northern Ireland—all the more important in the context of the marked decline of religious influence in public policy there recently in relation to same-sex marriage and abortion reforms (Gribben, 2021). There needs to be a real and imaginative commitment to developing

student teacher engagement with Scripture, with Liturgy and with Catholic Social Teaching. Catholic teacher training needs to listen to, understand better and engage with the lives of these typical students. Perhaps the "spiritual but not religious" cast of mind of many student teachers, if imaginatively engaged with during teacher formation, may in time offer a route which will allow many of them to delve more deeply into their faith and find a path back into that very tradition.

2. Both the neo-liberal education policies of government and the marketization of education at all phases are marked characteristics of Northern Ireland society (Hagan, 2016). Government policy is more materialistic and technocratic, focused on trying to meet the needs of technological, knowledge-based economy resulting in a growing trend to define the common good of education in terms of the economy rather than culture. This constitutes a grave challenge to the specific character of Catholic education since human capital is replaced by knowledge capital, an explosion of managerialism and an unhealthy emphasis on testing, measurement of progress and audit trails "to the detriment of support for individual growth and the broader social goods of education" (Conway, 2015, p. 262). Growing levels of accountability to government in Northern Ireland mean that Catholic schools which are increasingly focused on being compliant with state requirements rather than drawing more deeply from the wells of a Catholic philosophy of education and thus being innovative in their approach to teaching and learning. This means that there is a real concern. Catholic teacher education must be alert to these trends and committed to forming teachers for the future who can model a holistic approach to teaching and learning, one which will involve the formation of the whole person and offers and education in all areas of life (Tuohy, 2013).

2.6 Conclusion

While religion in Northern Ireland is important to personal and political identity in ways that have long vanished in most of Western Europe, including the Republic of Ireland, the same secularizing and individualizing trajectory, just somewhat slower, is at work there too. Faith-based schools, overwhelmingly Catholic ones, continue to be valued in Northern Ireland for their excellence academically and pastorally. But Northern Ireland is a society where all schools are subjected to league tables and many, including Catholic ones, are succumbing to pressure to focus exclusively on the commodification of educational outcomes. This is a tragedy: Catholic schools everywhere need to demonstrate that they work out of a broader and deeper vision, a distinctive and different one, intent on achieving something more. Catholic teacher formation in Northern Ireland, both initial and ongoing among established teachers, if it is to be fit for its specific purpose of forming present and future educators for such Catholic schools, must be wholeheartedly committed to offering their students an intellectual, personal, professional, social and religious formation which will equip them to maintain and enhance the distinctive vision of Catholic education locally. Those who lead, teach in and administer institutions connected with Catholic teacher formation, at primary, secondary and tertiary levels, in addition to attending to academic and sporting success, need to ensure that they are also working, even in these most secular of times, to find new ways to cultivate in student teachers (and already qualified teachers too) a greater love for the Word of God, tools for theological enquiry, experience in prayer, a solicitude for the work of social justice and care for the poor, the suffering, the newcomer and the earth. If tempted to despair by the cold winds of secularization and the damage wrought by abuse in the Catholic Church, we need to remind ourselves that the spiritual thirst of humanity will never die and that there is so much that we can do now to form future generations of Catholic teachers who will keep alive the distinctive flame of Catholic education.

References

Barnes, P. L. (2005). Religion, education and conflict in Northern Ireland. *Journal of Beliefs and Values, 26*(2), 23–38.

Bauman, W., et al. (2014). Teaching the millennial generation in the religious and theological studies classroom. *Teaching Theology and Religion, 14*(4), 301–322.

Catholic Schools Trustee Service. (2021). *Welcome*. Retrieved from https://www.catholiceducation-ni.org/#

Coll, N. (2013). Religious pluralism and educational practice in Northern Ireland. In G. Byrne & P. Kieran (Eds.), *Toward mutual ground: Pluralism, religious education and diversity in Irish schools* (pp. 157–164). The Columba Press.

Conway, E. (2015). Vatican II on Christian education: A guide through today's 'educational emergency.' In N. Coll (Ed.), *Ireland and Vatican II: Essays theological, pastoral and educational* (pp. 253–273). The Columba Press.

Cochrane, F. (2020). *Brexit and Northern Ireland*. Manchester University Press.

Department of Education of Northern Ireland (DENI). (1989). *The education reform (Northern Ireland) order 1989*. Retrieved from https://www.legislation.gov.uk/nisi/1989/2406/contents

Donaldson, A. (2007). Catholic education at the crossroads: Issues facing Catholic schools in Northern Ireland. In G. R. Grace & S. J. O'Keefe (Eds.), *International handbook of Catholic education: Challenges for school systems in the 21st century*, Part One (pp. 231–248). Springer.

Duffy, G., & Gallagher, T. (2017). Shared education in contested spaces: How collaborative networks improve communities and schools. *Journal of Educational Change, 18*, 107–134.

Emerson, N. (2021). North needs a new policy on integrated education. *The Irish Times*, April 1.

Foster, R. F. (2008). *Luck and the Irish*. Penguin.

Franchi, L., & Rymarz, R. (2017). The education and formation of teachers for Catholic schools: Responding to changed cultural contexts. *International Studies in Catholic Education, 9*(1), 2–16.

Francis, L. J., McKenna, U., & Lewis, C. A. (2020). (2020) Shifts in denominational differences in student attitude toward Christianity in Northern Ireland 1979–2011. *Journal of Religious Education, 68*, 409–415.

Gallagher, E., & Worrall, S. (1982). *Christians in Ulster 1968–1980*. Oxford University Press.

Gallagher, T. (2005). Faith schools in Northern Ireland: A review of research. In R. Gardner, J. Cairns, & D. Lawton (Eds.), *Faith schools: Consensus or conflict?* (p. 2005). Routledge.

Gracie, A. J. (2021). Healing the scars of conflict: Teaching religious education in post-conflict Northern Ireland. In Z. Matevski (Ed.), *The role of religion in peace and conflict* (pp. 65–77). Cambridge Scholars Publishing.

Gribben, C. (2021). *The rise and fall of Christian Ireland*. Oxford University Press.

Hagan, M., & Eaton, P. (2020). Teacher education in Northern Ireland: Reasons to be cheerful or a 'Wicked Problem'? *Teacher Development, 24*(2), 258–273.

Hagan, M. (2016). Learning and teaching in a Catholic college: the importance of ethos. A study in Northern Ireland. *International studies in Catholic education, 8*(1), 102–119. https://doi.org/10.1080/19422539.2016.1140425

Hansson, U., & Roulston, S. (2020). Integrated and shared education: Sinn Féin, the Democratic Unionist Party and educational change in Northern Ireland. *Policy Futures in Education, 19*(6), 730–746. https://doi.org/10.1177%2F1478210320965060

Hughes, J. (2011). Are separate schools divisive? A case study from Northern Ireland. *British Educational Research Journal, 37*(5), 829–851.

Hurley, S. J. M. (2002). Northern Ireland and the Post-Vatican II ecumenical journey. In D. Keogh & B. Bradshaw (Eds.), *Christianity in Ireland: Revisiting the story* (pp. 259–270). The Columba Press.

Jackson, A. (2010). *Ireland 1798–1998* (2nd ed.). Wiley.

Kieran, P., Parker-Jenkins, M., & Ryan, A. (2022). Religions and beliefs in changing times: perspectives of student stakeholders in third-level educational contexts in the Republic of Ireland and Northern Ireland. British Journal of Religious Education, 44(1), 38–52. https://doi.org/10.1080/01416200.2020.1775552

McGrath, M. (2000). *The Catholic Church in Northern Ireland. The price of faith*. Irish Academic Press.

McKeever, M. (2017). *One man, one God: The peace ministry of Fr Alec Reid CSsR*. Redemptorist Communications.

McKeown, D. B. (2011): *Address at the launch of Northern Ireland Catholic schools week 2011*. Retrieved from http://www.catholicbishops.ie/2011/01/24/address-by-bishop-donal-mc-keown-at-northern-ireland-launch-of-catholic-schools-week-2011/

Meredith, R. (2019). *Catholic teaching qualification offered by Stranmillis, June 7*. Retrieved from https://www.bbc.com/news/uk-northern-ireland-48559429

Moran, A. (2012). Crises as catalysts for change: Re-energising teacher education in Northern Ireland. *Educational Research, 54*(2), 137–147.

O'Leary, B. (2019), *A treatise on Northern Ireland, Volume 3: Consociation and confederation*. Oxford: Oxford University Press.

Pick and mix: Northern Ireland's segregated schools (2021). *The Economist*, July 31, 17–18.

Richardson, N. (2019). *Education and reconciliation: reflections on the journey*. Corrymeela Press. Retrieved from N-Richardson-Reflections-on-Journey.pdf (corrymeela.org)

Robinson, P. (2010): In G. Moriarty (Ed.), NI education system a 'form of apartheid', says Robinson, *The Irish Times*, October 16.

Scull, M. M. (2019). *The Catholic Church and The Northern Ireland troubles, 1968–1998*. Oxford University Press.

Smith, C., et al. (2014). *Young Catholic America: Emerging adults in, out of and gone from the Church*. Oxford University Press.

St Mary's University College. (2021). *Religious education certificate*. Retrieved from https://www.stmarys-belfast.ac.uk/academic/re.asp

Taylor, C. (2007). *A secular age*. Harvard University Press.

The Catholic Bishops of Northern Ireland. (2001) *Building peace shaping the future*. Retrieved from https://www.catholicbishops.ie/wp-content/uploads/images/docs/buildingpeace_october.pdf

Transforming Education—Ulster University Briefing Paper. (2021). *Community division and student separation in initial teacher education*. Retrieved from https://www.ulster.ac.uk/research/topic/education/unesco-centre/research/transforming-education

Trueman, C. R. (2020). *The rise of the modern self: Cultural amnesia, expressive individualism and the road to sexual revolution*. Crossway.

Tuohy, D. (2013). *Denominational education and politics: Ireland in a European context*. Veritas

Twenge, J. (2017). *iGen: Why today's super-connected kids are growing up less rebellious, more tolerant, less happy- and completely unprepared for adulthood (and what this means for the rest of us)*. Atria Books.

Niall Coll is a priest of the Diocese of Raphoe in Ireland serving in Donegal Town. He is a former senior lecturer in Religious Studies and Religious Education at St Mary's University College, Belfast (a College of Queen's University Belfast). He is the author of *Christ in eternity and time: Modern Anglican perspectives* (2001), Dublin: Four Courts Press; the co-editor (with Paschal Scallon CM), *A Church with a Future: Challenges to Irish Catholicism today* (2005), Dublin: The Columba Press; the editor, *Ireland and Vatican II: Essays theological, pastoral and educational* (2015), Dublin: The Columba Press. He is a member of the Irish Inter-Church Committee. His research areas of late concern the Second Vatican Council and its reception in Ireland and interreligious education. niallcoll30@gmail.com

Chapter 3
Catholic Teacher Formation in Scotland

Roisín Coll and Stephen Reilly

Abstract Catholic Teacher Education in Scotland contributes to an internationally recognised and acclaimed national education system, in one of the few countries in the world where denominational education is fully supported and funded by the state. The Catholic Teacher Education mission is located within the School of Education of one of Scotland's ancient universities, which accepts the responsibility as 'sole provider' of teachers for Scottish Catholic schools despite the university's secular character. This chapter explores the tensions and mutual benefits inherent in such a partnership between Church and university. It charts the opportunities arising from the national policy shift towards teaching as a Masters-level profession and the scope for intercultural dialogue amongst Catholic students and their peers. It also appraises the challenges to the ongoing Catholic identity of teacher education, the maintenance of a critical mass of committed and highly qualified Catholic teachers and the strategy required to inspire the next generation of Catholic teacher educators who will carry forward the mission.

Keywords Catholic Teacher Education · Intercultural dialogue · Catholic teacher identity · Mission integrity · Catholic educational philosophy

3.1 Introduction

Catholic Teacher Education in Scotland continues to be of interest to those engaged in academic discourse on the nature and value of Catholic education owing to its locus and contribution to an internationally recognised and acclaimed national education system. It is worth acknowledging the significance of the wider educational context in Scotland given it is one of the few countries in the world where denominational

R. Coll · S. Reilly (✉)
St Andrew's Building, 11 Eldon Street, Glasgow G3 6NH, UK
e-mail: Stephen.Reilly@glasgow.ac.uk

R. Coll
e-mail: Roisin.Coll@glasgow.ac.uk

education is fully supported and funded by the state. This rare characteristic differentiates Catholic Education in Scotland from other countries for a range of reasons including the wide variety of social backgrounds of the community that Catholic schools in Scotland and those working within them serve (Paterson, 2020). This distinctiveness has attracted the attention of academic scholars from within the field of Catholic Education and beyond.

Despite recent PISA reports indicating a shift in performance in certain subject areas, Scotland continues to be recognised globally as a country that performs at "a consistently very high standard" in terms of education, and a particular stage of the education of Scotland's teachers—its induction scheme—has been admired internationally and praised as being "world-class" (OECD, 2007). Teacher Education is regularly in the spotlight when discussing or assessing the achievements of education systems and international evidence suggests, unsurprisingly, that the "foundations of successful education lie in the quality of teachers and their leadership" (Donaldson, 2010: 3). In Scotland, all student teachers are subject to academically rigorous undergraduate or postgraduate Initial Teacher Education (ITE) programmes, and Catholic Teacher Education is located within such programmes. Given Catholic schools in Scotland educate nearly a quarter of the country's school children, Catholic Teacher Education's relationship with Initial Teacher Education in Scotland is of national interest and therefore worthy of continued reflection, discussion and review. This chapter provides a welcome opportunity for doing just that.

3.2 History

McKinney and McCluskey (2019) and others have traced the history of Catholic education and schooling in Scotland, placing its origins as far back as the mid sixth century to the establishment of monasteries and seminaries by St Columba and possibly even further back to St Ninian. Whilst other forms of education evolved over subsequent centuries, one of the most significant developments in the history of Scottish Education was the establishment of the universities of St Andrew's, Glasgow and Aberdeen in the fifteenth century—all of which were founded as "ecclesial institutions" and given university status by a series of Papal Bulls (*ibid*: 14). Education in Scotland continued to develop at all levels, but it isn't until the end of the 18th century when historians report that Catholic schools were established (Prunier, 2009), and it is not until the nineteenth century that the discipline of *Catholic Teacher Education* in Scotland comes sharply into focus and is highlighted as a pressing need.

The nineteenth century influx of Irish to Scotland, searching for employment or fleeing famines, resulted in a significant rise in the Catholic population—almost doubling it—and the need to provide appropriate education. Dilworth (1978) tracked the wave of religious orders that were encouraged to come to Scotland during this century to engage in Catholic schooling, yet, despite their dedication to Catholic education and the positive impact this had, there was still a notable shortage of qualified Catholic teachers. This was intensified by the 1872 Education (Scotland) Act which established a National Education System in the country, and despite the Catholic Church withholding the transfer of its schools for another 46 years (to protect their denominational status), education became compulsory, and simultaneously, the expectation of the quality of teaching in the country was raised. McKinney and McCluskey (2019) report that during this period, there was considerable strain placed on the Catholic school regarding Catholic teacher supply, and in trying to address the matter, there was an over-reliance on an unsustainable 'pupil–teachers' system which had been set up support children's early education (p. 20). Some wealthy families were able to send members to teacher training establishments run by religious orders in England; however, the turn of the century saw a further change in Scotland's expectation of teacher education (two years study at a college or university) which meant that an English qualification was no longer acceptable in Scotland (Fitzpatrick, 1995). The arrival of the Sisters of Notre Dame de Namur in Glasgow and their establishment of a Catholic Teacher Training College in 1895 began to address the shortfall of appropriately qualified Catholic teachers. Dowanhill in the west end of Glasgow was chosen as the site for this residential college. The location of the college was significant for a number of reasons: Glasgow and the surrounding area was a hub of Catholicism and contained many Catholic schools requiring the support and service of teachers, but the insightful and ambitious Sisters of Notre Dame de Namur chose to situate a national Catholic teacher training college a few streets away from one of the most influential educational establishments in the country—the University of Glasgow—giving the sisters and their students access to its extra-mural courses (Kehoe, 2019). The sisters were committed to a vision of education with a distinctive Catholic identity but one that also engaged with the world, welcomed and debated secular knowledge and embraced both tradition and modernity. It is evident then that academic rigour and excellence were key features of the emerging vision of Catholic Teacher Education for this country.

The passing of the 1918 Education (Scotland) Act is arguably one of the most significant events in the history of Catholic education in Scotland since it has safeguarded the denominational character of Catholic schools in the country for over a century and resulted in the social mobilisation and integration of Catholics into Scottish society. The Church had made the decision not to transfer its schools to the national system in 1872; however, in 1918, it accepted a very different invitation—to transfer *and* keep the distinctive faith character of the school. It remained in control of the RE curriculum and the *selection* of appropriately trained teachers (in terms of their 'belief and character'), but the state now assumed responsibility for all financial concerns including the employment of staff (Scotch Education Department, 1918). This resulted in class sizes being smaller and teachers in Catholic schools having equal pay to those teaching in the nondenominational sector. The ramifications of the passing of this Act for the Catholic community have been well documented particularly in relation to its social mobility (see, for example, Cullen, 2019; Fitzpatrick, 1995; O'Hagan, 1996; O'Hagan & Davis, 2007), but perhaps, one consequence of the passing of this Act that has been understated is how Catholic Teacher Education suddenly became of national significance. This new partnership between Church and state was to play out not only in relation to what happened in schools but what happened in the Catholic teacher educational establishments that were—or would be in the future—producing teachers for these schools. Notre Dame, along with all other teacher education institutions, was placed under the control of the National Committee for the Training of Teachers. A healthy and respectful working relationship with the state already existed since the Sisters had established quite skilfully a "collaborative and harmonious" rapport based on a mutual understanding of the necessity for a high standard of teacher training and education (O'Hagan, 2006, p. 245). Such a relationship would prove to serve them well when control on these matters eventually passed to the state.

After the 1918 Act, the standardised national expectations of teachers coupled with the high aspirations of such highly skilled teacher educators—the Sisters of Notre Dame—resulted in Catholic women being educated into 'white-collar' positions in Scottish society for the first time in history (O'Hagan, 2006). This contributed to the raising of expectations of the Catholic community, and Catholic schools began to flourish across the country. Now that salaries for Catholic teachers were elevated to be on a par with that of others, and paid for by the state, teaching became an attractive option for many. No longer did the Church have to rely on religious men and women to teach in Catholic schools which had helped to keep costs to a minimum. The reduction in class size and the expansion of Catholic education, particularly in the secondary sector, resulted in an urgent need for more qualified Catholic teachers, and in 1920, the Scotch Education Department agreed to the establishment of a second Catholic teacher training College in Edinburgh, Craiglockhart, which was founded by the Sisters of the Society of the Sacred Heart.

3.3 From College to University Provision

Two mergers have occurred since the establishment of these teacher training colleges, developments that have had a significant impact on the status of Catholic Teacher Education in Scotland. Both Notre Dame and Craiglockhart continued to produce Catholic teachers for the Catholic state sector until the 1970s, when retaining, while a national review of teacher training in the country proposed the number of institutions be reduced (McKinney, 2020). After considerable deliberation, it was agreed by the Church and the secretary of State for Education that the two Catholic colleges would merge to become one national Catholic College–St Andrew's College of Education. It was opened in Bearsden, Glasgow, in September 1981 and educated student teachers for almost twenty years.

St Andrew's College then merged with the University of Glasgow (UoG) in 1999 after two years of negotiations. Emerging funding pressures on the Scottish Higher Education Funding Council throughout the 1990s, allied with an increased perception of the advantages of teacher education entering the university system, resulted in all of the Scottish colleges of education merging with their university neighbours in that period (Humes, 2020). In the case of Glasgow, the merger engendered much trepidation on both sides, with fear of a loss of Catholic identity by voices in the Catholic educational community, and worry on the part of the existing UoG Department of Adult and Continuing Education about a wholesale takeover of the current educational provision by St Andrew's structures and staff, as well as interference by the institutional Catholic Church. Such fears resulted in "very public and sometimes heated interchanges." (McKinney, 2020, p. 174).

The merger document established the new Faculty of Education as the 'sole provider' of Catholic teachers for Catholic schools in Scotland, thus establishing a new partnership between the Catholic Church in Scotland and the university. Therein lay an obvious advantage for the Church, that the teaching staff of Catholic schools would comprise graduates of a highly prestigious Russell Group university, one which regularly ranks as amongst the top 100 universities in the world (THE, 2022). Nonetheless lingering doubts remained about the ability to sustain the Catholic identity of ITE for Catholic students.

As part of the merger agreement, smooth relations between the new faculty and the Scottish Catholic Church would be managed and fostered by a Board of Catholic Education, consisting of representatives from all stakeholders: head teachers, bishops, university management, and Faculty staff and students. The board continues to monitor all aspects of Catholic Teacher Education including courses, student admissions, and school practicum. Subsequently, in 2010, the newly renamed School of Education (SoE) established the St Andrew's Foundation for Catholic Teacher Education as "the home of Catholic Teacher Education in Scotland": to oversee the formation of Catholic Initial Teacher Education students, to stimulate research and scholarship, foster ongoing formation and leadership amongst Catholic teachers and act as guardian of Catholic educational heritage (University of Glasgow, 2021). The foundation is composed of School of Education staff members, including a Director, and a Co-ordinator of Spiritual and Pastoral Formation who is a Catholic priest.

The Board and Foundation reflect the specific history and mission of the SoE and the recognition on the part of university and Church of the need for clarity of roles, structural stability and a forum for dialogue in maintenance of the unique mission to Catholic education. As noted, the board's existence also reflects the fraught atmosphere surrounding the merger negotiations and the need to maintain trust and transparency amongst stakeholders both then and now. In addition, the establishment of the Foundation demonstrates the difficulty of maintaining a distinct Catholic identity over a number of decades in the midst of a large secular university, without a dedicated body to promote it.

3.3.1 Fulfilling the Mandate

Initial Teacher Education (ITE) at the SoE is undertaken via one of three programmes: the 5-year undergraduate-integrated Masters in Primary Education (MEduc), the 5-year undergraduate-integrated Masters in Technology Education

(MTech), and the Postgraduate Diploma in Education (PGDE). Cognisant of the sole provider status and the mission to Catholic education, the School offers the possibility of studying for the Catholic Teacher's Certificate in Religious Education (CTC)—which qualifies graduates to teach RE in Catholic schools—during the programme of study. An MEduc student would, for example, follow an integrated pathway through their studies which would include mandatory courses in Theology in Education, Catholic Teacher Formation, and Catholic religious educational pedagogy, as well as undertaking school practicum in Catholic primary schools including a school visit by a university tutor to assess their teaching of RE. PGDE students undertake a partially integrated pathway which consists of an Applied Theology and RE pedagogy courses plus Catholic school practicum and assessed RE teaching. MTech students gain the CTC via the long-standing online certificate in Religious Education by Distance Learning (Credl) course offered by the School.

The past few years have seen the growth of a multiplicity of extra routes to gain the CTC, entailing flexibility and creative thinking. Until 2017, students and qualified teachers could gain the CTC in only two ways: by studying at Glasgow University, or via the online Credl course. In that year, negotiations opened with the Schools of Education at the Universities of Aberdeen, Edinburgh and Strathclyde to offer the CTC to their PGDE students, with Glasgow staff travelling to those universities' campuses to teach the course. The course has subsequently been extended to the University of Dundee and the University of the West of Scotland. The UoG SoE also took over an existing course for qualified teachers run by the Scottish Catholic Education Service, entitled Setting Out on the Road, which is taught via intensive teaching days and monthly journal tasks. These developments have caused the annual number of CTC awards to multiply threefold, increasing the number of suitably qualified Catholic teachers and strengthening the position of the foundation. At the same time, they have raised inevitable questions around UoG admissions policy and the inability of Catholic students to study on UoG programmes: questions often aired at the Board of Catholic Education on behalf of the Bishops' Conference and Catholic schools.

3.3.2 Masters-Level ITE Provision

A further mark of the current ITE scene in Scotland is the increasing expectation of masters-level qualification amongst teachers and the response of ITE providers to this trend (Kennedy & Carse, 2020). Amongst the recommendations of the highly influential Donaldson report, entitled 'Teaching Scotland's Future' was an increased focus on postgraduate study amongst teachers to enhance professionalism and increase professional development (Donaldson, 2010). In a further development, Scottish Government policy throughout the late 2010s encouraged universities to enable students to complete a masters degree either during their ITE studies or within their induction year.

The Scottish Schools of Education have responded to the masters agenda in various ways, with one of the most striking responses being the SoE at Glasgow. As well as the majority of credits in the one-year PGDE programme being taught at masters level (90 credits at SQF Level 11), the school has established an integrated 5-year masters programme, entitled MEduc, to replace the Bachelor in Education as the standard undergraduate teacher education programme. Whilst students can exit after 4 years with an Honours degree in education with teaching qualification, the expectation is that they complete the programme by submitting a masters dissertation. Such a development at Glasgow further enhances the potential of Catholic schools in Scotland to be staffed by very highly qualified graduates. It might be noted, however, that the students graduating via the MEduc programme are in the minority vis-a-vis those pursuing the PGDE programme, and that (as Kennedy and Carse note), the evidence that masters-qualified graduates make better teachers is sparse.

Nonetheless, the turn towards masters-level provision in ITE opens an exciting space to encourage students to engage in deeper study of the Catholic educational tradition. The Foundation has recently established an elective course in Catholic educational philosophy in the 4th year of the MEduc programme, with a view to encouraging students to write their masters dissertation on a Catholic educational theme. The results of this encouragement remain to be verified in future years.

3.4 Challenges and Opportunities

The overview of the history of the merger and the development of the St Andrew's Foundation and ITE for Catholic students at Glasgow in early twenty-first century has thrown into relief the many challenges and opportunities ahead. The first set revolves around the location of ITE provision for Catholic students within the secular university, extending now to multiple universities around Scotland.

3.4.1 In but not of the Secular University

The SoE lies fully within the wider secular university structure yet retains a particular mission to Catholic education. As we have seen, the merger of St Andrew's College with the university was not a simple relocation but a merger with an existing educational unit of the university, meaning that the former college was immediately positioned in a secular negotiated space rather than carving a Catholic enclave, a situation not always understood in the Scottish Catholic educational community. Nonetheless in the early post-merger years, the staff, culture and historical memory of the new SoE was dominated by the college. Over the past 20 years, the retirement of former—and recruitment of new—staff coupled with the inevitable alignment with UoG policies, initiatives and structures has changed the face of the SoE. The composition of the student body has also evolved so that the majority of ITE students are no longer Catholic (decreasing from around 95% Catholic in the 2000s to around 40% today).

As noted, the establishment of the St Andrew's Foundation both served to acknowledge the reality of such a progressively secular cultural realignment and also provided a structure around which the Catholic intellectual and pastoral presence could coalesce. As Gerald Grace notes, faith-based educational bodies are vulnerable to mission drift, "an unintentional historical process which causes a school in its practices to move away from its foundational mission principles," overtime when held to secular standards and promised secular rewards (2009, p. 490). Maintaining what Grace calls 'mission integrity', requires intentionality and vigilance backed by policy, personnel and structure (2002). His definition of mission integrity—"fidelity in practice and not just in public rhetoric to the distinctive and authentic principles of Roman Catholic education" (2002, p. 498)—underlines that in order to survive and to fulfil its mission to the students, a key challenge for the Foundation is the formulation, articulation and dissemination a vision of Catholic educational philosophy.

3.4.2 Catholic Educational Philosophy

Rooted in revelation and expressed in magisterial documents and the work of Catholic educational scholars, Catholic educational philosophy rests on a vision of the human person and of the good life. Much as grace builds on nature, it embraces sound secular educational theory but, "expands and infuses it with a particular sensibility rooted in Catholic, rather than secular, philosophy and anthropology" (Morey, 2012, p. 397). Lydon summarises its essential pillars as the dignity of the individual, the call to human flourishing, and the promise of divine destiny (2018, ix).

To this, we might add the following characteristics of its educational vision:

- it is rooted in a Catholic ontology—understanding of what is real—and epistemology—how the real can be known (McKinney, 2011). Its hallmark is an optimistic faith in the data of the senses and the ability of the human mind to apprehend, study and grasp knowledge, thus becoming an affirmation of academic integrity (Kieran & Hession, 2005).
- it affirms the basic unity of knowledge since all that is real has its origin in God, and there are 'seeds of the Word' everywhere. It is therefore sceptical of the post-modern atomisation of knowledge and the temptations to overly favour specialisation in 'silos' in the university faculty over a humanising synthesis at the service of the common good and ethical ends.
- it contextualises conceptions of human achievement and the Good Life within the universal call to holiness, eternal life, communion and community, rooted in the Trinity as source all that exists. It thus promotes holistic growth which includes the spiritual and religious dimensions of the person.

- in Catholic schooling, it assists rather than replaces the parents and family as primary educators so that "The school is the community where the family is assisted in the integral education of the child" (Rymarz & Franchi, 2019, p. 15).
- Jesus Christ at placed at centre of the educational project, as a model to "teach us the art of living" (Hession, 2015, p. 72), and as the Way to the Father.

As members of university staff and also passionate advocates of Catholic education, Foundation staff can bring the Catholic vision into dialogue with other educational philosophies in the School of Education and also serve the Catholic educational community by articulating its spiritual and theoretical foundations. As engagement with parish life and liturgy dwindles in the Scottish Catholic community—as elsewhere in the global North—and as Catholic disaffiliation grows (Bullivant, 2019), a solid understanding of the distinctive basis and aims of Catholic schooling may increasingly serve to justify the existence of the sector.

The Foundation and Board also contain the potential to model the maintenance of an outward-looking but hard-fought negotiated space for Catholic education within the secular sphere, a space also inhabited by Catholic schools, being entirely state funded and subject to state policy, agendas and priorities.

3.4.3 Tools for Dialogue Amongst Students

As noted above, the CTC allows to some degree for a Catholic pathway through ITE for the Catholic students. Nonetheless the overall educational vision studied will be that common to Catholic and nondenominational schools, within programmes in which the Catholic students will be a minority. Although the minority status may seem a disadvantage, therein lies a fruitful opportunity, one which reflects recent thinking within the Congregation for Catholic Education. Its 2013 document invites Catholic schools to be sites of respectful intercultural dialogue, recognising that Catholic schools globally welcome students of varying faiths. The document also wisely notes that in dialogue, we become more aware of our own beliefs, as they have to be articulated rather than presumed (Congregation, 2013, paras 13–18). It behoves the foundation, the Catholic schools in which the students undertake practicum, and the wider Catholic community, to foster a vision, a language and a vocational awareness that will allow Catholic ITE students to dialogue and grow alongside their nondenominational colleagues, whilst also equipping them for the challenges of Catholic teaching.

Nonetheless the work of Coll and Franchi/Rymarz has helped to crystallise the challenges in equipping Catholic ITE students with tools for dialogue. Coll's studies of Scottish Catholic ITE students unveiled a lack of intentionality in choosing to teach in Catholic schools, where the choice was considered somewhat automatic, due more to their own social and familial background in the Catholic community and their attendance at Catholic schools as pupils (2007a, 2007b). Clearly, such lack of reflection and the sense of drift into the only system they have known, will hamper

Catholic students in explaining and debating the merits of Catholic schools and in forming their own mission identity. As one response, the essential importance of imbuing the courses leading to the Catholic Teachers' Certificate with a Catholic educational philosophy has already been explored. Another fruitful avenue consists of students being exposed to the history of Catholic schooling in Scotland during their studies, allowing a practical appraisal of Catholic schools' value, and aiding students in developing their identity as Catholic teachers. As McKinney and McCluskey note, "The historical narrative which any community inherits is often closely tied to that community's shared sense of identity" (2020, p. 2). In their survey of the post-1918 historical development of Scottish Catholic schools, they trace the role of schools in transforming a poor, unskilled immigrant community into one integrated into the Scottish mainstream. Paterson, in a study of schooling outcomes from 1950 to 2010, further specifies the strong role of Catholic state secondary schools in closing the attainment gap with nondenominational schools in terms of post-16 school completion and academic attainment in the comprehensive school system era, thus increasing attainment and social mobility amongst their graduates (2020). An awareness of the successful history of Catholic state schooling in Scotland allied to a familiarity with Catholic educational philosophy may provide a powerful approach to building mission identity amongst Catholic ITE students, whilst helping to form their own educational philosophy. The foundation's pastoral, spiritual and community-building activities can also contribute to identity formation and the initiation into a community of practice (Reilly & Lappin, 2020; Reilly et al., 2019).

Franchi and Rymarz have raised another challenge for Catholic ITE students as they seek to build their professional identity and construct tools for dialogue: a lack of theological language and literacy. In drawing conclusions for Catholic education from their overview of worldviews amongst young Catholics and the precipitous decline in participation in faith practice, they call for a substantial investment in the theological education of Catholic student teachers (2017). Their subsequent empirical research amongst beginning Catholic teachers in Australia found an enthusiasm for working in a Catholic school and for teaching RE. Nonetheless, the teachers' lack of specialist religious knowledge and confidence leads the authors to recommend ongoing religious preparation and support, coupled with the fostering of a supportive faith network often lacking out with school (2019). In similar vein, Coll specifically references the current Scottish RE syllabus 'This is Our Faith', whose catechetical style and rigour demands a breadth of theological knowledge and expertise from the teacher, leading her to recommend the establishment of a national structured system of professional ongoing development on the part of Church, schools and state (2015).

The need for serious theological study as part of Catholic ITE preparation is thus highlighted. Whilst the CTC courses at Glasgow are heavily theological, it would seem prudent to reframe the development of theological literacy as a lifelong task, aided by the current national educational policy focus on continuous professional learning and supportive networks. A challenge and opportunity for the Foundation and the wider Catholic educational community could be to build and support career-long theological and pastoral formation opportunities. The Foundation's recent development of knowledge transfer events such as its Theology Thursdays series for non-specialist participants is a welcome move in this direction towards ongoing formation, but a refreshed career-long professional learning catalogue and Catholic Masters programme would also respond to this emerging need for lifelong theological growth.

3.4.4 Maintaining Critical Mass

A further challenge for those engaged in Catholic Teacher Education in Scotland is the need to maintain a critical mass of appropriately qualified teachers for the Catholic sector. The issue is not in relation to the number of applicants for the ITE courses, which remains healthy; however, the significant expectations of the University of Glasgow of its students coupled with its global reputation result in a highly competitive application process for its programmes. Such high aspirations for the teaching profession are reflected in the entry tariffs elsewhere in the country, but the attraction of studying a degree at an ancient Russell Group University, in a School of Education that sits in the top 50 in the world, is reflected in the quality and quantity of applicants. The pool of potential students to be educated for the Catholic sector is reduced by the high expectations of both Church and university—essentially, only, the highest achieving, practising Catholics have the chance of receiving an offer. Furthermore, there are other competing career choices with similar entry tariffs for such high-fliers in the Catholic community, and many have more attractive salary propositions (see Healy's recent study (2020) which highlights the continued rise of young Catholics in the legal and medical professions in Scotland).

Had the Sisters of Notre Dame, in 1894, known that over a century after the opening of their college in Dowanhill, Catholic Teacher Education in Scotland would be the concern of one of the world's leading academic establishments; there is no doubt they would have considered this a substantial accomplishment. However, such an achievement is not without its challenges, and the decline in numbers of those securing a place on an ITE programme has raised questions about the adequate provision of teachers in Catholic schools for the future. One way of addressing this matter would be to reduce the entry requirements for Catholic applicants; however, this would signal to Scottish society a lower expectation of academic standards of the Catholic teacher workforce compared with their nondenominational counterparts. This is unacceptable for a number of reasons, particularly in a climate where there is a continuing emphasis, post Donaldson (2010), on enhancing teacher professionalism as has been illustrated in the masters-level ITE qualifications referred to earlier. To reconsider the expectation of faith adherence of teachers in Catholic schools would be to change the purpose, nature and vision of Catholic Education in Scotland and of Religious Education too. Other Catholic school systems across the world operate successfully without the requirement for staff to be Catholic, instead reserving that condition for certain posts—usually in senior management—however, studies have concluded that maintaining a distinctively Catholic identity can be challenging in such schools (Pollefeyt & Bouwans, 2012). Safeguarding the distinctive faith identity of Catholic schools has been a driver of the Catholic Church in Scotland since its first schools were established and its current expectation that all head teachers, depute head teachers, and teachers of religious education (which includes all primary teachers) in the Catholic school are committed members of the Catholic faith has ensured the continued strength of that distinctive faith identity.

Of course, this raises questions as to what is meant by faith *commitment*? And what is meant by the term 'practising Catholic'? In recent years, the St Andrew's Foundation recognised the vast range of levels of faith commitment of those applying for the Catholic Teacher's Certificate. This has been further illuminated owing to the honesty of the applicants who seek guidance when trying to obtain a reference from a priest (part of the application process requires a statement from a priest who is asked to attest to the applicant's suitability to teach in the Catholic school). This, for many potential students, has been a stumbling block, and by way of supporting the applicants, the Foundation has delayed the submission of the reference from the point of application to halfway through the course. This has given students the space to reengage with their faith and has enabled a period of discernment where they have been encouraged to have conversations with a priest about their faith journey and commitment. Anecdotally, this space has been of benefit to many, and rather than considering the reference as a potential barrier to being accepted onto a programme, it has been used as a supportive mechanism for helping students to reengage with their faith and parish community. The testimony from the priest can also be viewed as a helpful reminder to the students that, when they do eventually qualify as a teacher and wish to seek employment in the Catholic sector, they will require another reference from their priest to enable the diocese to approve them to work there. Some of the ramifications of asking for a reference at the student stage of their Catholic teacher journey include it operating as a tool to initiate a conversation and trigger a relationship with the priest and parish, a rapport that may continue through to NQT stage and beyond.

3.4.5 Building Capacity

A recent shift in the working of the Board of Catholic Education has enabled some of the above challenges to be discussed and, in some cases, addressed. In between the triannual meetings, smaller working parties convene to deliberate particular aspects of the Board's remit (i.e. admissions and recruitment, staff development, monitoring of courses and quality assurance, and student placements). This very positive modification to how the BCE functions has enabled focussed, strategic conversations about key areas of Catholic Teacher Education, many of which consider its future. One such discussion has been the need to build capacity and to anticipate a new generation of committed and well qualified Catholic teacher educators. Currently, the majority of those responsible for teaching Catholic ITE students have been educated to postgraduate masters or doctoral level, many of whom are members of the university's professoriate. The legacy of having highly skilled and well-educated teacher educators remains intact, but there is a responsibility for the current cohort of Catholic teacher educators to instil in the new generation of Catholic teachers an appetite for research in the field and a desire to engage in postgraduate studies and international academic collaborations. The challenge then is to nurture any evident enthusiasm and passion for Catholic education and to carve academic pathways for those demonstrating a commitment to, and interest in, the field. The undergraduate 4th year elective referred to earlier is one such example of how such an eagerness to learn more about Catholic education can be encouraged and supported. However, Catholic student–teachers have a range of areas for potential focus in terms of their elective choice and masters dissertation emphasis. Catholic Education, as a field of study, must compete with these and may not be the first choice for many. It is, therefore, a fundamental objective for current Catholic teacher educators to continue to present to students Catholic Education as an interesting, rigorous and stimulating option, worthy of study. (At the time of writing, the 4th year undergraduate Catholic education elective is full! This is testimony to its reputation, established by current staff.)

3.5 Conclusion

Scotland is in an enviable position in terms of its Catholic Teacher Education provision; however, the contemporary challenges presented in this chapter demonstrate the necessity to avoid complacency but rather to emulate the vision, academic drive and pragmatism fostered by the first Catholic teacher educators at the end of the nineteenth century. The University of Glasgow has established excellent working relationships with both the Bishops' Conference of Scotland and the Scottish Government, predominantly through the work of the St Andrew's Foundation for Catholic Teacher Education and the Board of Catholic Education. It will continue to work with these key partners and stakeholders and address operational challenges affecting its provision as they arise. As it grapples with some of the internal philosophical challenges, an important focus for St Andrew's Foundation is to continue to be outward looking—to engage in dialogue on such matters in an international forum and to listen to and learn from those colleagues committed to Catholic Teacher Education from around the world.

References

Bullivant, S. (2019). *Mass exodus: Catholic disaffiliation in Britain and America since Vatican II*. OUP.

Coll, R. (2007a). Student teachers' perception of their role and responsibilities as Catholic educators. *European Journal of Teacher Education, 30*(4), 445–465.

Coll, R. (2007b). The struggle for the soul. Implications for the identity of Catholic teachers. *Journal of Religious Education, 55*(3), 46–53.

Coll, R. (2015). Catholic religious education in Scotland: bridging the gap between teacher education and curriculum delivery. In: M. T. Buchanan & A.-M. Gellel (Eds.), *Global perspectives of catholic religious education in schools* (pp. 179–193). Springer.

Congregation for Catholic Education. (2013). *Educating to intercultural dialogue in Catholic schools—Living in harmony for a civilization of love.* Retrieved February 14, 2021, from http://www.vatican.va/roman_curia/congregations/ccatheduc/documents/rc_con_cca theduc_doc_20131028_dialogo-interculturale_en.html

Cullen, M. (2019). 1918: A panacea for Catholic education in Scotland? Open House Issue No 279, December 2018/January 2019, pp. 5–6. https://openhousescotland.co.uk/downloads/back_i ssues/22-1642953797.pdf

Donaldson, G. (2010). *Teaching Scotland's future—Report of a review of teacher education in Scotland.* Retrieved February 14, 2021, from http://www.gov.scot/resource/doc/337626/0110852. pdf

Fitzpatrick, T. A. (1995). *No mean service: Scottish Catholic teacher education 1895–1995.* St Andrew's College Publications.

Franchi, L., & Rymarz, R. (2017). The education and formation of teachers for Catholic schools: Responding to changed cultural contexts. *International Studies in Catholic Education, 9*(1), 2–16.

Grace, G. (2002). Mission integrity: contemporary challenges for Catholic school leaders. In K. Leithwood & P. Hallinger (Eds.). *Second international handbook of educational leadership and administration.* Kluwer Academic Press.

Grace, G. (2009). Faith school leadership: A neglected sector of in-service education in the United Kingdom. *Professional Development in Education, 35*(3), 485–494.

Healy, F. (2020). Survey of a diasporic Irish community using a social network. *National Identities, 22*(1), 63–89.

Hession, A. (2015). *Catholic primary religious education in a pluralist environment.* Veritas.

Humes, W. (2020). Re-shaping teacher preparation in Scotland: Curricular, institutional and professional changes, 1920–2000, in R. Shanks (Ed.), *Teacher preparation in Scotland.* Emerald Publishing Limited.

Kehoe S. K. (2019). Women Religious and the development of Scottish education. In S. McKinney & R. McCluskey (Eds.), *A history of Catholic education and schooling in Scotland.* Palgrave Macmillan.

Kennedy, A., & Carse, N. (2020). Masters-level teacher preparation. In R. Shanks (Ed.), *Teacher preparation in Scotland* (pp. 137–150). Emerald Publishing Limited.

Kieran, P. & Hession, A. (2005). *Children, Catholicism and religious education.* Veritas.

Lydon, J. (Ed.) (2018). *Contemporary perspectives on Catholic education.* Gracewing.

McKinney, S. J. (2011). A rationale for Catholic schools. In L. Franchi & S. J. McKinney (Eds.), *A companion to Catholic education* (pp. 147–161). Gracewing.

McKinney, S. J. (2020). Catholic teacher preparation. In R. Shanks (Ed.), *Teacher preparation in Scotland* (pp. 165–178). Emerald Publishing Limited.

McKinney, S. J., & McCluskey, R. (2019). Introduction. In S. McKinney & R. McCluskey (Eds.), *A history of Catholic Education and Schooling in Scotland* (pp. 1–12). London: Palgrave Macmillan. https://doi.org/10.1057/978-1-137-51370-0_1

McKinney, S. J., & McCluskey, R. (Eds.). (2020). *A history of Catholic education and schooling in Scotland: New perspectives.* Palgrave MacMillan.

Morey, M. (2012). Education in a Catholic framework. In J. J. Piderit & M. Morey (Eds.), *Teaching the tradition: Catholic themes in academic disciplines* (pp. 397–415). Oxford Scholarship Online.

O'Hagan, F. J. (1996). *Change, challenge and achievement: A study of the development of Catholic education in Glasgow in the nineteenth and twentieth centuries.* Glasgow: St Andrew's College Press.

O'Hagan, F. J. (2006). *The contribution of the religious orders to education in Glasgow during the period 1847–1918.* Lewiston, N.Y.: Edwin Mellen Press.

O'Hagan, F. J., & Davis, R. A. (2007). Forging the compact of church and state in the development of Catholic education in late nineteenth-century Scotland. *The Innes Review, 1*(1), 72–94. https://doi.org/10.1353/inn.2007.0010.

Organisation for Economic Cooperation and Development. (OECD). (2007). OECD Annual Report 2007: A comprehensive report on OECD activities in 2006–2007. https://doi.org/10.1787/annrep-2007-en

Paterson, L. (2020). Social inequality in Catholic schools in Scotland in the second half of the twentieth century. *British Journal of Sociology of Education, 41*(8), 1115–1132.

Pollefeyt, D., & Bouwens, J. (2012). *Identity in dialogue: Assessing and enhancing Catholic school identity. Research methodology and research results in Catholic schools in Victoria, Australia.* Catholic Education Commission of Victoria and Katholieke Universiteit Leuven.

Prunier, C. (2009). They must have their children educated some way': The education of Catholics in eighteenth-century Scotland. *The Innes Review, 60*(1), 22–40.

Reilly, S., Crichton, H. & Lappin, M. (2019) Pilgrimages: fruitful sources of faith formation for Catholic student teachers? In: M. T. Buchanan & A.-M. Gellel. (Eds.), *Global perspectives on Catholic religious education in schools. Volume II: Learning and leading in a pluralist world* (pp. 203–215). Springer.

Reilly, S., & Lappin, M. (2020) Formation of the heart: Memory, liturgy and the identity of Catholic student teachers. *EducA: International Catholic Journal of Education, 6*, 94–110. https://educa.fmleao.pt/no6-2021/formation-of-the-heart-memory-liturgy-and-the-identity-of-catholic-student-teachers/

Rymarz, R., & Franchi, L. (2019). *Catholic teacher preparation: Historical and contemporary perspectives on preparing for mission.* Emerald Publishing.

Scotch Education Department. (1918). Education Scotland Act (1918). https://digital.nls.uk/exams/browse/archive/143486136#?c=0&m=0&s=0&cv=0&xywh=-992%2C-83%2C2927%2C2342

Times Higher Education. (2022). *World university rankings 2022.* Times Higher Education (THE).

University of Glasgow. (2021). *The St Andrew's foundation for Catholic teacher education.* Available at https://www.gla.ac.uk/research/az/standrewsfoundation/

Roisín Coll is Director of the St Andrew's Foundation for Catholic Teacher Education at the University of Glasgow and has oversight of Catholic Teacher Education programmes in Scotland. She has taught, written and presented widely on initial teacher education, Catholic school leadership, professional and spiritual development of Catholic teachers and prayer in the Catholic school setting. She is a mother to two girls, both of whom attend a Catholic primary school. Roisin.coll@glasgow.ac.uk

Stephen Reilly is Co-ordinator of Spiritual and Pastoral Formation at the School of Education at the University of Glasgow. He teaches on many Initial Teacher Education courses in Catholic theology, curriculum and pedagogy. His research interests include the religious and spiritual development of young people, the role of the family in catechetics, the spirituality of pilgrimage and Catholic educational philosophy. He is a former parish priest, school chaplain, diocesan RE advisor, seminary teacher and pastoral centre director. Stephen.reilly@glasgow.ac.uk

Chapter 4
Catholic Teacher Formation in America

Max T. Engel

Abstract The lack of best practice standards for Catholic school teacher formation in the United States amplifies the challenge posed by the fact that most Catholic school teachers in the United States are trained in public, secular institutions, and the teachers themselves reflect the contemporary values of a secularized American culture. A large number of prospective and current teachers are therefore unprepared to teach in a school with a Catholic identity and mission. This chapter summarizes the history and current tensions of the Catholic Church in the United States and how these challenges relate to Catholic school teacher formation. The chapter proposes a process to develop Catholic school teacher formation standards based on the development of the *National Standards and Benchmarks for Effective Catholic Elementary and Secondary Schools* (NSBECS).

Keywords Catholic school · Teacher formation · Standards · United States

4.1 Introduction

The challenges of Catholic school teacher preparation and formation in the United States historically and currently reflect tensions for the American Catholic Church. A significant contemporary challenge for Catholic schools in the United States is forming Catholic school teachers in an ecclesial context that is uncertain how to coherently and consistently define what it means to be Catholic and American today. This chapter summarizes the history of Catholic school teacher preparation and formation in the United States and briefly presents current practices to prepare and form Catholic school teachers. It then posits the fundamental challenge to religious faith inherent in a contemporary worldview. This worldview is manifest in the symptoms of Catholic disaffiliation, diminished personal relevance for Catholicism, and polarized responses to these symptoms, which further exacerbate the challenges.

M. T. Engel (✉)
Creighton University, Eppley Building, 441, 2500 California Plaza, Omaha, NE 68178, USA
e-mail: MaxEngel@creighton.edu

© The Author(s), under exclusive license to Springer Nature Singapore Pte Ltd. 2022
L. Franchi and R. Rymarz (eds.), *Formation of Teachers for Catholic Schools*, Catholic Education Globally: Challenges and Opportunities 1,
https://doi.org/10.1007/978-981-19-4727-8_4

The chapter concludes by proposing a process to develop best practice standards for Catholic school teacher induction and formation to address this fundamental challenge and its symptoms.

4.2 History of Catholic Identity and Formation in the United States

Despite the U.S. Bishop's decrees in 1852 for every parish to have a school and 1884 for parents to send their children to a Catholic school, Walch (2016) notes the reality of the school was always based on individual parish circumstances including the city, ethnic identity, and finances of the parish. For the parishes that met this mandate, vowed religious and clergy staffed the majority of principal and teaching roles through the middle of the twentieth century (Walch, 2016). Religious faith formation for the faculty of Catholic schools was therefore largely under the aegis of the religious orders sponsoring and teaching in the schools. The paramount concern for these teachers was their pedagogical training (Walch, 2016). Though the idea of "Catholic normal schools" operated by dioceses or centralized institutes floated around for decades, these initiatives for Catholic school-specific preparation never gained financial support to make them viable (Walch, 2016). In 1902, the Catholic University of America (CUA) in Washington D.C. started an "Institute of Pedagogy" for priests and brothers teaching in Catholic schools; a few years later, CUA started a separate program for sister-teachers (Walch, 2016). Nevertheless, Walch explains, drawing heavily on Veverka (1988), that most teaching religious orders operated their own normal schools to train their sister-teachers: By the 1920s, approximately, 17,000 sister-teachers were enrolled in over 90 religious-community-run normal schools. Simultaneously, the "craft" or apprenticeship model where a novice religious was mentored by an experienced member of the order while both mentor and novice teacher taught full time was widely employed (Walch, 2016). Walch (2016) notes this pleased the religious superiors because it kept their novices under their purview and satisfied the bishops because there was little cost to the diocese; however, given the widely varying quality of pedagogical preparation, this arrangement had few supporters among Catholic educators. By the 1930s, the necessity for state certification for teachers became more prevalent, and therefore, vowed religious began to be prepared in Catholic college training programs and very occasionally in secular public institutions (Walch, 2016).

In 1950, 90.1% faculty and administration of Catholic P-12 schools were vowed religious, though by 1960 the percentage was 73.8% due to the dramatic "Baby Boom" enrollment increase that necessitated hiring lay people to staff the schools (Watzke, 2002). The percentage of lay school leaders and teachers has been on a trajectory upwards since the 1960's. During the 2020–2021 school year, Catholic school staffs were 97.7% lay men and women and 2.3% vowed religious or clergy (National Catholic Education Association, 2021).

4.3 Catholic School Teacher Preparation, Induction, and Ongoing Formation in the United States

There are no standards or criteria for the preparation, induction, or ongoing formation of Catholic school teachers in the United States. For publicly funded P-12 schools, i.e., public schools, teacher certification criteria vary based on the state, so teacher preparation programs in each of the 50 states, including those in Catholic institutions, design their programs to at least meet the criteria for their state. Approximately, 170 post-secondary Catholic institutions in the United States offer programs to prepare and certify future P-12 school teachers (Watzke, 2002). Responses to a survey in the early 2000's showed that roughly 30% of the faculty in American Catholic college or university teacher preparation programs had experience in Catholic schools (Watzke, 2002). Over 80% had faculties where fewer than half had any experience in Catholic schools (Watzke, 2002); only, 15% indicated that the foundation of their mission was for Catholic schools. Approximately, 33% of the respondents did not offer any preparation for Catholic P-12 education. A respondent stated: "Catholic school teachers are prepared in the same manner for certification as are public school teachers" (Watzke, 2002, p. 146). Another wrote: "We prepare students to become teachers in all schools, public, and private. We do not offer special programs or courses for teaching in Catholic schools. We do not distinguish between preparing students for Catholic schools and public schools" (Watzke, 2002, p. 146).

Currently, fourteen institutions sponsor teacher preparation programs in the University Consortium for Catholic Education (UCCE) explicitly for Catholic schools. UCCE programs have graduated roughly 8000 teachers since 1994 and currently graduate approximately 400 teachers each year that administrators hope will be a core of future Catholic school leaders, education program directors, and scholars (University Consortium for Catholic Education, 2021). Regrettably, teachers formed in these Catholic school-oriented programs are a small number of the 142,977 full-time Catholic school staff during the 2020–2021 school year (National Catholic Education Association, 2021). Even if there were standards for pre-service teachers preparing for Catholic schools, there is presently minimal commitment—outside of the UCCE programs—to implement such standards in teacher preparation programs. As a partial response to the fact that relatively few applicants for teaching positions in Catholic schools are specifically prepared for the Catholic school identity and mission, multiple Catholic school administrators referenced their preference to hire Catholic high-school graduates rationalizing that these teachers are more likely to understand and embody the identity and charisms needed for Catholic education (K. Wessling, personal communication, June 24, 2021; C. Sepich, personal communication, June 23, 2021; J. Bopp, personal communication, June 23, 2021). (Note: all personal communication referenced in this chapter is with building or diocese-level Catholic school administrators.)

The responsibility to form teachers for Catholic schools falls to dioceses and individual schools and is often combined with new teacher orientation or induction programs after these individuals have been hired and assigned duties. Orientations and inductions should be different processes with distinct objectives though they are frequently conflated. Orientations introduce new teachers to procedures and information related to school operations from grading policies to parking spots and are usually completed in a day or two. Inductions connect new teachers to the unique identity and mission of their specific school as well as Catholic education as a whole and serve as an early step in the ongoing formation of Catholic school teachers that continues as long as the teacher is in the school.

An anecdotal review of Catholic schools across a number of dioceses indicates that orientation, induction, and ongoing formation for Catholic school teachers varies (M. Green, personal communication, June 23, 2021; J. Schulte, personal communication, June 22, 2021; C. Sepich, personal communication, June 23, 2021). For example, some dioceses provide an orientation for all new Catholic school teachers at a centralized location, while others expect individual schools to orient and induct their new teachers (V. Kauffold, personal communication, June 24, 2021). The content of these orientations generally includes a philosophical introduction to Catholic schools as well as a pragmatic explanation of teaching in general.

New teacher induction programs have been recognized as crucial for new hires in all schools (Hobson et al., 2009), but this is particularly true in Catholic schools given their distinct ecclesial identity and mission (Brock & Chatlain, 2008). Two of the "emerging themes" from Brock and Chatlain are relevant here. First, they found that diocesan induction frameworks "varied widely in structure and comprehensiveness, ranging from minimal to highly-structured programs" (p. 375). Diocesan orientations were usually part of new teacher inductions, but the content and time allotted ranged between a half-day to three days. Second, the "Catholic dimension" of the induction that oriented new teachers to the religious dimension of Catholic schools was of the highest importance (p. 378).

For example, an archdiocese with a significant number of Catholic schools hosts a required initial eight-hour orientation for teachers new to Catholic schools (V. Kauffold, personal communication, June 24, 2021). The published schedule is as follows:

> Mass
> Social time—getting to know one another, build community
> What does it mean to be a Catholic school teacher?
> Professional ethics
> Diversity and equity awareness
> Lunch provided
> Best practices, including classroom management, learning objectives, formative assessments, and methodology related to core instructional practices.

Three more sessions hosted by the diocese for 2.5 h each are mandated over the course of the school year, for a total of 15.5 h. It is unclear how much of the remaining 7.5 h will focus on teacher formation related to the identity and mission of Catholic schooling. Beyond these sessions, each individual school is free to implement their own procedures to induct new teachers. Some schools assign a mentor teacher to beginning teachers or teachers new to the building, with expectations and structure varying by school and in some cases by circumstances within a school (C. Sepich, personal communication, June 23, 2021).

Ongoing veteran teacher formation for this archdiocese consists of 24 h of formational experience within a given school year. In recent years, the model for this formation has been presentations to faculty on theological topics, and the archdiocese has contracted with an outside entity to provide these presentations. This year, schools can choose an alternative process such as inviting a local pastor or deacon to lead presentations or incorporate a different method where faculty independently watch a series of online presentations before gathering in small groups to reflect on the content for their own teaching and lives (V. Kauffold, personal communication, June 24, 2021).

Typically, independent religious order-sponsored schools have latitude to develop their own induction and ongoing formation initiatives and do not participate in diocesan programs. For instance, Jesuit high schools in the USA Upper Midwest Province induct new teachers and staff with a multi-year formation program with assigned readings and discussion seminars every semester, mandatory retreats, meetings with administrators related to their role in the school, and multiple presentations to their cohort and administration related to their role supporting the Jesuit and Catholic identity of the school (J. Schulte, personal communication, June 21, 2021).

4.4 Historical and Current Tensions for Catholicism in the United States

Catholic Americans' view of themselves and the world has changed since John F. Kennedy was elected the United States' first Catholic president in 1960, the Second Vatican Council, and the social revolution of the 1960's (McGreevy, 2003). The challenge of preparing and forming Catholic school teachers is part of the American Catholic Church's larger challenge to respond to these profound changes in contemporary worldview. The abstract macro-problem facing the Church becomes a concrete micro-problem in terms of Catholic school teacher formation. This is similar to the challenges prior to the 1960's because they reflect and distill tensions in American culture and the American Catholic Church; however, the challenges are new, and the Church's ability to respond has changed.

Broadly speaking, the history of Catholics in the United States begins as a religious minority viewed with suspicion by the dominant White Anglo Saxon Protestant culture (Dolan, 2002). Since the 1960s and not coincidentally the Second Vatican Council, while external suspicions about Catholicism generally have subsided, intra-Catholic uncertainty mirroring larger cultural polarization has increased significantly (McGreevy, 2003). This internal tension about what it means to be Catholic in the early decades of the twenty-first century might be exemplified in the current debate over Joe Biden, elected the United States' second Catholic President in 2020, sharing in communion during Mass (Sawyer, 2021). Throughout this history from colonial times to the present, American Catholic school teacher formation has reflected larger religious and cultural tensions in American society and the American Catholic Church.

The American Catholic Church had always been unified in differentiating between an external existential threat, which roughly prior to the 1960's was the Protestant American culture, from an internal matter of debate, such as whether Catholic schools were the best response to the influence of Protestantism specifically or a generic Americanism typified by disassociation from one's cultural or religious heritage (Bryk et al., 1993; McGreevy, 2003; Walch, 2016). The external tensions were two-fold. First, Catholic practices such as the Latin Mass, abstaining from meat on Fridays, a celibate clergy, maintaining the real presence in the Eucharist, allegiance to a foreign pope, and use of a different translation of the Bible distinguished Catholics from the religious mainstream in the United States. Further, Catholic organizations served the social, recreational, educational, and healthcare needs of Catholics literally from birth to death, all of which promoted clear religious identification of an "us" and "you" based on one's perspective. In other words, for Catholics, "we" maintain these practices, which distinguishes us from "you" non-Catholics. Alternatively, from the dominant Protestant view, "we" don't have the same practices "you" Catholics do. The second tension between Catholics and larger American culture related to the first: If Catholics maintained all those practices that distinguished themselves from mainstream Protestant American life, were they truly American? (Dolan, 2002; McGreevy, 2003).

Viewed today, the lines of demarcation seem simplistic, but one result was clarity of identity for Catholics, which made formation and preparation for teaching in Catholic schools straightforward. Catholic school teachers were expected to educate and form the next generation of Catholics to maintain identity and allegiance to a larger Catholic "us" that was defined by the distinctive Catholic practices and doctrines that delineated them from non-Catholics. Whether the teacher was a vowed religious or lay-person, this teacher was coming from a "thickly" Catholic culture that socialized one into a Catholic worldview and identity through mutually reinforcing faith practices and communal cultural norms (Smith et al., 2014, p. 26, as cited in Franchi & Rymarz, 2017, p. 2). Catholic schools were also tasked with making sure Catholic youth could access the same political, economic, social, and cultural opportunities afforded white Protestant Americans at the time. This responsibility necessitated using contemporary teaching pedagogy to provide an outstanding education, so students would be prepared to thrive in influential positions in the United States. Commitment to Catholic identity both sustained and was sustained by Catholic schools, which enculturated an allegiance to being both "Catholic" and "American" for the generation that came of age before the 1960's (Walch, 2016).

Today, frustration is growing in the United States evident in a distinct but unattributable sense of cultural malaise, social discontent, and political gridlock. It is not that no one can identify the cause, it is that everyone identifies a different cause. There is little consensus, only argument. Addressing this paralysis, Canadian

Catholic philosopher Charles Taylor theorizes that we live in a "secular age" characterized by an "immanent frame" that impedes our understanding of who we are in relation to the God who created us (Taylor, 2007). This materialist and exclusively scientific worldview is the contemporary default or "natural" order that is contrasted with a worldview that recognizes the world as charged with God's grace in a way that transcends empirical explanation. Smith (2014) interprets Taylor thusly: "Some inhabit [the world] as a closed frame with a brass ceiling; others inhabit it as an open frame with skylights open to transcendence" (p. 93). It is not a question of knowledge or belief, but how one lives. If Taylor is right, the busy and distracted lives that disconnect Americans from their inner selves, one another, and God is not the cause but symptoms resulting from the limiting, pervasive, and unconscious worldview that impedes acknowledging God's transcendence in the mystery of individual and communal lives. This is the changed cultural context that is at the root of the challenge to all American institutions today, especially organized religions like Catholicism.

The initial challenge of this pervasive worldview to Catholicism and the preparation and formation of Catholic school teachers is that it at least coincides with the "decline of the cultural religious paradigm" in the Anglosphere (Franchi & Rymarz, 2017, p. 3). Franchi and Rymarz (2017) summarize two major trends in response to this decline that are present in the United States (p. 4). First, the outright disaffiliation from Catholicism is increasing in the United States (McCarty & Vitek, 2018). Second, a significant percentage of young people may identify as Catholic, but Catholicism's relevance in their lives is minimal, and they interpret and live their faith identity in their own terms (Clydesdale & Garces-Foley, 2019). It is this pool of Catholics from which Catholic school teachers are drawn today (Franchi & Rymarz, 2017). These teachers are not arriving in Catholic schools formed as Catholics able to witness and pass on the faith tradition and Catholic worldview because they themselves do not have foundational understandings or lived practices to support such a view. They need to be religiously formed, and this formation needs to recognize and respond to the default materialist worldview they have adopted.

Responding to this initial challenge of incompletely religiously formed, teachers manifests a polarization in the American Catholic Church that is another characteristic of contemporary American society (Steinfels, 2003). The same forces of exclusive secular materialism sustaining the contemporary worldview simultaneously decenter the individual from shared centers of meaning such as religious traditions. In place of shared centers of meaning that cohere communities is an ethic of individualism that makes the self and one's own perceived needs the center of meaning and value. This individualism closes people off from collective wisdom rendering them susceptible to shallow cultural fads, quick-fix solutions, and demagoguery, all of which results in a polarization infecting social, political, and ecclesial institutions in the United States, including the Catholic Church. The American Catholic Church struggles with factionalism and has been unable to satisfactorily respond to the disintegration of the Catholic cultural paradigm, deterioration of Catholic practices and understanding, and ultimately disaffiliation from the Catholic Church (Avella, 2019). Such paralysis further deepens the anxiety that already motivate the polarizing forces within the laity and hierarchy. In short, Catholic school leaders and teachers are in a cultural and religious context where religious identity and worldview cannot be taken for granted, and there is no consensus for how to respond to this challenge.

4.5 Responding to the Challenge

The United States Conference of Catholic Bishops (2005) wrote: "The preparation and ongoing formation of new administrators and teachers is vital if our schools are to remain truly Catholic in all aspects of school life" (p. 10). To attain this, the attributes of these Catholic school leaders and teachers must be enumerated and the best practices and procedures to form these teachers identified. A process is therefore needed to develop standards for initial induction and ongoing formation of Catholic school teachers for their ministry in Catholic schools. The development of this process is important because there must be support from bishops, Catholic school leaders, and Catholic school scholars to develop and use these standards. The recent successful process to create and promulgate the *National Standards and Benchmarks for Effective Catholic Elementary and Secondary Schools* (NSBECS) provides a template to develop Catholic school teacher formation standards (Ozar & Weitzel-O'Neill, 2012).

The NSBECS document is the result of a process initiated in 2009 with conversation among Catholic school leaders, the National Catholic Education Association (NCEA), and Catholic school university scholars. Supporters of the initiative "voiced the conviction that collectively endorsed national standards supported and advocated by the Bishops offer the opportunity for the Catholic community to: clarify the 'brand' of 'Catholic school'" (Ozar & Weitzel-O'Neill, 2012, p. vi). For over two years, an eight-person task force developed the document; this collaborative process went through multiple revisions and was reviewed by Catholic school leaders, bishops, university scholars, and teachers. A similar process to develop Catholic School teacher formation standards is envisioned.

The NSBECS document itself provides a rough template for what is needed. The NSBECS is based on the standards-based reform movement that recognizes clearly articulated standards motivate changes in schools. Standards are not magic wands, but they provide a starting point for revisions to school practices and culture (Ozar et al., 2019). The introduction explains that it "is intended to describe how the most mission-driven, program effective, well managed, and responsibly governed Catholic schools operate" (Ozar & Weitzel-O'Neill, 2012, p. vi). The standards and benchmarks are intended to provide measurable criteria to "determine how well a school is fulfilling its obligation to those who benefit from its services" (Ozar & Weitzel-O'Neill, 2012, p. vi). School communities are expected to implement the standards within their own context.

With the process to develop the NSBECS and the standards themselves as a model, the following is a proposal to develop Catholic school formation standards for use in United States Catholic schools.

- Enumerate essential attributes of Catholic school teachers.
- Once the essential attributes have been enumerated, the process needs to identify best practices to inculcate and enhance these attributes in teachers for Catholic schools.
- These attributes and best practices should be distilled into standards for "What Catholic school teachers need to know" and "What Catholic school teachers need to experience" and then broadly promulgated.
- Resources in both English and Spanish need to be aggregated and widely distributed to assist schools incorporating these guidelines as they implement induction and ongoing formation initiatives.
- Formation initiatives based on the guidelines should be evaluated for their efficacy; the guidelines can then be revised based on the outcomes.

The core of the resulting standards as envisioned could be the twin domains "What Catholic School teachers need to know" and "What Catholic school teachers need to experience." A number of anticipated foundational premises for the standards in these domains are proposed below, though they will need to be evaluated by the committee developing the standards.

First, per the NSBECS, the initial defining characteristic of a Catholic school is that it is "Centered on the Person of Christ." Specifically:

> Catholic education is rooted in the conviction that Jesus Christ provides the most comprehensive and compelling example of the realization of full human potential... In every aspect of programs, life, and activities, Catholic schools should foster personal relationship with Jesus Christ and communal witness to the Gospel message of love of God and neighbor and service to the world, especially the poor and marginalized. (Ozar & Weitzel-O'Neill, 2012, p. 2)

Starting with Jesus Christ will not automatically bring back a Catholic cultural paradigm or heal polarizing tendencies in the American Catholic Church, but it is the essential and integrating place for all commitment, conversation, and conversion to begin.

Second, everyone's faith story is dynamic, so the Catholic context of the school and the teacher's background and experience must be taken into account. Some teachers may need additional guidance in understanding their role in a Catholic school. As explained by a Catholic high school Dean of Faculty Formation: "Everyone has a faith story and we need our faculty to understand that. Even those that claim no faith need to participate in our faculty formation programs" (J. Schulte, personal communication, June 21, 2021). The guidelines should provide a basis for these conversations.

Third, an ongoing formation process for the length of a teacher's time in Catholic schools is anticipated. One is always journeying toward God; one is never "finished." However, the guidelines should recognize phases in one's formation for Catholic schools. An initial phase could be an introduction to the school and Catholic education during the hiring and orientation process; a second induction phase includes approximately the first three years of teaching (Williby, 2004); ongoing formation fulfills the third phase.

Fourth, the format for ongoing education and formation is crucial. Relying solely on a presenter giving information to faculty every few months, though well-intentioned and efficient, is not an effective model for faculty formation. The guidelines should incorporate modes of encounter beyond direct instruction such as discussion, faith sharing, and personal mentorship. Additionally, ongoing self-reflection, adjustment of practice and disposition, and personal evaluation are integral parts of Catholic school teacher formation.

The benefits of Catholic school teacher formation standards are obvious. Consistent expectations across dioceses would foster collaboration, lower costs, and increase effectiveness of ongoing formational initiatives, especially among smaller dioceses and schools. For example, if every Catholic school teacher were expected to have highly similar educational and formational experiences, publishers and consultants would be better able to provide resources to support the standards. Additionally, teacher preparation programs at Catholic institutions would have a guide to enhance existing initiatives or develop new programs for pre-service formation of those aspiring to teach in Catholic schools.

The challenges to develop and promulgate the above proposal are equally clear. A process to develop guidelines as envisioned above takes a significant commitment of resources. Developing the NSBECS and the accompanying Catholic School Standards Project (CSSP) was a multi-year endeavor that only funded the development of the standards and the first phase of research on their implementation. For instance, lack of resources has indefinitely delayed the anticipated subsequent research into the standards' relationship to measurable outcomes (Ozar et al., 2019; Ozar, personal communication, July 15, 2021). Another challenge is the lack of time in some schools to support even a modest commitment to develop procedures to induct new teachers and facilitate ongoing formation. This has proven true for implementing the NSBECS (Ozar et al., 2019).

4.6 Conclusion

A coherent and consistent articulation of what a Catholic school teacher needs to know and experience in initial and ongoing formation would be a small step toward helping Catholic school teachers recognize and live God's grace through their roles in Catholic schools. When convicted teachers do this, they provide witness for the next generation of Americans and Catholics. The internal tensions of polarization in the American Church will not be immediately overcome, but standards for Catholic school teacher formation similar to the NSBECS based on Jesus Christ and the Church's collective wisdom are the core that grounds everyone in the foundation of our Church.

References

Avella, S. M. (2019). Since Vatican II: American Catholicism in transition. In P. O. Killen & M. Silk (Eds.), *The future of Catholicism in America* (pp. 108–152). Columbia University Press.

Brock, B. L., & Chatlain, G. (2008). The status of teacher induction in Catholic schools: Perspectives from the United States and Canada. *Catholic Education: A Journal of Inquiry and Practice, 11*(3), 370–384.

Bryk, A., Lee, V., & Holland, P. (1993). *Catholic schools and the common good.* Harvard University Press.

Clydesdale, T., & Garces-Foley, K. (2019). *The twentysomething soul: Understanding the religious and secular lives of American young adults.* Oxford University Press.

Dolan, J. P. (2002). *In search of an American Catholicism: A history of religion and culture in tension.* Oxford University Press.

Franchi, L., & Rymarz, R. (2017). The education and formation of teachers for Catholic schools: Responding to changed cultural contexts. *International Studies in Catholic Education, 9*(1), 2–16. https://doi.org/10.1080/19422539.2017.1286905

Hobson, A. J., Ashby, P., Malderez, A., & Tomlinson, P. D. (2009). Mentoring beginning teachers: What we know and what we don't. *Teaching and Teacher Education, 25*(1).

McCarty, R. J., & Vitek, J. M. (2018). *Going, going, gone: The dynamics of disaffiliation in young Catholics.* St. Mary's Press.

McGreevy, J. T. (2003). *Catholicism and American freedom: A history.* W.W. Norton.

National Catholic Education Association. (2021). *Catholic school data: United States Catholic elementary and secondary schools 2020–2021.* https://www.ncea.org/NCEA/Who_We_Are/About_Catholic_Schools/Catholic_School_Data/NCEA/Who_We_Are/About_Catholic_Schools/Catholic_School_Data/Catholic_School_Data.aspx?hkey=8e90e6aa-b9c4-456b-a488-6397f3640f05

Ozar, L. A., & Weitzel-O'Neill, P. (2012). *National standards and benchmarks for effective Catholic elementary and secondary schools.* The Catholic School Standards Project. https://www.catholicschoolstandards.org/

Ozar, L. A., Weitzel-O'Neill, P., Barton, T., Calteaux, E., & Yi, S. (2019). Making a difference: The promise of Catholic school standards. *Journal of Catholic Education, 22*(1), 154–185. https://doi.org/10.15365/joce.2201102019

Sawyer, S. (2021, June 22). Catholics are talking past each other in the Biden-communion debate. *America Magazine.* https://www.americamagazine.org/faith/2021/06/22/communion-debate-bishops-hyprocrisy-gospel-240911

Smith, J. K. A. (2014). *How (not) to be secular.* Eerdmans.

Steinfels, P. (2003). *A people adrift: The crisis of the Roman Catholic Church in America.* Simon & Schuster.

Taylor, C. (2007). *A secular age.* Harvard University Press.

United States Conference of Catholic Bishops. (2005). *Renewing our commitment to Catholic elementary and secondary schools in the third millennium.* https://www.usccb.org/beliefs-and-teachings/how-we-teach/catholic-education/upload/renewing-our-commitment-2005.pdf

University Consortium for Catholic Education. (2021, June 12). *History.* http://www.ucceconnect.com/history.html

Veverka, F. B. (1988). *For God and country: Catholic schooling in the 1920's.* Garland Publishing.

Walch, T. (2016). *Parish school: A history of American Catholic parochial education from colonial times to the present: Revised and expanded edition.* NCEA Press.

Watzke, J. (2002). Teachers for whom? A study of teacher education practices in higher education. *Journal of Catholic Education, 6*(2). https://doi.org/10.15365/joce.0602022013

Williby, R. (2004). Hiring and retaining high-quality teachers: What principals can do. *Catholic Education: A Journal of Inquiry and Practice, 8*(2), 174–192.

Max T. Engel teaches courses in both the Education and Theology departments at Creighton University, in Omaha, NE, USA. He researches in the areas of religious formation and instruction in Catholic schools as well as the identity of Catholic schools. Recent publications include co-authoring "Why inclusion isn't coming, it is already here: Catholic schools and inclusive education" in the *Journal of Catholic Education*; the lead author of *Name It, Claim It, and Build on It: Your School's Catholic Identity*; and he is a co-author of the book *On the 8th Day: A Catholic Theology of Sports*. MaxEngel@creighton.edu

Chapter 5
Catholic Teacher Formation in the Republic of Ireland

John-Paul Sheridan

Abstract The denominational nature of teacher education in Ireland stems from its establishment in the nineteenth century by religious orders and congregations, and while their presence is no longer evident in the colleges of education, the denominational paradigm remains. Coupled with this is the still strong association of the primary school with the Catholic Church. Religious education has always been under the care of the Churches both in its curriculum and syllabus, including the catechetical and formational dimension which encompasses the sacramental preparation of children. This system is one which has become increasingly under pressure in the last decades of the twentieth century and into the present.

Keywords Religious orders and congregations · Syllabus · Catholic culture · Religious identity

5.1 Introduction

For the purposes of this chapter, I have confined the discussion to the primary sector in the Republic of Ireland, although I have continued to use the term "Ireland". While the island of Ireland is divided between the Irish Republic and the Province of Northern Ireland (which is part of the UK), in ecclesiastical terms, Ireland is one area, with the Archbishop of Armagh as Primate of All Ireland.

The chapter is in two sections. The first section begins with some insights from the development of denominational teacher education in Ireland. This is followed by a survey of both Catholic Education and Teacher Education in Ireland, which also encompasses the current provision of religious education in Irish primary school and the requirements expected of primary teachers in respect of the qualification for teaching primary religious education. The second section offers some of the challenges associated with teacher formation. They can be divided into three subsections. First are the challenges of contemporary Ireland and the rapidly changing Irish social

---

J.-P. Sheridan (✉)
St. Patrick's Pontifical University, Maynooth, Republic of Ireland
e-mail: JohnPaul.Sheridan@spcm.ie

© The Author(s), under exclusive license to Springer Nature Singapore Pte Ltd. 2022
L. Franchi and R. Rymarz (eds.), *Formation of Teachers for Catholic Schools*, Catholic Education Globally: Challenges and Opportunities 1,
https://doi.org/10.1007/978-981-19-4727-8_5

and political landscape of the last twenty to thirty years—the period into which these student teachers were born and grew up. Following this are the challenges of the Catholic school in Ireland today and how this might have a bearing on the formation of student teachers. There are many positive changes in schools today—the presence of a rich multicultural and multireligious pupil profile which makes for a rich and varied school experience. There are also changes in terms of government legislation and curriculum development which might be seen to undermine the mission of the Catholic school in terms of Catholic education, religious education, and catechesis. The final challenge is the internal dynamic of religious identity. This section is partly based on research undertaken several years ago into the religious identity of primary school student teachers.

5.2 Insights from the History of Catholic Education in Ireland

The first directions in teacher education had been the establishment in 1811 of the Church of Ireland Training College (or Kildare Place Training Institution) and in 1838, the opening of the Marlborough Street Training College in Dublin. As religious congregations became more established in the education landscape, they turned their attention to teacher education. With the support of the Archbishop of Dublin, the Vincentians established a training college in 1875 at Drumcondra and the Sisters of Mercy their college at Baggot St. in 1877 (Coolahan, 1981). The Irish Christian Brothers established a college of education at Marino in Dublin in 1881. It was principally for the training of Christian Brothers and did not admit lay students until 1972. The De La Salle brothers founded a college in Waterford in 1894, and in 1898 the Sisters of Mercy founded Mary Immaculate College in Limerick. The Congregation of Dominican Sisters founded the last of the colleges of education: Belfast in 1900 and Froebel College of Education in 1943 in Dublin.

These colleges have evolved through various changes and amalgamations over the course of their respective histories. Froebel College of Education had been an associated college of Trinity College, Dublin, along with Marino and the Church of Ireland College of Education. In 2010, it began its move to Maynooth University and eventually was established on the Maynooth Campus in 2013. In 2016, St. Patrick's College became part of Dublin City University along with the Church of Ireland College of Education, Mater Dei Institute of Education, and All Hallows College. St. Mary's in Belfast (established in 1949) continues its association with Queen's University Belfast. Mary Immaculate College is linked to the University of Limerick and Marino College of Education maintains its link with Trinity College, Dublin. The most recent provider of teacher education is Hibernia College of Education, which was established in 2000 and is the first college to facilitate online learning as the predominant paradigm of education provision.

5.3 Catholic Education in the Republic of Ireland Today

Several documents have been issued on the subject of Catholic Education by the Irish bishops in the last number of years, many in response to the ongoing debate regarding the continuing provision of denominational education and as an Irish response to documents coming from the Congregation for Catholic Education, in particular, *Vision 08: A Vision for Catholic Education in Ireland* (2008).

Apart from its management role in Irish education, the Catholic Church has been responsible for the provision of the curricula and syllabi for the teaching of religious education in the primary school classroom.

The dioceses of Ireland have a network of primary diocesan advisors who will visit schools and offer advice and support to teachers in the work of religious education and catechesis. The approach is always to assist the teaching of religious education and to support the teacher. Some dioceses will also offer some continuing professional development (CPD) especially in the area of new programmes and sacramental preparation. This is not easily achieved, however, as releasing teachers for courses and CPD days are rarely sanctioned by the Department of Education and Skills (DES).

5.4 Catholic Teacher Formation Pathways

Qualification for primary teachers in Ireland takes two forms. Most students come through a four-year bachelor of education (B.Ed.) from one of the colleges of education. The second route towards primary teaching is a two-year Professional Master of Education, and again the religious education dimension is integrated into the programme.

As part of their education, they will undertake a certification in religious education and religious/theological studies. This programme varies from college to college, but since 2011, the Irish Episcopal Conference has laid down the criteria for qualification and now there is a certain uniformity in the programmes undertaken.

For a teacher with an initial teacher education degree to be recognised to teach in a Catholic school, they should have one hundred and twenty contact hours in religious education, to include an exploration of catechesis and Catholic Religious Education (hours of religious education and associated theological subjects, in the B.Ed. or other degree), and of Religious or Theological Studies (often taken in an additional certificate) (Irish Episcopal Conference, 2018, p. 9). Except for Maynooth University, the religious education certification is integrated into the four-year programme, in various ways. The students at Maynooth University avail of a Certificate in Catholic Religious Education and Theological Studies at St. Patrick's Pontifical University, Maynooth.

The two-year Professional Masters is similar in its expectation, with the exception that these students are required to have a minimum of fifty contact hours (Irish Episcopal Conference, 2018, p. 11).

As to the content of these programmes of teacher education, the undergraduate student should be qualified to demonstrate knowledge, understanding, and appreciation in the following fields of study:

- God: Faith, Creed, and Trinity
- Jesus Christ and Discipleship
- Scripture
- Prayer, Sacraments, and Liturgy
- Ethics, Social Justice, Spirituality, and Human Rights
- Church and Mission, Ecumenism, and Inter-Religious Dialogue.

These themes allow for inclusion of many current issues, such as social justice; peace and reconciliation; gender; ethics; ecology; equality; disability; sexuality; racial, cultural, and religious diversity, and citizenship (Irish Episcopal Conference, 2018). The postgraduate programme has similar expectations.

Several colleges also offer a part-time programme of certification in religious education to assist student teachers who have undertaken their studies in the UK.

Further education and CPD around Catholic education are offered by a few the colleges of education. These include a Certificate in Christian Leadership in Education, a M.Ed. in Educational Leadership and Management, and a M.Ed. in Religious Education at Mary Immaculate College, Limerick. Marino offers a Master in Education Studies (Leadership in Christian Education).

5.5 Challenges for Catholic Teacher Formation

To call what Ireland has experienced over the last fifty years 'a changing landscape' does not come close to encapsulating how much it has changed in terms of culture, identity, and society. Much of that change has happened in the lifetime of current student teachers. There has also been change in the educational landscape and in the gradual, if glacial, pace of increasing diversity in provision of primary schooling. Finally, there has been a seismic change in the position of the Catholic Church in Irish society. Some of this is the result of an emerging liberal society, but one can never forget the revelations that have damaged the Catholic Church with regard to child sexual abuse. The part played by religious congregations in the neglect and abuse of children in schools, orphanages, industrial schools, and Magdalene laundries has irreparably damaged the noble ideals of founders and the tradition of education that they began (Barkham, 2019). In his letter to Ireland in 2010, Pope Benedict referred to the manner in which congregation members were "suffering as a result of the sins of our confreres who betrayed a sacred trust or failed to deal justly and responsibly with allegations of abuse" (Pope Benedict XVI, 2010).

In this context, attention to the challenges of teacher formation might be approached from three distinct angles. The first and broadest challenge comes from the changing religious and cultural landscape of Ireland, which has had a profoundly erosive effect on Catholic Education in Ireland, beginning in the latter part of the last century and continuing to the present. The second area of challenge is the school and its changing landscape. This comprises the evolving demographic of the Irish nation and its effect on the primary school. It also encompasses the teaching of the religious education programme and issues around catechetical formation and sacramental preparation. The final challenge is the changing religious identity of the student teacher. There are links between these three areas, but attention to these external and the internal challenges will not only give us occasion to pause for thought, but also offer some pointers for the direction teacher education and formation might take into the future.

5.5.1 Challenge I. Changing Society and Cultural Landscape

The changing Irish landscape can also be seen within an external/internal framework. Regarding the external, the Irish population has been gradually changing with the addition of immigrants from other countries, fuelled by the economic boom of the 1990s and the early 2000s. Ireland has also welcomed asylum seekers and refugees over the last decades. The 2016 Census had this to say on the diversity of the Irish population:

> The 535,475 non-Irish nationals living in Ireland in April 2016 came from 200 different nations. Polish nationals were the largest group with 122,515 persons followed by 103,113 UK nationals and 36,552 Lithuanians. Just twelve nations each with over 10,000 residents – America, Brazil, France, Germany, India, Italy, Latvia, Lithuania, Poland, Romania, Spain and the UK – accounted for 73.6% of the total non-Irish national population. (CSO, 2017a, b)

In the same census, Roman Catholicism was still the largest professed religion, but the second largest group was those who professed no religion (468,421), a jump of 73.6% on the previous census. There was also a significant increase in the numbers of both Muslims and Orthodox Christians by 28.9% and 37.5%, respectively, on the previous census (CSO, 2017a, b).

This changing demographic has been one of the reasons for the increasing call for a greater diversity in school type, moving away from the traditional denominational schooling to a more multicultural model, as espoused by the Educate Together patronage model (Darmody & Smyth, 2018; Faas et al., 2016, 2018). This call for greater diversity has also been heard among the Irish bishops, including the now retired Bishop Leo O'Reilly who, at the (2007) launch of the document, *Catholic Primary Schools: A Policy for Provision into the Future* stated:

> The Catholic Church has no desire to be the sole provider of education for whole communities. However, it does wish to respond to the desire of those parents who want a Catholic education for their children.

This desire to balance the needs of education into the future and the constitutional rights of parents as the primary educators of their children led the former Taoiseach, Garret FitzGerald, to observe:

> On the one hand the guarantee of parents' rights to primary education of their choice is firmly embedded in the Constitution, but on the other hand the State cannot be expected to provide for an indefinite multiplication of different types of school throughout the country. (FitzGerald, 2003, p. 141)

The internal dynamic can be seen in the changes that have been brought about by government legislation and constitution change. This includes legislation which, while having no direct effect on education, still has a huge resonance in the profile of the nation, and legislation which is concerned directly with education and schooling. A significant legislative agenda of successive Irish governments has mirrored the changing Irish population and the changing Irish attitudes towards various social and moral issues. In 1979, contraception became available; in 1993, homosexuality was decriminalised, and in 1995, divorce was legalised. The two most significant changes in recent years were the 2015 amendment to the constitution which recognised marriage between two people regardless of their gender and in 2018 the successful plebiscite to repeal the eighth amendment to the constitution and the legalisation of abortion.

In the opinion of many, Ireland's liberal agenda was evidence of a nation catching up with the rest of Europe (O'Toole, 2009). Ireland has become increasingly secular both in its social mores and its politics. The Church's role and voice in recent debates around constitutional changes have been stymied by its record regarding child sexual abuse. Apart from which, for many, it has become a voice that is no longer relevant when speaking about these issues, apart from the fact that people were moving away from organised religion (Littleton, 2008, 14).

Irish governments have also legislated to reflect the demographic and religious changes in schools. In 2011, it established the Forum on Patronage and Pluralism to ascertain how best to serve a diverse population and how to divest schools of patronage where necessary. The final report of the Forum was released in 2012 (Coolahan et al., 2012). In 2016, the Minister for Education and Skills revoked Rule 68, which had stated:

> Of all the parts of a school curriculum Religious Instruction is by far the most important as its subject matter, God's honour and service, includes the proper use of all man's faculties, and affords the most powerful inducements to their proper use.

This rule had placed religious education above all other subjects in the primary school curriculum. In 2018, the government announced a plan with the aim of establishing four hundred multi-denominational and non-denominational school by 2030 (DES, 1965; 2016; 2018). In the same year, the Education (Admission to Schools) Bill was enacted. It meant that Catholic schools could not have an admissions policy which gave priority to Catholic children. This issue arose in a small percentage of certain primary schools in urban areas which were oversubscribed.

5.5.2 Challenge II. The Changing Landscape of the Catholic School

All primary school student teachers are educated at secular institutions regardless of their religious identity or affiliation. As members of religious congregations disappear from these institutions, the possibilities for maintaining an anchor with the founding ethos and identity will become more and more difficult. Furthermore, opportunities for a formational dimension to teacher education are limited, especially when it comes to their identity as Catholic teachers.

This is especially true when considering the Catholic school in Ireland through the lens of the aspirations of successive documents from the Congregation for Catholic Education. *Educating Together in Catholic Schools* states, "educators must dedicate themselves to others with heartfelt concern, enabling them to experience the richness of their humanity" (Congregation for Catholic Education, 2007, 24). Galioto and Marini's (2021) vision of a school as the locus for the integration of faith, culture, and life might display the ideal, but the reality can be far from that. Creating a distinctive Catholic culture within a school requires in the first place teachers and leaders who are sure of what that particular culture is. The identity of a Catholic school is sometimes reduced to the external indicators (iconography, the liturgical year, and its religious education programme) without delving deeper into the Catholic school as a place which creates "a synthesis between faith, culture and life" (Congregation for Catholic Education, 2007, 3).

The ability to immerse a student into a Catholic culture takes more than merely attempting to lecture on the ethos and identity of a Catholic school. This is an area which requires a more formative dimension, and the way student teacher education is carried out leaves little room for teacher formation. In their study of teacher formation, O'Connell & Meehan found only one viable course which offered the opportunity to explore the spirituality of teachers (2012, pp. 201–202).

When applying for a position at a Catholic school, the Catholic Primary School Management Association (CPSMA) requires the applicant to provide a copy of either their certificate or college transcript as evidence of completion and competence in the subject of religious education. (However, this certificate is sometimes forgotten or not asked for. The insistence on this qualification can vary from diocese to diocese.) The certification is an inadequate indication of the beliefs of the prospective teacher, and while an interview panel might ask about a candidate's knowledge of Catholic education and the religious education programme, it is not permissible (and rightly so) to ask about their own faith. Unlike some places, a candidate does not need a reference from a parish priest to begin the religious education certification at university, which makes it increasingly difficult to differentiate between those who are happy to teach in a Catholic school as opposed to those who might see their role as forming the faith of students. (Jamieson, 2013, p. 13). The former might suggest a *laissez-faire* approach; the latter has a much stronger sense of the overall vocation of the Catholic school. There can also be a laissez-faire attitude to teaching religious education, as it becomes pushed more and more to the periphery of the curriculum in Irish schools as in their counterparts in the rest of Western Europe (Gellel, 2019).

Newly qualified teachers are required to undergo an induction programme when beginning their teaching career known as *Droichead* (NIPT, 2021). While I am sure religious education is part of this framework, there exists no similar programme or framework from the Catholic Church.

There is a challenge in the fact that teachers often find themselves teaching religious education with negligible support from parents and sporadic support from parish personnel. While parents might be interested in the academic ability and achievements of their children, it is an interest that is often not evident when it comes to religious education and sacramental preparation (INTO, 2003, p. 15). The lack of interest displayed by some parents in being part of the transmission of religious identity and commitment is eroding the ability to pass religious identity on to another generation. It can also erode the teacher's belief that what they are doing in religious education is a sustainable and worthwhile activity. Teachers find this happening most in the area of sacramental preparation when the bulk of the responsibility falls to the school.

Another challenge in primary religious education is the relationship between religious education and catechesis. The *Grow in Love* programme is very clear in delineating the difference between learning outcomes and faith formation goals (Council for Catechetics of the Irish Episcopal Conference, 2019). Without getting tangled up in the debate about the merits of the information/formation debate in religious education, the Irish programme sets store by the integration of the two dimensions. The strong academic tradition that exists in the colleges of education can equip the student for the information dimension of religious education, but students sometimes have difficulty with the formational dimension. Added to this, when this formational dimension is done without a strong support from the home and the parish, it not only becomes difficult but often impossible. Perhaps it might be suggested that difficulty with the formational dimension is because of a student teacher's own particular religious identity and attitude to this dimension of religious education. It is something that might be rectified by a formative dimension to their own education.

The role of the school principal is central to life and mission of the Catholic school. Coll (2009) has emphasised the importance of a values-driven leadership, especially when it comes to leading probationary teachers. Sugrue (2009) has shown how the role of principal in Irish primary schools has changed over time. Stynes and McNamara (2019) outline extremely well the role of the principal in keeping all the elements of school life and leadership in balance at the same time.

If the role of the principal is paramount in driving the ethos and identity of the school, and if the principal sees this as low on their long list of priorities, then there is often a decline in the visible manifestations of the Catholic identity of the school. If religious education is not being taught, this can often go unchecked. Coupled with this, if parents are less concerned about the religious component of the school day, then there is less likely that complaints will land on the principal's desk than if English, Irish, or Maths was not being taught.

School leadership is certainly an important driving force in Catholic education, and those in senior management as well as those aspiring to promotion and management need to undertake qualifications in Christian Leadership in schools. To addressing this challenge, and returning to the idea of a formative dimension to teacher education, it might be easier to undertake this at the postgraduate level. While the colleges of education will always strive to produce the best qualified primary school teachers, it is at Masters level that school leaders could be formed. A greater recognition of postgraduate programmes offered by some of the colleges of education would assist, whereby the patronage and management bodies would require a prospective candidate for a position of leadership in a Catholic school to hold an appropriate qualification in Catholic school leadership. Not only would it prepare teachers to be effective leaders in Catholic schools, but it would also create a climate whereby these qualifications would be honoured and sought after.

Colleges of education find it difficult to recruit students for Master's programmes in Christian Leadership. They need assistance from all involved in Catholic education—dioceses, patron bodies, religious congregations. The move into leadership education might begin with CPD. I mentioned previously the role of dioceses in offering professional development around new catechetical programmes, but this could be expanded to short courses on the ethos and identity of the school and the role of the teacher and future leader in this school, which might in turn lead towards the programmes offered by the colleges of education. Attention to the CPD needs of teachers as laid out by Byrne & Sweetman (2019) might assist the colleges of education to recognise potential gaps in their curricula and the attitudes to teaching religious education, and it might also assist dioceses to create relevant programmes for teachers.

The final recommendation of the Forum on Patronage and Pluralism is for the development of a new curriculum on education about religion and beliefs and ethics, and this has been a lightning rod for discussion about the future of a denominational religious education programme in school. It remains to be seen how much of an effect the addition of this new curriculum with have on the Catholic religious education programme (Kieran & McDonagh, 2021).

5.5.3 *Challenge III. Religious Identity*

In the end, and at the heart of the educational endeavour, is the teacher. Standing before the class and teaching, the complex and sophisticated spectrum that is the identity of the teacher comes to the fore. This has been described as follows:

> a loose cluster of complementary, sometimes competing, contributions from social psychology, social anthropology, sociolinguistics, and philosophy that focus on the self in practice; on the various interdependencies among person, context, history, and others; and on the situated, continuous nature of self-development. (Olsen, 2008, p. 4)

Religious identity forms part of that cluster, and, as I have already suggested, the student cannot but be aware of the way Ireland has changed and how attitudes to the Church and Catholic education have changed. The external challenges of religious belief and affiliation are matched by the internal dynamic of personal religious identity and the acknowledgement of that identity as part of the teaching self. This can be a challenge because while all who teach in a Catholic primary school should have the relevant certification, the content with its attendant faith formation components might be problematic for those who do not share the same religious beliefs (Heinz et al., 2018).

In research conducted and published a few years ago (Sheridan, 2013), the emerging identity of student teachers could be viewed across a spectrum of emerging adults' religious identity typologies (Jensen Arnett & Jensen Arnett, 2002): conventional religious, creatively religious, and deist and atheist/agnostic.

For students, religious identity is very individuated, and there is a separation of the spiritual from the religious. They see the significance of the "other", and community is still very important. This community is usually located in places other than the parish. There is a gradual generational decrease in religious practice, which was seen as a matter of choice rather than obligation, and while the religious practice of parents and grandparents is admired, it is not something to be emulated. Many students were still well disposed to the Catholic Church and an important facet of Irish life. Traditional issues like divorce or contraception were hardly mentioned, leaving one to surmise that they are not issues that the students have a problem with.

Some students had difficulty in articulating Christian thought or sentiments, and there was a lack of religious language/articulation. This might be attributed to poor religious education at primary and secondary levels:

> God is present in their lives as they seek to make meaning of their spiritual side. God is present as they move along the transitioning moments of their lives, and is present in their moments of happiness and trouble. Their understanding is at times shallow and on occasion profound. They struggle to make meaning and sense of the transcendent, but it is the willingness to enter the struggle which is the strongest evidence for the presence of God in their lives. (Sheridan, 2013, p. 319)

The challenge of teacher education and formation must attend to the very real lived experience and beliefs of teachers, to support where necessary and to challenge at other times. However, it would require a more intentionally formative dimension in their time in the colleges of education.

5.6 Conclusion

Among those charged with teacher formation, there are perhaps other challenges and perspectives that could be addressed. It might be suggested that each of these challenges merits a longer exposition.

While some of the challenges seem insurmountable, others are not. A need to create a better understanding of the Catholic education endeavour would help to instil in student teachers a more refined narrative of what it means to teach in a Catholic school. Furthermore, a sophisticated understanding of the place of the Catholic school in a multicultural and multireligious society would assist them in seeing that the two are not mutually exclusive. Finally, finding opportunities for a more intentional formation for students will be the best and most sustainable way to ensure the place of Catholic education in the Republic of Ireland in future.

References

Barkham, P. (2019). The brothers grim. *The Guardian.* https://www.theguardian.com/world/2009/nov/28/christian-brothers-ireland-child-abuse

Byrne, G., & Sweetman, B. (2019). CPD and RE: What do RE teachers in Irish Catholic schools say they need? In M. Buchanan & A.-M. Gellel (Eds.), *Global perspectives on Catholic religious education in schools* (pp. 231–243). Springer.

Central Statistics Office. (2017a). *2016 Census—Migration and diversity.* https://www.cso.ie/en/csolatestnews/pressreleases/2017pressreleases/pressstatementcensus2016resultsprofile7-migrationanddiversity/

Central Statistics Office. (2017b). *2016 Census—Irish travellers ethnicity and religion.* https://www.cso.ie/en/csolatestnews/presspages/2017b/census2016profile8-irishtravellersethnicityandreligion/

Coll, R. (2009). Catholic school leadership: Exploring its impact on the faith development of probationer teachers in Scotland. *International Studies in Catholic Education, 1*(2), 200–213.

Congregation for Catholic Education. (2007). *Educating together in Catholic schools.* Typoglotica Vaticana.

Coolahan, J. (1981). *Irish education: Its history and structure.* Institute of Public Administration.

Coolahan, J., Husse, C., & Kilfeather, F. (2012). *The Forum on patronage and pluralism in the primary sector: Report of the Forum's Advisory Group.* Department of Education and Skills.

Council for Catechetics of the Irish Episcopal Conference. (2019). *Grow in Love 8—Teacher's Manual.* Veritas.

Darmody, M., & Smyth, E. (2018). Religion and primary school choice in Ireland: School institutional identities and student profile. *Irish Educational Studies, 37*(1), 1–17.

Department of Education and Skills. (2016). *Address by Jan O'Sullivan, Minister for education & skills to IPPN Annual Conference.* https://www.education.ie/en/Press-Events/Speeches/2016-Speeches/SP2016-01-28.html

Department of Education and Skills. (2018). *Minister Bruton commences plan to increase provision of multi- and non-denominational schools.* https://www.education.ie/en/Press-Events/Press-Releases/2018-press-releases/PR18-05-28.html

Department of Education. (1965). *Rules for national schools.* The Stationery Office.

Faas, D., Darmody, M., & Sokolowska, B. (2016). Religious diversity in primary schools: Reflections from the Republic of Ireland. *British Journal of Religious Education, 38*(1), 83–98.

Faas, D., Smith, A., & Darmody, M. (2018). The role of principals in creating inclusive school environments: Insights from community national schools in Ireland. *School Leadership & Management, 38*(4), 457–473.

FitzGerald, G. (2003). *Reflections on the Irish State.* Irish Academic Press.

Galioto, C., & Marini, G. (2021). The integration of faith, culture and life in Catholic schools: Keys to understanding and pedagogical orientations. *International Studies in Catholic Education, 13*(1), 124–151.

Gellel, A.-M. (2019). Rethinking Catholic religious education in the light of divine pedagogy. In M. Buchanan & A.-M. Gellel (Eds.), *Global perspectives on Catholic religious education in schools* (pp. 39–49). Springer.

Government of Ireland. (2016). *Education (Admission to Schools) Bill*. https://www.oireachtas.ie/en/bills/bill/2016/58/

Heinz, M., Davison, K., & Keane, E. (2018). 'I will do it but religion is a very personal thing': Teacher education applicants' attitudes towards teaching religion in Ireland. *European Journal of Teacher Education, 41*(2), 232–245.

Irish Episcopal Conference. (2008). *Vision 08: A vision for Catholic education in Ireland*. Veritas.

Irish Episcopal Conference. (2018). *Recognition of qualifications to teach Catholic religious education in Catholic primary schools on the Island of Ireland*. Veritas.

Irish National Teachers' Organisation. (2003). *Teaching religion in the primary school*. I.N.T.O.

Jamison, C. (2013). God has created me to do him some definite service': Vocation at the heart of the Catholic curriculum. *International Studies in Catholic Education, 5*(1), 10–22.

Jensen Arnett, J., & Jensen Arnett, L. (2002). A congregation of One: Individualized religious beliefs among emerging adults. *Journal of Adolescent Research, 17*(5), 451–467.

Littleton, J. (2008). Being a Catholic in Ireland Today. In J. Littleton, & E. Maher, (Eds.), *Contemporary Catholicism in Ireland—A critical appraisal* (pp. 12–24). Columba Press.

McDonagh, K. (2021). The centre cannot hold: Decolonising the RE curriculum in the Republic of Ireland. *British Journal of Religious Education, 43*(1), 123–135.

National Induction Programme for Teachers. (2021). https://www.teacherinduction.ie/en/

O'Connell, D., & Meehan, A. (2012). Exploring the spiritual dimension of the school curriculum. In T. Grenham, & P. Kieran, (Eds.), *New educational horizons in contemporary Ireland: Trends and challenges* (pp. 93–211). Peter Lang.

O'Reilly, L. (2007) *Remarks at the launch of Catholic Primary Schools: A policy for provision into the future*. https://www.catholicbishops.ie/2007/10/02/bishop-leo-o%e2%80%99reilly-chairman-bishops%e2%80%99-commission-education-remarks-maynooth-media-launch-policy-document-catholic-primary-schools-policy-provision-future/

O'Toole, F. (2009). *Ship of fools: How stupidity and corruption sank the Celtic Tiger*. Faber & Faber.

Olsen, B. (2008). Introducing teacher identity and this volume. *Teacher Education Quarterly, 35*(3), 3–6.

Pope Benedict XVI. (2010). *Pastoral letter of the Holy Father Pope Benedict XVI to the Catholics of Ireland*. https://www.vatican.va/content/benedict-xvi/en/letters/2010/documents/hf_ben-xvi_let_20100319_church-ireland.html

Sheridan, J. P. (2013). I believe in the God that I believe. In *The religious identity of primary school student teachers*. Lambert Academic Publishing.

Stynes, M., & McNamara, G. (2019). The challenge of perpetual motion: The willingness and desire of Irish primary school principals to juggle everything. *Irish Educational Studies, 38*(1), 25–42.

Sugrue, C. (2009). From heroes and heroines to hermaphrodites: Emasculation or emancipation of school leaders and leadership? *School Leadership and Management, 29*(4), 353–371.

John-Paul Sheridan is a Roman Catholic priest from Ireland. He was ordained in 1990 and served in several parishes in the diocese of Ferns. He worked as a diocesan advisor for Primary School Catechetics (1997–2014) and joined the staff at St. Patrick's Pontifical University at Maynooth in 2014 as a lecturer and a coordinator of educational programmes. He lectures in Religious Education and Catechesis, along with modules in Liturgy, Systematic Theology and Homiletics. John-Paul holds undergraduate degrees from NUI Maynooth (B.A.) and the Pontifical Gregorian University (STB) and postgraduate degrees from Boston College (M.Ed.), Maynooth College (STL), University of Dublin at Trinity College (Ph.D.), and the King's Inn (Advanced Diploma in Education and Law). JohnPaul.Sheridan@spcm.ie

Chapter 6
Catholic Teacher Formation in England and Wales

Sean Whittle

Abstract There are many and complex issues surrounding the formation of Catholic teachers (who work in Catholic schools) in England and Wales. At the surface level, formation is related to the historical attempts in England and Wales to educate and train Catholics to teach in Catholic schools. For very practical reasons, Catholic schools have always been highly reliant on non-Catholic teachers. As a result, there are two distinct strands to the formation of teachers in relation to English and Welsh Catholic schools. The first strand is the formation in relation to those teachers who are Catholic Christians. The second strand is in relation to the high proportion of teachers in Catholic schools who are not Catholic Christians.

Keywords Formation · Catholic teacher · Catholic education in England and Wales · Catholic schools

6.1 Introduction

At the first glance, the task of describing the challenges and opportunities facing Catholic teacher formation in England and Wales would appear to be straightforward. It would involve presenting an overview of the various ways in which Catholic teachers are trained, prepared, inducted and supported in their ongoing work within Catholic schools throughout England and Wales. However, whilst it will be possible to do this, it will be argued that there are some complex difficulties that make this a challenging endeavour. Much of the complexity is rooted in the ambiguities surrounding both what is meant by the term "Catholic teacher" and the very notion of "formation". As a result of these ambiguities, it is far from a straightforward task to describe the situation facing Catholic teacher formation in England and Wales. Given this, the analysis in this chapter will operate at different levels. The first of these will be at the surface level, built around a description of the historical attempts in England and Wales to educate and prepare Catholics to teach in the growing number of Catholic

---

S. Whittle (✉)
Visiting Research Fellow, St Mary's University, Twickenham, London, UK
e-mail: sean.whittle@stmarys.ac.uk

© The Author(s), under exclusive license to Springer Nature Singapore Pte Ltd. 2022
L. Franchi and R. Rymarz (eds.), *Formation of Teachers for Catholic Schools*, Catholic Education Globally: Challenges and Opportunities 1,
https://doi.org/10.1007/978-981-19-4727-8_6

schools opened during the nineteenth and early twentieth centuries. Going beyond this, the analysis will delve to a deeper level, to unpick the theological issues at play around what it might mean to be a Catholic teacher as opposed to a teacher who works well and effectively in a Catholic school. As a result, it will be proposed that there are two distinct strands to the description of the formation of teachers in relation to English and Welsh Catholic schools. The first strand is the formation in relation to those teachers who are Catholic Christians. The second strand is in relation to the high proportion of teachers in Catholic schools who are not Catholic Christians. Obviously, making sense of how these teachers are or even could be "formed" for their work in Catholic schools is fraught with difficulties.

6.2 The Historical and Contemporary Reality in England and Wales

Before going further, it is important to briefly attend to the historical context of Catholic education in England and Wales. Approximately, 10% of all schools in England and Wales are designated as "Catholic". It is important to appreciate that the involvement of the Church in providing state education in England and Wales is closely bound up with the restoration of the Catholic hierarchy following the Reformation. In the centuries after Henry VIII and Elizabeth I, the plight of Catholic Christians in England was a tough one, with both periods of persecution and the introduction of specifically anti-Catholic legislation. It was only in the wake of the Irish Potato Famine that the presence of growing numbers of Irish immigrants triggered a steady increase in the number of Catholics in England. The presence of a critical mass of these immigrants, as well as a growing openness to tolerance in matters of religion, led to the eventual emancipation of Catholics. This meant they could enjoy religious freedom in society at large. The influx of Catholic immigrants during the eighteenth century coincided with the move towards an expansion of mass education that was taking place towards the end of the Industrial Revolution. The emergence of mass education (provided free of charge by the state) proved to be an effective way of providing some degree of child care, and this suited the needs of employers who wanted to have a readily available workforce (one partially freed from the demands of child care). In 1850, the Catholic hierarchy was restored and very early on the English bishops realised the importance of providing Catholic schools. This is aptly summed up in the declaration of the first synod of the province of Westminster in 1850: "We prefer the foundation of good schools to every other work (including the building of parish churches)" (quoted in Grace, 2002, p. 8). Establishing and maintaining a rich provision of primary and secondary Catholic schools has involved a huge commitment of human and financial resources on the part of the Catholic Church.

In England and Wales, like in other countries, the Catholic Church has been an important partner in facilitating and enabling universal state education to come into existence. It played an important role in educating and helping to assimilate into the wider culture life of Britain the poor immigrant Irish workers who arrived throughout the nineteenth century (Hornsby-Smith, 1978). For well over a century, a central aim of Catholic Church leaders in England and Wales has been to provide a place for every Catholic parent who wants to send their child to a Catholic school. In the light of this commitment to Catholic education, the result is that throughout England and Wales a nationwide network of Catholic primary and secondary schools has been established.

A corresponding aim has been to have sufficient numbers of Catholic teachers working in and leading these schools. Alongside opening schools, a number of Catholic teacher training colleges were established in order to ensure that there were enough Catholic teachers to work in these schools. These colleges are the origins of the four contemporary English Catholic universities: St Mary's in London, Liverpool Hope, Leeds Trinity and Newman University in Birmingham. However, despite this effort to provide enough Catholic teachers for Catholic schools, a golden period where this is achieved has never come to pass. The reality is that Catholic schools in England and Wales have always struggled to get to a situation where the overwhelming majority teachers in these schools are Catholic. The focus has been on recruiting suitably qualified staff, and it is this which has been the primary goal. If these teachers happened to be Catholic, this has been seen as a bonus.

The historical realities in England and Wales have resulted in an intriguing set of issues in relation to the formation of teaching staff in Catholic schools. Over the past five decades, government policy in England and Wales towards teacher training has taken a number of dramatic shifts. An earlier focus on Initial Teacher Education (ITE), which was part-and-parcel of the drive to make teaching a graduate-only profession, has given way to Initial Teacher Training (ITT), where the focus is on equipping entrants to the profession with the practical skills to be competent and effective classroom practitioners. For the past decade, the emphasis has been firmly on acquiring the necessary skills or competencies required to gain Qualified Teacher Status (QTS). For the majority of primary school teachers in Catholic schools, this has been through a four-year undergraduate course, which combines general degree studies (typically in education) with extended placements in schools. In contrast for secondary school teachers, the traditional way of gaining QTS status has been through completing the university based one year Postgraduate Certificate in Education (PGCE) after successfully completing undergraduate studies. A small number of secondary teachers complete the four-year undergraduate pathway, just as smaller proportion of primary teachers gain QTS through the PGCE route.

6.3 Teacher *Training* or Teacher *Formation?*

In England and Wales, the shift away from teacher education (located in the university) towards competence-based training (located in the school) has become a very significant challenge. It is important to appreciate the profound changes involved with shifting from ITE to ITT, particularly in relation to the concept of formation of Catholic teachers. Entrants to the profession were traditionally given a solid induction to central educational disciplines (the sociology, philosophy, psychology and history of education). This sort of teacher education could more easily be designated as a time of intense academic formation, coming at the start of a beginning teacher's entry to the profession. However, with the shift towards ITT, it becomes much harder to characterise training and skill development (in pedagogic practices and competences) as a process of either education or formation. In effect, a paradigm shift has occurred in relation to entry to the teaching profession in England and Wales, one in which the primary goal is on training rather than education or formation. With each passing year, an increasing proportion of the teaching profession in Catholic schools has received ITT, as opposed to ITE and almost inevitably this detracts from the presumption that becoming a teacher is in itself an educative process in which some element of formation is an integral part.

The practical realities of ITT have meant that the idea of being formed to be a teacher who works in a Catholic school might have little immediate resonance with newly trained teachers. At best, there might be a benign lack of awareness of the need for formation, and at worst, there might an explicit tension between training to be a teacher who has QTS and is thus able to work in a Catholic school, with the idea that being a Catholic teacher is someone who has undergone a process of formation, in which their faith is interwoven with their professional practice.

Another challenge facing the English and Welsh context is engaging with the ambiguity around what counts as a "Catholic teacher" and what to make of the theologically rich metaphor of formation in relation to Catholic teachers. This debate is not unique to England and Wales, but some broad sketching of the issues at play will offer a richer context for the more focused discussion below.

It is not uncommon to hear advocates of Catholic education refer to someone being a Catholic teacher when discussing what the characteristics of Catholic education are. A common assumption is that Catholic schools are or ought to be staffed by Catholic teachers. This assumption rests on an implicit argument that alongside pedagogic expertise, the Catholic teacher will be able to draw on their faith in range of ways for the benefit of the students. One of these might be in providing living role models of loving service and demonstrating or witnessing to what it means to put faith into action. As well as informing and underpinning their teaching skills and practice, the hope would be that Catholic teachers might see themselves as having something like a God-given vocation.

However, what counts as being Catholic is more ambiguous. Someone who has been baptised, confirmed and made their First Communion as a Roman Catholic Christian has completed their full initiation into the Church, and they are considered to be de facto "Catholic". However, not all baptised Catholics will practise their faith on anything like a regular basis in terms of attending weekly Sunday Eucharist. People in this situation are often described as "lapsed" Catholics, and there are many subgroups nested under this heading: for some, there has been a clear decision to reject the formal practice of the Catholic faith, perhaps because of no longer believing in God's existence or a rejection of other aspects of belief. For others, the issue might be to do with the practical discipline of regular practice set against the mundane practicalities of life, yet they remain keenly aware of having a Catholic identity.[1] These would be people who have not been baptised but yet live in such a way that their values and openness to the will of God align with what it is to be a Catholic. This is something (in Rahnerian terms) that the individual concerned may well be totally unaware of, and this is the sense in which they can be described as "anonymous members" of the Church.

Of course when these varieties of being Catholic are coupled with the concept of being a teacher, it can be challenging to work out what the implied relationship is between the two. For the practising Catholic, their job as a school teacher in a Catholic school would in all likelihood be wrapped up with their faith. As such, the decision to enter the teaching profession might then be described in terms of being their vocation (Jamison, 2013; Lydon, 2011). It is of course possible that a practising Catholic teacher does not see their teaching job, even in a Catholic school, in terms of being a vocation.[2] However, when it comes to both the lapsed and Rahnerian "anonymous Catholic", the senses in which their religious vocation is to be a teacher are not at all obvious or clear. It might well be that a lapsed Catholic teacher has been able to use the fact that they were baptised as an infant as a helpful way of being called for interview and making them a more appealing candidate. The interview panel might assume that all Catholic appointees will be supportive of the school's mission and ethos.[3] For the sake of expediency, such as the need for a job, a lapsed Catholic might seek out a teaching post in a Catholic school, despite having serious misgivings about Catholic Christianity. Moreover, in England and Wales, employment legislation means that there are very few "protected posts" in Catholic schools, which are reserved exclusively for practising Catholics. Other than when appointing head teachers or deputy head teachers, the appointment processes for teachers to Catholic schools need not necessarily include explicit religious criteria.

Not only is there ambiguity over what counts as a Catholic teacher, but there is a complexity built into the theologically rich metaphor of formation. The modern concept of formation has some of its etymological roots in the Latin *formation*, which is to do with shaping and the creation into patterns. There can be naturally occurring patterns, such as the formation of rock types or cloud types, and there can be the fabrication or making of a shape or pattern, which can range from physical objects to ideas. For those who join Religious Congregations or seek ordination, it has become commonplace to refer to their period of preparation or training as a time of formation, where the individual is nurtured and guided to a point where they are able

---

[1] Thanks to the insights of the theologian Karl Rahner (1976), there is a further layer of complexity, with the conviction that there are some who could be considered to be "anonymous" Catholic Christians.

[2] Although there are many in favour of describing teaching in a Catholic school as a vocation, such as Lydon (2011) and Jamison (2013), I have argued elsewhere (Whittle, 2021a, b) that there are some significant drawbacks and problems with this approach. There are negative connotations associated with the theology of vocation (Watkins, 2018) that need to be appreciated.

[3] A normal part of the interview process in Catholic schools is to ask the applicant if they are willing to support the ethos and values of the school.

to commit to the Rule of the Congregation or to make the vows of ordination. Here the metaphorical force of formation is used in relationship to the individual being called by God to the ordained ministry or to religious life within the church. Through prayer, study and engagement with others, the person is shaped and prepared to take on this new role and way of being in the Church. This is distinct from mere training or skill development because it is a more holistic concept.[4]

In the light of the complexity built into the concept of formation,[5] it becomes clearer that exploring what is involved in the formation of Catholic teachers is a multi-levelled challenge. It will involve describing what the formation of the different types of Catholic teacher might involve. At one level, when focusing on practising Catholic teachers, the formation can take a very explicit shape, informed by the theologies of vocation and baptism. At another level, when considering lapsed, or even "anonymous Catholic" teachers, the sense in which explicit formation might be involved can become more nebulous and perhaps problematic.

Given that the expansion of Catholic schools in England and Wales has outstripped the supply of Catholic entrants to the teaching profession, there has been little practical opportunity to focus on careful study of the many issues around how we understand formation. Instead, almost inevitably the focus has had to be on a pragmatic acceptance of the government policy in relation to teacher training. Catholic schools have been dependent on being staffed by high proportions of teachers who are not Catholic and who have not received their training in Catholic Higher Education institutions.[6]

6.4 Challenges in England and Wales

It is relatively easy to realise that there might be formation needs for of all teachers who work in Catholic schools. It is not just those who are baptised Catholic Christians who stand in need of some post-ITT formation. However, the real challenge is to tease out what this would involve for the whole teaching body in the Catholic school—both

---

[4] Another aspect of the etymology of the word formation is its links to Plato's *Theory of the Forms*, in which he played on the everyday idea of a "form" to develop his distinctive epistemology and account of reality. For Plato the Forms are the abstract, perfect, unchanging ideals and concepts (such as Truth, or Beauty or Justice). Plato insists that reality lies with these ideal Forms, rather than the changing physical world we perceive with our senses. In using *eidos*, or ideal, Plato was alluding to the blue-print or perfect model which the master craft person would make first. The craft person or their apprentices would use this model as their pattern to make the subsequent copies. A skilled crafter would make an exact or almost perfect copy. Whilst formation is typically classified as a noun, it is also verb-like in being a process in which something or someone undergoes being shaped into a highly specific and recognisable pattern or way of being.

[5] See Whittle (2021a, b) where concerns are raised about using the metaphor of "formation", and it is argued that it has the potential to lead discussions about Catholic education down some unhelpful directions.

[6] Research by Mihovilovic (2021) has focused on the important role played by non-Catholic teachers in sustaining the Catholic secondary schools in the UK.

Catholic and non-Catholic. Much pivots on whether or not being a Catholic teacher mean something fundamentally different to being a teacher in some more general sense. At one level, it might function merely as an identity marker, by referring to a teacher who identifies as a Catholic Christian. Alternatively, it might mean that the teacher understands their role in overtly religious terms, regardless of what subject they teach. This could be in terms of seeing their role as a teacher in overtly catechetical terms, in that they are seeking to play their part in nurturing the faith of students. It might also serve as a way of asserting that being a Catholic teacher is a vocation—in terms of being a God-given calling. However, at the same time it is not clear how being a Catholic would have any formal impact on the actual role and practice of being a teacher in a Catholic school. Perhaps the only possible exception might be for the subject of Religious Education, but even in relation to teaching this part of the curriculum in a Catholic school, it would be matter for debate.[7] Thus, even in the practical terms of teaching, there is a lack of clarity over what is meant or being referred to in using the designation "Catholic teacher".

The issue here relates to the wider debate around what the distinctive characteristics of Catholic education are. In the past, it was assumed that the overwhelming majority of both students and staff in Catholic schools in England and Wales were Catholic Christians. This is because Catholic schools had been established to serve the desire and right of Catholic parents to educate their children in accordance with their religious faith. Inevitably, this fuelled an unexamined set of correlations between creating a child's Catholic identity, belonging to a Catholic school, the staffing of Catholic schools, and what are often taken to be the primary aims of Catholic education. There are assumptions that Catholic schools are primarily for Catholic children and that part-and-parcel of this would be ensuring that the teachers are Catholic.

However, the assumptions and correlations at play here can be seriously challenged at a number of levels (Whittle, 2014, 2018, 2021a, b, 2022). At the obvious level, the composition of Catholic schools is steadily changing. In England and Wales, the annual census data from the *Catholic Education Service* (which represent the interests of the Catholic bishops in relation to Catholic education) indicate a year-on-year slow decline in the proportion of those who are baptised Catholic Christians attending Catholic schools. Whilst it is true that Catholic schools remain a popular choice amongst parents, it seems more and more the case that these parents are no longer Catholic ones. At the theological level, Catholic Church documents, such as Vatican II's *Gravissimum Educationist*, describe how Catholic schools are not just for Catholics. More explicitly, the 1977 Vatican document, *The Catholic School*, states that "First and foremost the Church offers its educational service to the poor" (1977, par. 58). It is service to the poor rather than being a privilege or perk for Catholic parents. It might well be that Catholic schools actually need very few of either its teaching staff or the student body to be Catholic Christians. Perhaps the experience and realities of Catholic schools in England and Wales in recent decades are an apt reminder that, going forward, there might not be a critical mass of Catholic teachers needed to safeguard or guarantee the Catholicity of Catholic schools.

---

[7] See Whittle (2014) which makes the case for a non-confessional theory of Catholic education.

6.5 Addressing the Challenges

Given that an increasing proportion of teachers working in Catholic schools have entered the profession under the ITT paradigm, it means that there is a need to use Continuous Professional Development (CPD) as a way of introducing and supporting the formation of Catholic teachers throughout their career. Over the past two decades, a range of practical ways of achieving this has been used in Catholic schools. When devising these, it has been necessary to be aware of the two differing strands of teachers in Catholic schools—those who are Catholic Christians (practising, lapsed and possibly anonymous) and those who belong to other faiths or who have no religious beliefs.

The most obvious response is in terms of school-based induction programmes for new teachers to the school. Teachers are introduced to the school's ethos and mission statement and how this shapes what it is to be a Catholic school. As well as enhanced duties, perhaps within the school's pastoral system, there are expectations and school-wide values which are underpinned due to the school being Catholic. The initial induction programme is supported through the school-wide CPD provision, which is typically organised around five days of In-Service Education and Training (Inset). During the five Inset days, teachers are relieved of their teaching duties and given time to attend to their CPD. Many Catholic schools devote an entire Inset day each year to a reconsideration and review of the school's ethos and guiding principles or mission statement. Often teachers are given opportunities to reflect on their professional practice in relation to the Catholic faith and the school's mission statement as a Catholic school. In addition to such school-based CPD, there is often provision offered at diocesan level, where there is a range of training available, including courses tailored to those who are not Catholic. Many dioceses will provide Inset that supports and seeks to inspire those who are Catholic teachers to take on leadership roles within Catholic schools. There are some other smaller organisations (and individuals) who have also sought to provide additional opportunities for CPD for teachers in Catholic schools. For example, the *Association of Catholic Religious Education Teachers* organises regular CPD opportunities.[8] Various helpful resources have also been published, such as *How to survive working in a Catholic school* by Raymond Friel (2013). This is an accessible guide designed to help all, especially non-Catholics, gain a grasp of what is distinctive and different about teaching in a Catholic school. Another provision, which is provided at diocesan or national level, is the well-established course known as the *Catholic Certificate in Religious Studies* (CCRS).[9] The CCRS is a course in adult theological education which although open to all people is frequently targeted at teachers in Catholic schools. This course equips teachers in Catholic schools with a working knowledge of key aspects of Catholic faith and belief. The course is awarded by the Board of Religious Studies on behalf of the Catholic Bishops' Conference of England and Wales but is taught in a number of institutions. It typically covers eight units, some compulsory and with some optional

---

[8] See atcre.org.uk for examples of CPD offered to Religious Education teachers in Catholic schools.
[9] See *The Final Report: CCRS Twenty-five Years On* by Dr Ross Stuart-Buttle (2019).

courses. It is designed as a basic qualification to teach Religious Education and is not evidence of a teacher's level of religious practice.

An increasingly popular way of accessing post-ITT formation is through the completion of Masters level courses. All the Catholic Higher Education institutions in England provide courses at this level (such as in Education or Theology) which are marketed at teachers working in Catholic schools.

One such course stands out as particularly influential: the successful Masters level course operated by St Mary's University in London, with the title *Catholic Education Leadership: Principles and Practices*. It has been running for over two decades, providing both education and a degree of formation around aspects of Catholic school leadership. It seeks to support the distinctive leadership development for people at all levels of Catholic education for those who aspire to leadership roles in a Catholic school, and it has become almost an expectation that this Masters course will have been completed applying for key leadership positions in Catholic schools throughout England. One intriguing way of attempting to support the ongoing formation of the Catholic teachers working in Catholic schools has been through the use of what are designated as "protected posts". These are posts within the school which are only open to Catholic Christians. In the past, the listing of protected posts included senior leadership posts alongside teachers of Religious Education. Now the protected posts are reserved just for the role of deputy head teacher and head teacher. Given that only practising Catholics are allowed to apply to these central leadership roles in Catholic schools, it provides an incentive for Catholic teachers (who aspire to these roles) to take their ongoing formation seriously. Failure to attend to their own formation could get in the way of being promoted to be the deputy head teacher or head teacher in a Catholic school.

6.6 Concluding Reflections on the Need for Formation

When it comes to the issue of post-ITT formation, there are two sets of needs in a Catholic school: those who are Catholic teachers and those who are not. For the former, the issue is not primarily around access to CPD but about being attentive to the guidance from the contemporary magisterium of the Church, which is most succinctly expressed in the two key constitutions of the Church from the Second Vatican Council: *Lumen Gentium* and *Gaudium et Spes*. Both draw attention to the centrality of the weekly Sunday Eucharist which is repeatedly described as the *source and summit of Christian life*. This makes the Eucharist the primary focus of formation for the Catholic teacher. The weekly imperative in the blessing at the end of the Eucharist is for every Catholic Christian (which includes the Catholic teacher) to love and serve the Lord with their lives. It is through a life of service and discipleship that this is achieved. It is in the weekly ebb and flow of the Eucharist that Catholic Christians are challenged to live out their baptism as a response to the universal call to holiness. This will involve teasing out the relevant aspects of the theology of baptism and the universal call to holiness described in *Lumen Gentium* (nos. 39–42). For those Catholic teachers who could be considered lapsed, the formation need could be on finding ways to re-engage or rekindle their nascent Catholic faith. For such teachers, this formation might come through opportunities for discussion, dialogue and reflection about the Catholic faith in relation to being a teacher.

The formation needs of teachers in Catholic schools who are not Catholic will be somewhat different. It is of course not a matter of rekindling their faith or even making an "anonymous" Catholic Christian teacher conscious of their true situation. The formation might be in terms of enhancing the induction process and being mindful that helping non-Catholic staff to navigate the Catholic approach to education (and life in general) is an ongoing process, and as such it should be an ongoing feature of school-based CPD. There is also the need to actively guard against creating a two-tiered system, in which the Catholic teachers are given an enhanced status over and above non-Catholic teachers. The research by Dr. Mary Mihovilovic (2021) has cast an important spotlight on the need to recognise the vital contribution made by non-Catholic teachers. At the obvious level, without the vast number of non-Catholic teachers, it would be impossible for the Catholic schools in England and Wales to operate. It is important to appreciate this contribution and to actively support the holistic development of these teachers in the Catholic school, and this way they too can be given some formation.

References

Congregation for Catholic Education. (1977). *The Catholic school*. Catholic Truth Society.
Friel, R. (2013). *How to survive working in a Catholic school*. Redemptorist Publications.
Grace, G. (2002). *Catholic schools: Missions, markets and morality*. Routledge.
Hornsby-Smith, M. (1978). *Catholic Education: The unobtrusive partner*. London: Sheed and Ward.
Hornsby-Smith, M. (1999). *Catholics in England: 1950–2000 Historical and sociological perspectives*. London: Cassell.
Jamison, C. (2013). 'God has created me to do him some definite service' (Cardinal Newman): Vocation at the heart of the Catholic curriculum. *International Studies in Catholic Education, 5*(1), 10–22.
Lumen Gentium. (1964). In Flannery, A. (Ed.), *Vatican council II: The conciliar and post conciliar documents* (Vol. 1, New revised edition, 1998). Costello Publications.
Lydon, J. (2011). *The contemporary Catholic teacher: A reappraisal of the concept of teaching as a vocation in the Catholic Christian context*. Lambert Academic Publishing.
Mihovilovic M. (2021). *Sustaining the system: Non-Catholic teachers in Catholic secondary schools*. In Whittle, S. (Ed.) Cited below.
Rahner, K. (1976). *Foundations of Christian faith: An introduction to the idea of Christianity* (Dych, W., Trans.). Crossroads Publishing.
Second Vatican Council, Gaudium et Spes. (1998). In A. Flannery, (Ed.), *Vatican council II: The conciliar and post conciliar documents* (Vol. 1, New revised edition). Costello Publications.
Second Vatican Council, Gravissimum Educationis. (1966). In W. Abbott, (Ed.), *The documents of Vatican II*. Herder and Herder.
Second Vatican Council, & Lumen Gentium. (1998). In A. Flannery, (Ed.), *Vatican council II: The conciliar and post conciliar documents* (Vol. 1, New revised edition). Costello Publications.
Stuart-Buttle, R. (2019). *Final report: CCRS Twenty-five years on*. Available at https://www.brs-ccrs.org.uk/images/CCRS-Twenty-Five-Years-On-WEBSITE.pdf

Watkins, C. (2018). In S. Whittle (Ed.) *Educational leadership in Catholic schools: A practiced based theology of vocation.*
Whittle, S. (2014). *A theory of Catholic education.* Bloomsbury.
Whittle, S. (Ed.). (2018). *Researching Catholic education.* Springer.
Whittle, S. (Ed.). (2021a). *Irish and British reflections on Catholic Education: Foundations, identity, leadership issues and Religious Education in Catholic schools.* Springer.
Whittle, S. (2021b) Gerald Grace and the Philosophy of Catholic Education. In S. Whittle (Ed.), *New thinking, new scholarship and new research in Catholic education: Responses to the work of professor Gerald Grace.* Routledge.
Whittle, S. (Ed.). (2022). *Newthinking, new scholarship and new research in Catholic Education.* London: Routledge.

Sean Whittle is Visiting Research Fellow at St Mary's University, London, and Research Associate with the Centre for Research and Development in Catholic Education, with Professor Gerald Grace. He also held a Fellowship at Heythrop College, University of London, for four years. Alongside these academic roles, he works part time as a secondary school RE teacher at Gumley House FCJ Catholic School in West London. His book, *A Theory of Catholic Education* (Bloomsbury 2014), presents a robust philosophy of Catholic education that draws heavily on insights from Karl Rahner. He has edited four books on Catholic education (*Vatican II and New Thinking about Catholic Education, 2016; Researching Catholic Education, 2018; Religious Education in Catholic schools in the UK and Ireland, 2018, Irish and British Perspectives on Catholic Education, 2021*), with a further edited book on the contribution of Gerald Grace to Catholic Education Studies to be published in 2022. In recent years, he has been collaborating with other academics working in the field of Catholic education in order to create the *Network for Researchers in Catholic Education* (NfRCE). In more recent years, he has worked as Postdoctoral Research Fellow at Brunel University on a Religious Literacy project and as Visiting Lecturer at Newman University. He is Secretary for the NfRCE and also serves as Chair of the academic association AULRE. sean.whittle@stmarys.ac.uk

Part II
Catholic Teacher Formation: Engaging with Current Topics

Chapter 7
Formation for Leadership in Catholic Schools

Ken Avenell

Abstract In a changing cultural context where modes of religious affiliation are increasingly diversified, the challenge to preserve and nurture distinctively Catholic schools is ever present. The role of school-based leaders in nurturing and sustaining this identity is critical. Future leaders will need to rediscover the vision that animates Catholic education and create and steward organisational cultures that are responsive to a call to service and to provide academic excellence. The approach to leadership formation in one particular context is given in this chapter as a departure point for further discussion on how best to form leaders in cultural contest, where the place and value of religious institutions are questioned. Several key documents and processes are highlighted as these give one framework for leadership formation in Catholic schools.

Keywords Leadership · Formation · Catholic schools · Mission

7.1 Introduction

Leaders of Catholic schools often serve as the foremost faith leaders of their community and are very visible and influential in their community regards the changing Catholic landscape. *"Through their daily interactions with parents, students, stakeholders, politicians, and community, their ability to articulate their Catholic identity as a school leader is imperative for the broader understanding of Catholic education"* (Pagnotta-Kowalczyk, 2018).

Leaders in Australian Catholic education stand on the shoulders of religious founders whose collective vision built some of the strongest educational institutions in the world. Yet, the intense focus on academic excellence and accompanying frequent drift of personal connection with Church presents contemporary challenges such that some leaders now neglect the distinctively Catholic vision that inspired the founders (Buckeye & Naughton, 2008).

K. Avenell (✉)
Toowoomba Catholic Schools, 29-33 Lawrence Street, Toowoomba 4350, Australia
e-mail: ken.avenell@bbi.catholic.edu.au

> Principals appear to be caught between multiple expectations. Not only do they have to prove the school's viability as an educational institution to their local community, they must also balance government accountability requirements with church expectations. In other words, principals in Catholic schools are required to balance an educational agenda with a religious mission. (Neidhart & Lamb, 2013, p. 70)

To preserve and nurture the qualities that make these institutions distinctively Catholic, the next generation of leaders will need to rediscover the vision of their roots and give it new life so that Catholic education leaders create and steward organisational cultures that hear and respond to a call to service and also achieve academic excellence.

Catholic schools are charged with a challenging mission to make the Reign of God a reality in the lives of our students, staff and families. This is an aspiration common to Catholic schools in a wide variety of cultural contexts. For Toowoomba Catholic Schools (TCS), for example, this mission has two pillars which support and guide the way we envisage our work.

The first is that schools are exemplary places of learning where every student experiences academic success. The second is that schools are nurturing places of spiritual life and Catholic faith where every student comes to know and experience the loving presence of Jesus in their lives. These two pillars provide the foundation of all we do (TCS, 2021).

According to Belmonte and Cranston (2009, p. 18), the Catholic principals' role is made challenging due to the dual (and sometimes competing) expectations that they are proficient in both professional and spiritual competence and that the faith dimension is often the one for which they feel most unprepared.

This paper examines leadership formation in a regional Catholic educational system. It suggests practical strategies to forming leaders who can sustain and develop the inspiring vision offered by Jesus Christ in such a way that these leaders live and flourish within an increasingly secular world.

Using formation as an invitational process, teachers and leaders articulate and integrate the spiritual insights of the Catholic Tradition into the organisational fabric of their schools. The structured yet personalised system approach to formation nurtures a community of leaders that genuinely identifies with core values, appreciates the distinctive richness of their ministry and advances an organisational culture that reflects the tradition's deepest aspirations for human flourishing.

In this chapter, Toowoomba Catholic Schools (TCS) shares insights and innovative practices in leadership formation of teachers and senior staff as they worked through the complex identity and practical concerns and responsibilities of a leader in Catholic education. It is an answer to their persistent call for intentional preparation to support the faith leadership dimension of their roles which require both professional and spiritual competence (Belmonte & Cranston, 2009).

7.2 Changing Australian Context

Australian Catholic schools educate one in five Australians (NCEC, 2019, p. 1) in a time when the shape of religion in Australia is undergoing significant change at both the institutional and individual levels. Pepper and Powell via the National Church Life Survey (2016) indicate that only 11% of Australian Catholics attend church regularly whilst nearly 50% never attend at all. Yet many of these "non-mass attenders" are associated with Catholic schools either as parents or teachers (Australian Catholic Mass Attendance Report, 2016). Too, the emergence of Australia as the most successful multicultural nation in the world (Rajadurai, 2018) has further challenged schools as large numbers of religious migrants present opportunity for creating a truly "katholik" or universal faith.

For many, it is no longer religious affiliation that largely determines school choice with Australian parents. Both McCarthy (2016) and Rymarz (2017) with data drawn from extensive Australian field research note that "parents send their children to Catholic schools because they offer a very good education". The Longitudinal Study of Australian Children (2016) similarly indicates that school choice is determined through reputation, academic performance, affordability, location and finally the philosophical or religious focus. And yet, as attested by Stevens (2014), the percentage of Australian children in private or Catholic schools is high by international standards.

Nevertheless, whether they are of the Catholic faith or not, "the Catholic school offers formation to all, and especially to those who experience old and new forms of poverty" (Congregation for Catholic Education 1998, The Catholic school on the threshold of the third millennium, 15).

Catholic schools have also been recently challenged by either involvement in or by vicarious association with, institutional failure to protect children from harm (Commonwealth of Australia 2017, Royal Commission into Institutional Responses to Child Sexual Abuse). Coupled with public contempt for many instances of organisational denial or cover-up and the parallel theological and ecclesial transformations of the post-Vatican II Church, the Catholic school now provides for many Australians, their only contact with a spiritual dimension of life when they cease their connection with Church.

This means at the practical level of school life, the vast majority of both parents and staff are either unchurched and/or unfamiliar with the contemporary teachings of Church or a Catholic worldview. Often within a school, it is only the leadership and new Australian families that have this familiarity. A proportion of these leaders see their presence in church as a corporate obligation that has to be met to keep employer expectations (Coughlan, 2009).

This all occurs in milieu where education continues to experience ecclesial, political and social comment to attempt to influence both the way schools are organised and function, and particularly, their teaching and learning priorities (Arbuckle, 1993; Rossiter, 2020).

Within Catholic school leaders, there is great disparity of awareness and sensitivity to the contemporary reality of "Catholic identity". Not all leaders recognise that drift has occurred, and not all who see it care. Some appear to be concerned almost exclusively with educational outcomes and enrolment share than aspects of their mission so that "Catholic" is an historical artefact, a social obligation to be remembered at particular times of the year (Gabbett, 2020; Grace, 2018).

Yet as revealed by Neidhart and Lamb (2013) in their Australian research, most Catholic school principals understand faith leadership as being integral to their role, and they indicate they could never "opt out" of these responsibilities and that such leadership could never be totally delegated other school leaders.

As summarised by the National Catholic Education Commission (NCEC, 2020), the fundamental purpose of Catholic education is dual and intended both for the person and for society. This is achieved by inviting students to find meaning in their lives through relationship with God and developing communal obligations and commitments as an expression of this. In doing so, Catholic schools emphasise a public good whose benefits enhance the whole community.

It is recognised that

> The challenges for Catholic schools will continue to change, but their overall goals and ethos will remain and be incorporated into a new vision which is more appropriate to the multicultural and pluralistic faith dimensions of modern Australian society. (NCEC, 2020 Homepage)

Hence, leaders in Catholic education have to now more than ever, engage the personal and institutional dimensions of leadership within a uniquely Catholic mission so that education is "centred on deeply meaningful vision and values and navigates the synthesis between culture and faith" (Congregation for Catholic Education 1998, The Catholic school on the threshold of the third millennium, 15). All of these factors contribute to a significant growth in the role of the school principal as an agent of faith development as staff and community become increasingly disengaged from Church.

Committing to what is "Catholic" about a "Catholic mission" requires both a philosophical and a theological dimension so that Australian Catholic schools can continue from their initial inception some 200 years ago, to contribute to an Australian community that is well educated, socially and culturally adept and willing to embrace critical analysis of social issues. Some of these citizens may well decide to attend Church, but that is neither the explicit intention, performance measure nor a prerequisite of a contemporary Catholic school (Rossiter, 2020).

7.3 Toowoomba Catholic Education

As a landlocked diocese, the approximate size of Spain, Toowoomba, has 31 Catholic schools hosting approximately 10,000 students and 1500 staff. Fifteen schools are located in close proximity to Toowoomba, whilst others are up to nine hours distant by car. Within the teaching fraternity, there are some 150 leadership roles encompassing Middle Leaders (ML), Assistant Principals Administration (APA), Assistant Principals Religious Education (APRE), Deputy Principals (DP) and Principals. Along with Aspirant Leaders, these role groups have each received longitudinal developmental attention with specific foci of religious and educative leadership.

As later recommended by Elliott and Hollingsworth (2020) as best practice, Toowoomba Catholic Schools in 2017 adopted a systematic approach to supporting school leaders so as to enhance collective efficacy to meet the complex challenges schools face.

Using *Leading for impact* (AITSL, 2017), the AITSL 2015 environmental scan for principal preparation programs (Watterston, 2015) and *Fundamentals of high-quality school leadership development programs* (Jensen et al., 2017) as evidence-based guidelines, TCS committed to the design and delivery of an integrated set of documents, polices and a suite of leadership programs for leadership formation and development across each leadership role group.

7.4 Initial Steps

Belmonte and Cranston (2009) identify that successful leadership in Catholic schools is highly influenced by the fundamental importance of both professional and spiritual competence, and Sinek et al. (2017) advise that systemic consistency is optimised when an entity is able to articulate their "why". Noting also that the core dimensions of Catholic leadership are religious and educative, extensive consultation, collaboration and iterations of drafts provided both a Toowoomba Catholic Schools Catholic Identity position paper and a Leadership and Capability framework.

The TCS Catholic Identity position paper (2019a) (https://twbcso.sharepoint.com/sites/intranet/PublishedDocuments/CatholicIdentityPositionPaper.pdf) provides a living expression of our Catholic world view and serves to shape the Catholic identity of our schools and office and is intended to permeate structures, procedures, relationships and the teaching and learning context in a way which offers students lifelong meaning and purpose.

Our stance is that being created in the image and likeness of God accords everyone an equal and inherent dignity and gives everyone unlimited potential. We believe in an innate original goodness, a universally shared dignity and that all should have a successful and flourishing life.

The TCS Catholic identity comes to life most authentically in our schools that reflect: a culture of dialogue; the integration of faith, life, teaching and culture; and a credible and connected belief system. Such that Toowoomba Catholic schools are called to be: welcoming and inclusive communities; places of faith and reason; places of meaningful prayer and liturgy; and places of care and service to the needs of others (TCS, 2019b) and provides deliberate connectivity to the TCS Leadership and Capability framework (2017).

The Dimensions, Indicators and Capabilities identified in the TCS Leadership Framework serve the core purpose of the Catholic school which is the formation, education and development of students in partnership with parents and parish within the evangelising mission of the Church. In doing so, the framework identifies, promotes and communicates the essential elements that constitute contemporary Catholic leadership at all levels. It aligns in parallel to the Australian Professional Standard for Principals (2014).

In this TCS framework, religious leadership and educative leadership are privileged as core dimensions and encompass the dual essential purposes of the Catholic school. These core purposes are served by the support dimensions, staff and community leadership, organisational leadership and strategic leadership. The support dimensions are not ends in themselves, but exist to support the core purpose.

Capabilities are those underlying personal characteristics and behaviours that are causally related to performance. The leader's capabilities underpin the five leadership dimensions of the Leadership Framework. The qualities, abilities and values are applied across the framework. The capabilities highlight the importance of the person of the leader in a Catholic school, growing out of the school's strong community context with a focus on the formation of students.

The TCS *Leadership Framework* is approached on a holistic basis. Toowoomba Catholic Schools recognise that leadership is an integrated activity and that the dimensions of this framework do not operate in isolation from each other or the environment but provide the synergy for the whole.

There is strong and deliberate interconnectivity between the TCS *Strategic Plan*, the TCS *Leadership Framework* and the TCS *Teaching and Learning Framework* (2018). The *Leadership Framework* also connects role descriptions, selection criteria, succession planning, performance and development including goal setting and review, summative appraisals and professional learning of leaders. These are approached both individually and collectively.

7.5 Leadership Formation

In developing the requisite knowledge and skills for effective leadership in the twenty-first-century Catholic schools, TCS adopted the informational and transformational learning approaches of Mezirow (2000) and Garvey-Berger (2012). This integrated the more traditional "reading and discussing" approach to leadership preparation with more complex, engaged and reflective learning scenarios that focused leadership development on navigating the complexities of educational and religious leadership. The method as championed by Duignan (2012) was to depth personal understanding of core values through a shared leadership approach and to pass on the conviction of the difference this makes in the lives of colleagues and students.

This approach of symbolic interactionism (Blumer, 1969; Charon, 2010) utilises the basic premise that people interact with things based on meanings they have for them; the derived meaning of things comes from our interactions with others and society; the meanings of things are interpreted by a person when dealing with things in specific circumstances; hence, the meanings of things differ from person to person.

All such leadership framing was based on the precepts of andragogy as originally delineated by Knowles (1994) and subsequently further developed by many and various writers such as Drago-Severson (2009), Hoare (2006), James and Nightingale (2005) and Kenner and Weinerman (2011). Influenced by the writings of Young (2015) and the leadership recruitment scenarios of Clarke and Wildy (2010), such an experiential methodology reflects the characteristics of an integrated TCS approach to adult learning such that:

- Leaders are involved in the planning and evaluation of their instruction
- Experience (including mistakes) provides the basis for the learning activities
- Learning has immediate relevance and impact to their work or personal life
- Learning is problem centred rather than content oriented using authentic and relevant activities
- A sequenced and varied range of work-based integrated activities is facilitated, and there is avoidance of "one-off" events
- All learning is very experiential, requires collaboration, interdependence, reflection and discussion and involves frequent synthesis and learner representation.

Inherent in these principles are implications for practice so that program facilitators:

- Set a cooperative climate for learning
- Discern learner's needs, interests and skill levels to develop learning objectives
- Design sequential activities to achieve the objectives
- Work collaboratively with the learner to select methods, materials and resources for instruction
- Evaluate the quality of the learning experience and make adjustments, as needed, whilst assessing needs for further learning
- Empower learners and make them responsible for their own learning
- Shift the perspective from classroom to school to diocesan level.

This experiential approach, characterised by discourse and dialogue, requires deliberately and continuously structuring and restructuring learners in groups of varying sizes so as to best maximise learning intentions.

Groups of any size can exist. However, the size of the group allows certain group behaviours to function best. The size of the group also influences the group dynamics and places limitations on the tasks and functions that it might be expected to perform. As a maxim, as the group becomes greater, the individual becomes separated and grows more alone, isolated and segmented. Social loafing increases with group size. In working with groups, we seek deliberate entitativity—the unity of a group for a particular purpose.

In very small groups, the addition or loss of one member can make a radical difference to the group process. Similarly, larger groups need to be managed in quite different ways from smaller ones. The larger the group, the greater is the pool of talent and experience available for solving problems or sharing the effort. On the other hand as the size increases, fewer members have the chance to participate, and indeed the differences in relative participation increase to the point where one or two members begin to dominate (Jacques & Salmon, 2007).

Attention therefore to social dynamics married with activity intent allows simultaneous deep engagement by leaders at greatly varying experiences and contexts (Cunningham et al., 2019). This constructivist perspective guides learners to understand their experiences (Dewey, 1938) and subsequently through reflection and discourse develop deep connections across theory, research and practice (Cunningham et al., 2019).

Given the challenging work of Catholic school leadership, it is critical that leaders are not only able to respond to routine problems from educational experience but also bring to bear the values-based ethos of a contemporary Catholic worldview. Development of such a skill set typically entails frequent engagement with authentic scenarios drawn from real school experiences. These scenarios all integrate and require attention to religious and educative leadership as practical applications of contemporary faith. Through framing, theoretical and research input, access to experts and significant peer collaboration, leaders are drawn into creating and customising solutions relevant to their own world. A commitment to reflective journaling and subsequent school-based action learning as a developmental extension of each leadership immersion is also a core aspect of such an approach.

Very deliberately, TCS reviews each leadership program to consciously avoid those practices as identified by Petrie (2014) and Gurdjian et al. (2014) and paraphrased by Jensen et al., (2017, 17) as extensively limiting leadership development, viz.

- Programs focus is too content-heavy and does not allow enough time for the process of development
- Programs have little connection to the context and work of the participant, creating problems of relevance and applicability
- Leadership development is isolated from key colleagues and stakeholders in the participant's professional life, with whom leadership and decision-making processes are shared
- Programs are too short and are too often one time "content events" that boost leaders through intensive and interesting content but provide little opportunity for reflection, experiential learning or the ability to practice the new ideas and behaviours.

Consequently, the TCS learning environments as the antithesis of these program limiters reflect the complex and dynamic working world of school leaders. In this way, the leadership formation programs are not simply content events but part of a longitudinal process, using learning activities premised on 360° feedback, collaboration, networks, mentoring and engaging in school-based action research.

7.6 Overall Outcomes

Each of the TCS formation programs noted in Appendix A has built into their core design the concept of collective efficacy (Donohoo, 2017), where the efforts and learnings of the individual are synergised within the group to increase engagement and ownership. Leadership here is enacted beyond the individual. It is focused on establishing collective community of schools. The TCS Professional Learning Community Framework (2019b) is a written expression of this engagement and anticipated process.

Internal review and continuous feedback from participants indicates that TCS formation programs:

- Build skills for a dynamic work environment
- Are tied to actionable problems from practice
- Empower and enable leaders to lead schools as professional learning communities
- Are collaborative and networked and taken as a process and not a product
- The method of delivery (experiential) not the actual content delivered is the key focus for leadership learning
- Continue throughout the iterations of each leader's career
- Structurally reflect the TCS vision for schools and Catholic identity.

Informal evidence offered by senior education leaders (the direct line managers of principals) suggests that school selection panels are recognising the abilities of and privileging those who have been through particular formation programs.

Specifically however, leaders as part of their contract renewal every four or five years undertake a 360° review process that assesses leadership capacity and capability. The composite data from longitudinal tracking of individual leaders from these reviews shows growth as perceived by staff, parents and clergy against the dimensions and capabilities of the TCS Leadership Framework. Similarly, diagnostic tools such as work culture, leadership styles, individual and team capabilities, all of which are employed iteratively by external consultants with participant supervisors, staff and peers, substantiate growth in most leaders over time.

Comprehensive school reviews are also conducted every four years via a panel of experts external to the school. These reviews examine ongoing collection, analysis and action based on student learning data and analysis and action based on school satisfaction surveys as well extensive interviews with a range of staff, students and community and include extensive comment and data on teaching and learning, and school mission and identity. These school reports consistently show the visibility of school leaders as Catholics and school cultures successfully intertwining the two distinct dimensions of "Teaching people religion and teaching people to be religious" (Elliot et al., 2020).

Additionally through the use of various formal and informal mechanisms (including feedback from course participants), TCS has continually sought to strengthen program design and respond to participant needs. Participants consistently report via exit feedback that they have a greater awareness and appreciation of the responsibilities and opportunities of leadership roles and feel more confidently prepared to work within current and future roles as representatives of the church and leaders of schools.

References

Arbuckle, G. (1993). *Refounding the Church*. Orbis.
Australian Institute for Teaching and School Leadership. (2014). *Australian Professional Standard for Principals and the Leadership Profiles, AITSL*. Melbourne.
Australian Institute for Teaching and School Leadership. (2017). *Leading for impact: Australian guidelines for school leadership development*. https://www.aitsl.edu.au/docs/default-source/national-policy-framework/leading-for-impact.pdf?sfvrsn=b67fff3c_8
Belmonte, A., & Cranston, N. (2009). The religious dimension of lay leadership in Catholic schools: Preserving Catholic culture in an era of change. *Catholic Education: A Journal of Inquiry and Practice, 12*(3), 294–319.
Blumer, H. (1969). *Symbolic interactionism; perspective and method*. Prentice-Hall.
Buckeye, J., and Naughton, M. (2008). The importance of leadership formation. *Journal of the Catholic Health Association of the United States*, March-April. Retrieved from The Importance of Leadership Formation (chausa.org) (https://www.chausa.org/publications/health-progress/article/march-april-2008/the-importance-of-leadership-formation). August 2021.
Charon, J. (2010). *Symbolic interactionism: An introduction, an interpretation, and integration* (10th ed.). Prentice Hall.
Clarke, S., & Wildy, H. (2010). Preparing for principalship from the crucible of experience: Reflecting on theory, practice and research. *Journal of Educational Administration and History, 41*(1), 1–16.
Commonwealth of Australia. (2017). *Royal Commission into Institutional Responses to Child Sexual Abuse*.
Congregation for Catholic Education. (1998). The Catholic School on the threshold of the third millennium. *Journal of Catholic Education, 2*(1). https://doi.org/10.15365/joce.0201022013
Coughlan, P. (2009). *The mission of the Catholic school and role of the principal in a changing Catholic landscape*. Doctoral dissertation, Australian Catholic University, Brisbane.
Cunningham, K., VanGronigen, B., Tucker, P., & Young, M. (2019). Using powerful learning experiences to prepare school leaders. *Journal of Research on Leadership Education, 14*(1), 74–97.
Dewey, J. (1938). *Experience and education*. Collier.
Donohoo, J. (2017). *Collective efficacy: How educators beliefs impact student learning*. Corwin Publishing.
Drago-Severson, E. (2009). *Leading adult learning: Supporting adult development in our schools*. Corwin.
Duignan, P. (2012). *Educational leadership: Together creating ethical learning environments*, 2nd edition. Cambridge University Press.
Elliott, K., & Hollingsworth, H. (2020). *A case for reimagining school leadership development to enhance collective efficacy*. Australian Council for Educational Research.
Elliott, M., Stower, L., & Victor, A. (Eds.). (2020). *Religious education P-12 curriculum* (2nd ed.). Catholic Education Archdiocese of Brisbane.
Gabbett, C. (2020). *Maintaining a balance between school improvement and Catholic distinctiveness—A trajectory of improvement in an Australian context*. Master Dissertation, St Mary's University, London.
Garvey-Berger, J. (2012). *Changing on the job: Developing leaders for a complex world*. Stanford Business Books.

Grace, G. (2018). Catholic schools self-evaluation: Five international challenges—An analysis for Governors, Headteachers and Teachers to discuss and take action. In J. Lydon, (Ed.), *Contemporary perspectives on Catholic education*. Gracewing.

Gurdjian, P., Halbeisen, T., & Lane, K. (2014, January). Why leadership-development programs fail. *McKinsey Quarterly*.

Hoare, C. (2006). Growing a discipline at the borders of thought. In C. Hoare (Ed.), *Handbook of adult development and learning* (pp. 3–26). Oxford University Press.

Jacques, D., & Salmon, G. (2007). *Learning in groups: A handbook for face-to-face and online environments*. Routledge.

James, K., & Nightingale, C. (2005). *Self-esteem, confidence and adult learning: A briefing sheet*. National Institute of Adult Continuing Education, Learning and Work Institute.

Jensen, B., Downing, P., & Clark, C. (2017). *Preparing to lead: Lessons in principal development from high-performing education systems*. National Centre on Education and the Economy.

Kenner, C., & Weinerman, J. (2011). Adult learning theory: Applications to non-traditional college students. *Journal of College Reading and Learning, 41*, 87–96.

Knowles, M. S. (1994). *Andragogy in action*. Jossey-Bass.

McCarthy, M. (2016). Parental choice of school by rural and remote parents. *Issues in Educational Research, 26*(1), 29–44.

Mezirow, J. (2000). Learning to think like an adult: Core concepts of transformation theory. In J. Mezirow (Ed.), *Learning as transformation* (pp. 3–33). Jossey-Bass.

National Catholic Education Commission. (2019). Australian Catholic Schools 2019. National Catholic Education Commission, Sydney. Available at www.ncec.catholic.edu.au

National Catholic Education Commission (2020) Homepage, at National Catholic Education Commission (NCEC): Australia's Peak Catholic Education Body (https://www.ncec.catholic.edu.au/index.php?option=com_content&view=article&id=16)

Neidhart, H., & Lamb, J. (2013). Forming faith leaders in Catholic schools. *Leading & Managing, 19*(2), 70–77.

Pagnotta-Kowalczyk, E. (2018). *Catholic educational leadership: Exploring overlapping consensus of Catholic identity through narrative inquiry*. Doctoral dissertation, University of Victoria.

Pepper, M., & Powell, R. (2016). *Australian community survey*. NCLS Research.

Petrie, N. (2014). *Future trends in leadership development*. Centre for Creative Leadership. http://insights.ccl.org/wp-content/uploads/2015/04/futureTrends.pdf

Rajadurai, E. (2018). *Success in diversity—The strength of Australia's multiculturalism*. McKell Institute.

Rossiter, G. (2020). Addressing the problem of 'Ecclesiastical drift' in Catholic religious education. *International Studies in Catholic Education, 12*(2), 191–205.

Rymarz, R. (2017). *Catholic school enrolment: Perspectives of school principals in Tasmania*. Australian Institute of Theological Education.

Sinek, S., Mead, D., & Docker, P. (2017). *Find your why: A practical guide to discovering purpose for you and your team*. Portfolio Books.

Stevens, R. (2014). Market value and equity in schools. In S. Gannon, W. Sawyer (Eds.), *Contemporary Issues of equity in Education* (pp. 22–38). Cambridge Scholars Press.

The National Centre for Pastoral Research. (2016). *Australian Catholic mass attendance report*.

Toowoomba Catholic Schools. (2017). *Leadership and Capability framework*. Diocese of Toowoomba.

Toowoomba Catholic Schools. (2018). *Teaching and learning framework*. Diocese of Toowoomba.

Toowoomba Catholic Schools. (2019a). *Catholic identity position paper*. Diocese of Toowoomba.

Toowoomba Catholic Schools. (2019b). *Professional learning community framework*. Diocese of Toowoomba.

Toowoomba Catholic Schools. (2021). *TCS strategic plan 2021–2024*. Diocese of Toowoomba.

Warren, D. (2016). *Parent Choices of primary school. Longitudinal study of Australian children*. Australian Institute of Family Studies.

Watterston, B. (2015). *Environmental scan: Principal preparation programs*. Australian Institute for Teaching and School Leadership.

Young, M. D. (2015). The leadership challenge: Supporting the learning of all students. *Leadership and Policy in Schools, 14*, 389–410. https://doi.org/10.1080/15700763.2015.1073330

Ken Avenell grew up as the son of a shearer in Longreach and long before he went to school, learnt to read and play chess from a host of post-war migrants. This multicultural mix has given him a passion for literature, poetry and music. Ken has had a long and distinguished career in senior leadership roles in Catholic education. His current position is the director of Formation and Identity Toowoomba Catholic Education. Ken has served as the national president of the Australian Council of Educational Leaders and has received numerous awards in recognition of his contribution to education, such as the 2015 Miller-Grassie Award for educational leadership. Ken.Avenell@twb.catholic.edu.au

Chapter 8
Reflections on the Vocation of the Teacher: Formation, Agency and Meditation

Julie Harvie and Kathleen Kerrigan

Abstract The increased secularisation of society, the general decline in Catholic cultures and lower levels of participation in the sacraments have resulted in recent generations of Catholic teachers having less experience in the traditions of the Catholic faith from which to draw to inform their practice. This chapter reflects upon Catholic teaching as personal vocation and proposes that the fulfilment of this vocation requires both professionalism and spiritual capacity. An ecological model of agency is used as a framework for exploring approaches to developing the professionalism and spiritual capital that Catholic teachers require in order to fulfil their mission as Catholic educators. Professional learning and the distinctive ethos of Catholic school cultures are found to play a significant role in their professional formation. Personal, reflective encounters with the person of Christ are identified as important to the process of faith formation, and approaches such as pilgrimage, reflection and Christian meditation are proposed as ways in which Catholic teachers can be supported in their development of spiritual capital and in the fulfilment of their Catholic teaching vocation.

Keywords Agency · Formation · Meditation · Pilgrimage

8.1 Introduction

The aim of this chapter is to reflect on the vocation of the Catholic teacher. The concept of "professionalism as a vocation" will be discussed and an ecological model of agency drawn upon as a way of understanding the importance of formation in teacher development. This conceptual model provides a framework for examining

---

J. Harvie (✉)
8 Peathill Avenue, Chryston, Glasgow G69 9NP, UK
e-mail: Julie.Harvie@glasgow.ac.uk

K. Kerrigan
8 Locksley Avenue, Cumbernauld, Glasgow G67 4EN, UK
e-mail: Kathleen.Kerrigan@glasgow.ac.uk

© The Author(s), under exclusive license to Springer Nature Singapore Pte Ltd. 2022
L. Franchi and R. Rymarz (eds.), *Formation of Teachers for Catholic Schools*, Catholic Education Globally: Challenges and Opportunities 1,
https://doi.org/10.1007/978-981-19-4727-8_8

factors which may influence the ability of teachers to realise their mission to "…promote human flourishing, through a call to centre everything on God" (Rymarz & Franchi, 2019, p. 15). In particular, there will be a focus on iterational factors which can be described as those involving the personal and professional experiences a person has had, which shapes how they come to view their role as an educator. Pilgrimage, reflection and Christian meditation will then be explored as forms of faith formation and usefulness in terms of enhancing the agency of the Catholic teacher.

8.2 Professionalism as a Vocation

Definitions of teacher professionalism are contested, constantly changing (Sachs, 2003; Porrit et al., 2017) and influenced by external forces such as government (Evans, 2008). Such definitions usually include features like autonomy and expertise; however, the influence of external pressures can result in tensions around the extent to which the teaching profession is able to exercise autonomy (Forde & McMahon, 2019). This tension is reflected in many education systems by the use of mechanisms such as professional standards which often serve to re-enforce external expectations of professionalism.

The Catholic Church views teaching as both a call to professionalism and to a particular vocation in which teachers are called to personal holiness and to an apostolic mission to develop, inspire and empower others in their faith. Catholic schools play a vital role in supporting the formation of young people in an increasingly secular society (Baum & Javierre, 1982). Catholic teachers contribute to this formation through their modelling of gospel values and in all the ways in which they execute their responsibilities as an educator and their contributions to developing a school culture which is characterised by Catholic values. Grace (2010) argues that, in order to fully realise the mission of Catholic education, those who teach in Catholic schools require a religious formation that is equal to their professional formation. Drawing from Bourdieu's forms of capital, he argues that Catholic educators require opportunities to develop "spiritual capital" which draw from resources of faith, values and theological understandings and will inform and sustain them in their vocation.

General life and professional histories including initial teacher education, professional learning and professional experience are recognised as important iterational factors which influence the agency of teachers (Priestley et al., 2015), and the concept of agency will be considered in more depth later in this chapter. However, the decline in thickly Catholic cultures and lower levels of participation in the sacraments mean that recent generations of Catholic teachers may not have a rich range of life and professional histories in the Catholic tradition to draw from and inform their practice as Catholic teachers (Franchi & Rymarz, 2017). Consequently, there is a need for Catholic teacher educators and Catholic schools to provide formative experiences in which Catholic teachers and school leaders can develop their spiritual capital and nurture their practice of the Catholic faith (Franchi & Rymarz, 2017; Grace, 2010).

8.3 A Responsibility to Grow and Develop

Professional learning is recognised as a key factor in improving teacher quality and thus securing school improvement (Opver & Pedder, 2011; Hargreaves & Fullan, 2012; Harris & Jones, 2017). The Organisation for Economic Cooperation and Development (OECD) identifies professional learning as a means by which teachers can keep abreast of developments in subject knowledge, pedagogy and communication and ensure that their knowledge and skills continue to equip them for the task of preparing young people for a rapidly changing world (OECD, 2016). The increasing use of terminology such as life-long learning and career-long professional learning signals a professional responsibility for teachers to actively engage in learning throughout their career.

The complexities of teacher learning are highlighted by Korthagen (2016) who asserts that learning takes place at various levels, involves cognitive, emotional and motivational dimensions and is largely an unconscious process. Given the multi-dimensional and individual nature of professional learning, opportunities for focussed "core" reflection such as coaching are thought to have the capacity to provide meaningful opportunities for professional reflection and an individualised approach to professional development. The need for professional learning in order to sustain and develop professional practice and the significance of individual reflection in this process aligns with the need for Catholic educators to develop and sustain faith and spiritual capital and also equip them with experiences that will ultimately result in the achievement of agency in their Catholic teaching vocation. Discussing the graces of teachers who are spiritual leaders, Shimabukuro (2008) asserts that the vocation of each teacher is highly individual and requires consistent contemplative and reflective practice to nurture and support the vocation. Teachers are exhorted to make time for an individual relationship with Christ, and reflective practices that might facilitate this include activities such as scripture study, sacraments, community, adoration and prayer (McVey & Poyo, 2019).

8.4 Collaborative School Culture

It is expected that the Catholic school will be a community of faith and learning where Christ is the foundation of its cultural identity and education is understood as a mission of love and a service to society (Laghi & Martins, 1997). The Catholic teacher is called to support this distinctive ethos.

A collaborative community in which members share a concern for what they do and learn to do it better as they interact is defined as a "community of practice".

Intentional and unintended learning can take place within such a community as participants learn from the practice of others (Wenger, 1998). It is widely acknowledged that one of the strongest influences upon teacher practice is the collaborative culture of the school (Franchi, 2016, Leithwood et al., 1998; Timperley, 2008). With Catholic values central to the identity of the Catholic school and permeating all aspects of its work (McVey & Poyo, 2019), a Catholic community of practice has the potential to provide intended and unintended opportunities for staff and pupils alike to encounter the person of Christ and to develop in their faith. The important role of school leaders in ensuring such a collaborative culture of faith and learning cannot be underestimated, and it is expected that those in leadership roles in Catholic schools will strive to model excellent practice in all aspect of their work, serving as a source of professional and spiritual inspiration for the extended Catholic school community (Baum, & Javierre, 1982). The concept of agency will now be considered in order to better understand the role that formation plays in the role of the Catholic teacher.

8.5 Agency

Agency is a concept which is growing in popularity within educational literature (Etelapelto, 2013; Priestley et al., 2013); however, many models and theories around this subject exist and the term could be described as somewhat amorphous. Discussions around agency can be categorised into four main theoretical domains, namely social sciences; post-structural; socio-cultural; and the identity and life-course approaches (Etelapelto et al., 2013). Each of these traditions perceives agency, and how it can be realised, in subtly different ways. For example, in the social science literature in this area there is a focus on social and economic structures and how these affect a person's ability to bring about social change (Hitlin & Elder, 2007). From this perspective, agency can be viewed as a factor which is weighted against powerful and influential structures in society. By way of contrast, the post-structuralist lens on this subject is skewed towards the construction of language and discourses in terms of how these can enhance or constrain an individual's ability to act. Some feminist post-structural research, for example, examines how language can create categories, hierarchies and classifications which disadvantage some genders while privileging others (St. Pierre, 2000). Alternatively, collective and social networks and environments are considered as being key to developing the ability of people to thrive and develop in socio-cultural ideologies (Archer, 2003). Identity and life-course approaches, on the other hand, see agency as something which people do, based on their previous experiences, present situations and future orientations (Etelapelto et al., 2013).

Much of the literature on agency conceptualises it as variable or capacity (Priestley et al., 2015). It is seen as a variable in terms of being measured against other factors such as structures (Hitlin & Elder, 2007), or capacity in terms of being perceived as an intrinsic quality or capability a person has which enables them to realise the outcomes they wish to achieve (Korsgaard, 2009). However, it could be argued that agency is an analytical category in its own right which warrants greater analysis. Emirbayer and Mische (1998), for example, go beyond what they argue are often one-sided points of view by theorising the relationships between the different dimensions of agency, namely iterational; practical-evaluative; and projective. They describe these key elements as " …a chordal triad of agency within which all three dimensions resonate as separate but not always harmonious tones" (Embriyer & Mische, 1998, p. 972). Here, agency is conceptualised as phenomenon rather than a variable or capacity with the three key factors interacting simultaneously and constantly as people go about their daily business (Priestley et al., 2015).

In their ecological model, Priestley and colleagues (2015) present "agency as phenomenon". It is viewed here as something which a person is able to achieve rather than a quality or capacity that they possess and is affected by the "chordal triad" (iterational, practical-evaluative and projective) as identified by Emirbayer and Mische (1998). See Fig. 8.1.

The practical-evaluative dimension of agency includes culture, structure and materials. Culture involves the values held, the discourses and language used. Structure includes social structures, relationships, power and trust. Materials can be resources and the physical environment. Projective factors are defined as the long-term and short-term objectives a person has, and iterational factors relate to a person's personal and professional life history. All of these elements are related, work together and interact with each other as indicated by the arrows in Fig. 8.1. Changes in any of these elements can have a negative or positive impact on agency.

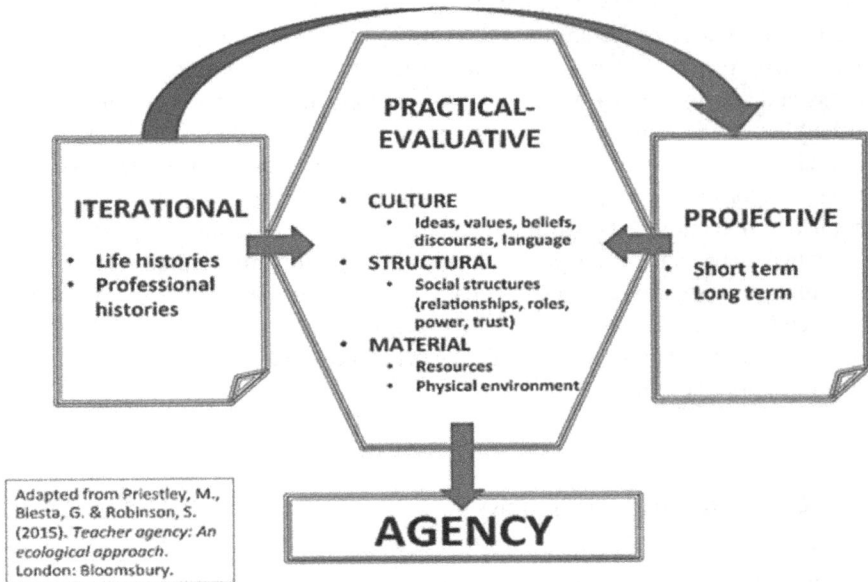

Fig. 8.1 Ecological model of agency (Breslin et al., 2021)

In considering the agency of the teacher in a Catholic school, it might be said that iterational factors are extremely important. These can be described as the personal and professional experiences a person has had, which shapes how they come to view their role as a teacher. They can involve formal professional learning as well as more informal activities such as dialoguing with colleagues on a day-to-day basis and taking part in the everyday routines of school life. The aspirations and beliefs that teachers develop about their role and the purpose of education are recognised by many as being strongly related to how they carry out their work (e.g. Nespor, 1987; Pajares, 1992; Priestley et al., 2015).

Biesta et al. (2015) assert that agency is enacted in the present, informed by the past and involves looking to the future. The ability to draw from a rich range of understanding and experience can enable teachers to imagine a wider range of possibilities for the future and consider a variety of potential solutions to problems that may arise. If the learning opportunities of the present are to become the experiences from which teachers draw to inform agency, the formative stages of teachers' careers must provide experiences and opportunities that reflect the capacities that we wish them to develop.

8.6 Pilgrimage

Recognising the challenges presented by the loss of thick Catholic cultures, Reilly et al. (2019) highlight the potential of pilgrimage as a means of faith formation for Catholic student teachers. In a study which explores the perspectives of student teachers with recent pilgrimage experience, pilgrimage is presented as a reflective process and a faith journey which aims to develop and strengthen spiritual capital and build confidence in the ability to witness to the faith. The results confirm that pilgrimage can result in a significant strengthening of personal faith offering student teachers opportunities to learn about aspects of the Catholic faith, opportunities for spiritual reflection and opportunities for peer influences on faith formation. The pilgrimage can provide strong, positive experience of belonging to a Catholic community which, in turn, can engender an eagerness to share experiences with family, friends and pupils, bearing witness to their personal encounter with the living Christ. It is a way of strengthening values and beliefs related to the iterational factors which can in turn promote agency.

8.7 Reflection and Interiority

Being a "reflective practitioner" can be viewed as one of the hallmarks of a teacher today and a benchmark for practice in many educational systems around the world (McMahon et al., 2019). In Scotland, for example, reflection is embedded in teachers' professional standards. There is also an expectation that school leaders reflect routinely as part of their leadership role and "..model good practice for staff, create a culture of critical reflection, and encourage staff to reflect on their teaching practice" (GTCS, 2012, 19). This emphasis on reflection as a key component of professionalism has resulted in a growing body of academic literature, and there are journals such as *"Reflective Practice"* which are now dedicated to the subject.

McMahon and colleagues (2019) observe that St. Teresa of Avila was an early proponent of reflection as practice. The need for interiority and meditative reflection was emphasised in her writings, and she viewed this as crucial in her role as a foundress and spiritual leader. For St. Teresa, self-knowledge was essential in her mission to know God and to carry out her work in leading others to Him. "I cannot know you, God, unless I know myself; but, I cannot know myself unless I know You" (Teresa of Avila, in Welch, online).

Catholic teachers then, in developing agency in their role of educating and leading others to Christ, can perhaps learn from St. Teresa of Avila who gave advice through her letters and collective writings. She advocated that to achieve the deep level of self-knowledge that will enable one to come to know God intimately, interiority is key (Welch and Carm, n.d.). In her book *The Interior Castle* (1556), this is encapsulated. Here, the saint describes the inner self as a mansion with different rooms where God dwells. The journey of becoming closer to God involves delving into one's own mansion through meditative prayer and passing through the rooms until God is encountered. For St Teresa of Avila, this was an active process which needed to be practised regularly and developed and she used metaphors, such as watering a garden, to illustrate this. For teachers then and school leaders, deep reflection which is critical and transformative similarly must be worked on because it does not occur accidently. The value and importance of such reflective practice need to be recognised in school by ensuring time is set aside and making resources and tools available for staff to engage in the process (McMahon et al., 2019).

8.8 Meditation

According to the *Catechism of the Catholic Church*, meditation is "…above all a quest. The mind seeks to understand the why and how of the Christian life, in order to adhere and respond to what the Lord is asking" (Catholic Church, 1994, 575). We know from scripture that Jesus often prayed on the mountain (Mt 14:23), alone and in seclusion (Lk, 9:18). Leon-Dufour (1973) argues that it would be a mistake to think that he was simply trying to obtain silent intimacy with the Father by doing this but that it was to do with his mission and the education of his disciples. The gospels inform us, for example, that Jesus was engaged in prayer before choosing the twelve apostles (Lk, 6:12) during the transfiguration (Lk 9:29) and before teaching the Our Father (Lk, 11:1). He also spent forty days in the desert as a preparation for the ultimate part of his mission on earth (Mt 4,7). Following the example of Jesus then, this type of silent, meditative prayer seems very relevant to the Catholic teacher's mission of leading and educating.

8.9 Christian Meditation in Schools

International interest in meditation and mindfulness practices in schools has been increasing in recent years (Campion & Rocco, 2009; Waters et al., 2014). While Catholic schools include opportunities for prayer, ritual and Liturgy, Christian meditation can be primarily conceptualised as a particular form of prayer, encouraging participants to take the opportunity to reflect and "be" in God's presence, affirming their faith through personal experience (Graham & Truscott, 2020a). In practical terms, teachers need to be trained in how to engage in the practice themselves and how to lead this within the classroom. The practice involves focussing the mind of participants through the use of a repeated, prayerful mantra during the meditation. Participants sit still, with eyes closed and focussing the mind. When carried out in schools, this is typically done with the whole class, with the teacher also participating where possible. The target length of the meditation is associated with students' age, for example, a target of seven minutes for students who are seven years old.

Some studies suggest that the regular practice of Christian meditation can have a variety of positive effects, not only for pupils but for teachers as well. Benefits cited include helping to create a calm classroom environment, improving student/student and student/teacher relationships and promoting general feelings of wellbeing (Bakosh et al., 2016; Campion & Rocco, 2009; Franco et al., 2010). After carrying out research within an Australian primary school, Graham and Truscott (2020a) concluded that their findings added to the weight of this growing body of literature when enhanced emotional wellbeing and improved socio-relations were observed and reported by both students and their teachers. They found that these benefits occurred in "…multiple, accumulative and often reciprocal ways" (Graham & Truscott, 2020a, 818).

While terms such as wellbeing and socio-relations can be considered as secular, Graham and Trusscot also found that some teachers explicitly said that the practice of Christian meditation had expanded their understanding of prayer and that through it they had come to recognise "…that prayer need not necessarily be about talking to God or asking for something, but was an opportunity just to sit in God's presence – and they felt very appreciative to have the opportunity to explore their spirituality and faith during work time" (Graham and Trusscot, 2020a, 815). Data from a similar study found that students' relationships with God were also nurtured through the use of Christian meditation. It was concluded that "In terms of connecting to God, it was clear that the practice had helped nurture, diversify or sustain many students' relationship with God ………. with some students describing quite profound experiences" (Graham and Trusscot, 2020b, 69). While small-scale studies like these might be criticised for their lack of generalisability, it could be argued that their value is in provoking thought in this area and supporting the conduction of further research in this field. They also provide some evidence that Christian meditation can be a useful tool in developing the agency of the Catholic educator in realising their mission to deepen their own relationship with Jesus Christ while also leading others to Him.

8.10 Conclusion

This chapter has presented the role of the teacher as a vocation which requires formative experiences to enhance personal faith and develop agency in terms of educating and leading others to Christ. An ecological model of agency has been drawn on to illustrate the importance of iterational factors in shaping practice and the need for faith formation to be considered as part of the professional development of the Catholic educator. The use of pilgrimage, reflection and Christian meditation has been explored as ways of providing valuable, experiential formation experiences to enhance agency in the vocation to teach.

References

Archer, M. (2003). *Structure, agency and the internal conversation*. Cambridge: Cambridge University Press.
Baum, W. & Javierre, A.M., (1982). *Lay Catholics in Schools: Witnesses to the Faith.* http://www.vatican.va/roman_curia/congregations/ccatheduc/documents/rc_con_ccatheduc_doc_19821015_lay-catholics_en.html
Bakosh, L. S., Snow, R. M., Tobias, J. M., Houlihan, J. L., & Barbosa-Leiker, C. (2016). Maximising mindful learning: Mindful awareness intervention improves elementary school students' quarterly grades. *Mindfulness, 7*(1), 59–67.
Biesta, G., Priestley, M., & Robinson, S. (2015). *Teacher agency: An ecological approach.* Bloomsbury Academic.
Breslin, M., Harvie, J., Leslie, B. and McLaren, E. (2021). Enhancing the agency of early career academics. *Journal of Perspectives in Applied Academic Practice, 9*(3), 32–40. https://oa.mg/work/10.14297/jpaap.v9i3.469
Campion, J., & Rocco, S. (2009). Minding the mind: The effects and potential of a school-based meditation programme for mental health promotion. *Advances in School Mental Health Promotion, 2*(1), 47–55.
Catholic Church. (1994). *Catechism of the Catholic Church.* Vatican City: Libreria Editrice Vaticana.
Leon-Dufour, X. (1973). *Dictionary of Biblical theology.* London, G. Chapman
Etelapelto, A., Vahasantanen, K., Hokka, P., & Paloniemi, S. (2013). What is agency? Conceptualising professional agency at work. *Educational Research Review, 10*, 45–65.
Evans, L. (2008). Professionalism, professionality and the development of education professionals. *British Journal of Educational Studies, 56*(1), 20–38.
Forde, C., & McMahon, M. (2019). *Teacher quality, professional learning and policy: Recognising, rewarding and developing teacher expertise.* Palgrave Macmillan.
Franchi, L. (2016). *Shared mission: Religious education in the Catholic Tradition*, Scepter (UK) Ltd.
Franchi, L., & Rymarz, R. (2017). The education and formation of teachers for Catholic schools: Responding to changed cultural contexts. *International Studies in Catholic Education, 9*(1), 2–16.
Franco, C., I., Mañas, A. J., Cangas, E., Moreno, & J. Gallego. (2010). Reducing teachers' psychological distress through a mindfulness training program. *The Spanish Journal of Psychology* 13(2): 655–666.
General Teaching Council Scotland. (2012) *Standards for leadership and management..* GTCS.
Grace, G. (2010). Renewing spiritual capital: An urgent priority for the future of Catholic education internationally. *International Studies in Catholic Education, 2*(2), 117–128.

Graham, A. & Truscott, J. (2020a) Meditation in the classroom: supporting both student *and* teacher wellbeing? *Education 3–13, 48*(7), 807–819.

Graham, A., & Truscott, J. (2020b). Exploring mystery: Can Christian meditation at school nurture students' relationships with God? *Journal of Beliefs & Values, 41*(1), 58–71.

Hargreaves, A., & Fullan, M. (2012). *Professional capital.* Routledge.

Harris, A., & Jones, M. (2017). Leading professional learning: Putting teachers at the centre. *School Leadership & Management, 37*(4), 331–333.

Hitlin, S., & Elder, G. H. (2007). Time, self and the curiously abstract concept of agency. *Sociological Theory, 25*(2), 170–191.

Korsgaard, C. M. (2009). Self-Constitution: Agency, identity and integrity. New York: Oxford University Press Inc.

Korthagen, F. (2016). Inconvenient truths about teacher learning: towards professional development 3.0. *Teachers and Teaching: theory and practice,* 1–19.

Laghi, P. & Martins, J. S. (1997). *The Catholic School on the threshold of the Third Millennium.* http://www.vatican.va/roman_curia/congregations/ccatheduc/documents/rc_con_ccatheduc_doc_27041998_school2000_en.html

Leithwood, K. A., Leonard, L. & Sharratt, L. (1998). Conditions Fostering Organisational Learning In Schools, *Educational Administration Quarterly, 34*(2).

Livingston, K. (2014). Teacher Educators: hidden professionals? *European Journal of Education, 49*(2).

McMahon, M., Harvie, J. and Kerrigan, K. (2019). A leadership lens on St Teresa of Avila. In J.C. Puente (Ed.), *Tendicial y retos en la formacion inicial de los docentes.* Universidad Pontificia Comillas.

McVey, M. K., & Poyo, S. R. (2019). Preparing Catholic Educators to Educate and Evangelize in 21st Century Schools, Action Research of an Analysis of Educator Preparation Program Requirements Including Professional and Pedagogical, Relational, Formational and Evangelistic Education for P-16 Students (PROFEss). *Journal of Catholic Education, 22*(2).

Nespor, J. (1987). The role of beliefs in the practice of teaching. *Journal of Curriculum Studies, 19*(4), 317–328.

Organisation for Economic Co-operation and Development (OECD). (2016). *Teacher professionalism* (Vol. 14). OECD Publishing.

Opver, V. D., & Pedder, D. (2011). Conceptualizing teacher professional learning. *Review of Educational Research, 81*(3), 376–407.

Pajares, M. F. (1992). Teachers' beliefs and pedagogical research: Cleaning up a messy construct. *Review of Pedagogical Research, 62,* 307–332.

Porrit, V., Spence-Thomas, K., & Taylor, C. (2017). Leading professional learning and development. In P. Earley & T. Greany (Eds.), *School Leadership and System reform* (pp. 121–130). Bloomsbury Academic.

Priestley, M., Biesta, G. J. J., & Robinson, S. (2013). Teachers as agents of change: Teacher agency and emerging models of curriculum. In M. Priestley & G. J. J. Biesta (Eds.), *Reinventing the curriculum: New trends in curriculum policy and practice* (pp. 187–206). Bloomsbury Academic.

Priestley, M., Biesta, G., & Robinson, S. (2015). *Teacher agency: An ecological approach.* Bloomsbury Academic.

Reilly, S., Crichton, H., & Lappin, M. (2019). Pilgrimages: Fruitful sources of faith formation for Catholic student teachers? Learning and leading in a pluralist world. In M. T. Buchanan & A. M. Gellel (Eds.), *Global perspectives on Catholic religious education in schools* (Vol. II, pp. 203–215). Springer Singapore.

Rymarz, R, & Franchi, L. (2019). *Catholic teacher preparation: Historical and contemporary.* Emerald (UK) Ltd.

Sachs, J. (2003). *The activist teaching profession.* Open University Press.

Seashore Louis, K., & Lee, M. (2016). Teachers' capacity for organizational learning: The effects of school culture and context. *School Effectiveness and School Improvement, 27*(4), 534–556.

Shimabukuro, G. (2008). Toward a pedagogy grounded in christian spirituality. *Journal of Catholic Education, 11*(4).
St. Pierre, E. A. (2000). Poststructural feminism in education: An overview. *Qualitative Studies in Education, 13* (5), 477–515.
Timperley, H. (2008) *Teacher professional learning and development.* International Academy of Education, Educational Practices Series 18. IBE, Publications Unit, Geneva. Available: http://www.ibe.unesco.org/fileadmin/user_upload/Publications/Educational_Practices/EdPractices_18.pdf. Accessed May 2021.
Waters, L., Barsky, A., Ridd, A., & Allen, K. (2014). Contemplative education: A systematic, evidence-based review of the effect of meditation Interventions in Schools. *Educational Psychology Review* 1–32. doi:https://doi.org/10.1007/s10648-014-9258-2.
Welch, J., O. Carm (online, n.d). Carmelite on going formation course the spirituality of St. Teresa of Avila: The Castle Journey. Available online at https://www.ocarm.org/en/content/ocarm/spirituality-st-teresa-avila. Last accessed 20 January, 2019.
Wells, M. (2014). Elements of effective and sustainable professional learning. *Professional Development in Education, 40*(3).
Wenger, E. (1998). *Communities of practice: Learning, meaning, and identity.* Cambridge University Press.

Julie Harvie is a Senior Lecturer in Educational Leadership and Programme Leader for the In and Into Headship programmes at the University of Glasgow. She is a member of the National Design Group for educational leadership within Scotland. Julie is the Depute of the Educational Leadership and Policy Research and Teaching Group and Quality Enhancement Officer for the School of Education. She supervises Ph.D., Ed.D. and Masters students and teaches on a variety of Initial Teacher Education courses. Julie previously held the role of Primary Head Teacher and also has experience of system leadership. She is an External Examiner for the University of Nottingham. Julie.Harvie@glasgow.ac.uk

Kathleen Kerrigan is a lecturer in Educational Leadership at the University of Glasgow, where she leads programmes in Middle Leadership and Teacher Leadership and is Deputy Director of the St Andrews Foundation for Catholic Teacher Education. Kathleen is a committee member of the Scottish Professional Learning Network and a Professional Learning Ambassador for the General Teaching Council, Scotland. Kathleen worked for many years as a teacher and middle leader in Scotland's schools. Prior to joining the University of Glasgow was Development Officer with the Scottish College for Educational Leadership (SCEL) where she contributed to the development and delivery of leadership learning opportunities for educators across Scotland. Kathleen.Kerrigan@glasgow.ac.uk

Chapter 9
Teacher Formation: An Augustinian Study in Learning Truth and Beauty

Renée Köhler-Ryan

Abstract Augustine's theory of education refers to principles of teacher formation that depend upon ongoing prayer and Scriptural study, as well as deep reflection on the fact that education is a way of opening up the intellect to divine light. These are both private and communal practices, ultimately emphasising that teachers are formed both by the act of teaching and by the activity of learning. One can derive Augustine's principles for teacher formation from *On the Teacher*, *De doctrina Christiana* (here called *Teaching Christianity*) and *Confessions*. Like all human formation, teacher formation means learning responsiveness to God's truth and beauty in creation and Scripture. More particularly, religious educators must also learn to communicate what God says, by becoming formed in the contemplation of Scripture and reflective practice. This includes formation in presenting ideas in dialogue so that students exercise their rationality in a virtuous community of learning, thereby preparing for Christ to illuminate the intellect with truth. Along with the student, the Christian teacher responds to beauty. Through teaching, the teacher is formed to be a better witness to truth and beauty.

Keywords Augustine · Formation · *De Magister* · *De Doctrina Christiana* · Liberal arts

9.1 The Elements of Teacher Formation

Whilst discussions of Augustine's understanding of education and of human formation abound, there is little extant literature on how he would approach the issue of formation of teachers (Clair, 2017; Kenyon, 2012; Topping, 2012). Yet, especially in *On Teaching Christianity* (*De doctrina Christiana*), such formation clearly preoccupies him (Augustine, 1996). There, the teacher is the one who knows Scripture and can communicate it to others, using the tools of the liberal arts tradition in

R. Köhler-Ryan (✉)
School of Philosophy and Theology, University of Notre Dame, Sydney, Australia
e-mail: renee.kohler-ryan@nd.edu.au

© The Author(s), under exclusive license to Springer Nature Singapore Pte Ltd. 2022
L. Franchi and R. Rymarz (eds.), *Formation of Teachers for Catholic Schools*, Catholic Education Globally: Challenges and Opportunities 1,
https://doi.org/10.1007/978-981-19-4727-8_9

which Augustine is trained. The teacher finds truth and expresses it beautifully—so that others can see its attractiveness and move towards it. The Christian teacher knows how important this is because he understands that God himself is truth and beauty—and that Christ is the one who illuminates the mind. As *Teaching Christianity* conveys, the teacher knows that this world is a place of pilgrimage, where everything is a sign that points to God. Teachers foster their ability to communicate these signs by reading and apprehending Scripture in community with others.

Two other texts are important for understanding Augustine's theory of the formation of teachers. Like *Teaching Christianity*, *On the Teacher* develops Augustine's theory of how language and signs point to God (Augustine, 1995). Perhaps more importantly, it demonstrates how the act of teaching forms the teacher. The reader appreciates this by seeing Augustine in action. As Augustine leads the dialogue with his son Adeodatus, we watch him witness the illumination of the pupil's mind. As teacher, he provides beautiful objects for contemplation, thereby creating a pathway for Adeodatus to comprehend truth.

In the *Confessions*, Augustine contrasts a good with a bad teacher, providing insight into how a teacher must be formed in the proper relationship between truth and beauty (Augustine, 1997). Faustus, the worst kind of teacher, is lazy, unconcerned with finding the truth, and unable to answer questions. Worse, he focuses all his energy on looking like he knows the truth, and "ensnares" others in his trap. His words may *seem* beautiful, but they cover over his lies. In contrast, Saint Ambrose's rhetoric leads Augustine towards truth and beauty as no other teacher has been able to thus far in his life. This Catholic bishop studies, prays, and then preaches beautifully, providing insight into the many levels through which God speaks through creation and Scripture. Unlike Faustus, Ambrose is so concerned to preach what is true that he spends much of his time in quiet contemplation.

It becomes apparent that the formation of teachers involves several different elements. Above all, the Christian teacher must desire truth and beauty and know that the quest for these comprises our earthly pilgrimage to God. Making one's way along the path to God entails the hard work of study and the practice of beautiful communication. The Christian teacher must study grammar, logic and rhetoric in order to understand Scripture and to teach it to others. This involves him in a tradition where teachers and pupils work together, and the teacher is an occasion, rather than a direct cause, of learning. That is to say, the teacher is the one who helps the pupil to prepare the way for Christ to illuminate the mind. As this happens, the teacher at the same time undergoes formation, by delighting all the more in the way that God loves and causes us to love, in an ordered way. The practical implications of Augustine's theory, for the formation of the contemporary religious educator, will be spelled out after closer examination of these main themes in *Teaching Christianity*, *On the Teacher*, and *Confessions*.

9.2 Teacher Formation is Human Formation in Truth and Beauty

Before discussing what Augustine thinks about the formation of the Christian teacher, one must understand his theory of human formation. Human formation is the personal response to God's love, as God calls to us through creation and revelation. Specifically, Augustine thinks of this formation as what he calls a reformation (Ladner, 1959). God's creation of the cosmos was the first formation. When Adam and Eve sinned, they became deformed, by choosing a disordered love. Putting themselves before God, they could no longer easily discern truth and beauty. Humans thereafter needed to learn, with the aid of divine grace, what it means to love properly, according to the order of love where God comes first, and then, all else falls into place. Loving well means responding to God, who is truth and beauty, and avoiding what might *seem* to be true and beautiful. In other words, the Christian is the one who can avoid those pleasures that cause us to stop seeking God, instead pursuing God through the signs he gives in the world. Using such signs well, the Christian can love appropriately—bringing truth and beauty into harmony.

Humans, then, undergo formation when they participate freely in their reformation. This is, properly speaking, religion for Augustine—whereby humans turn back to God, binding themselves to him freely through learning to love properly (Fiedrowicz, 2002). Thereby, they become capable of loving as they should—loving God first, thus enabling proper self-love, love of neighbour as self and then the rest of creation (Clair, 2016; Kohler-Ryan, 2020). This ordered love means that nothing else takes God's place, and only what leads to God is loveable. Formation, then, is a process of education, whereby the person learns how to pursue what is true, by avoiding what distracts from God and pursuing what leads to him. Such education describes Augustine's understanding of conversion, which is arduous, ongoing, and best pursued with others.

Like any other human, the Christian educator participates in her formation by increasingly finding joy in the truth, particularly when she responds to divinely configured beauty. In addition, as a teacher, she is able to convey what she knows to others, with the main goal of helping them to open their hearts and minds to God. Above all, she has the task to communicate the joy that comes from being in relationship to Christ. The source of the educator's joy is God's love, which expresses itself to the human heart and mind through the beauty of creation. Whilst her formation as educator is quintessentially human, she is especially tasked with learning how to convey her joy to others, through constant witness. This means developing an insight into the truths that God conveys to us through the beautiful world. At the same time, it entails learning the art of rhetoric (Augustine, 1996). Above all, the teacher must witness to the way that the Christian can discriminate between what God gives us as a means to reach him, and God himself. The Christian knows how God uses beautiful signs to convey his love. The Christian educator needs to become particularly adept at teaching the danger of mistaking a sign for God.

Finally, formation of the teacher is, for Augustine, a communal activity. It depends on speaking and listening, and above all understanding that learning and teaching are never solely human activities. In fact, learning and teaching are "something that we receive from God and then share with others, rather than something which comes from ourselves" (Harrison, 2013). Learning and teaching are essentially acts of love—in the highest sense of charity—towards others, and teachers have the responsibility to undergo the right kind of formation for such activities. An important aspect of the formation of the teacher occurs during the activity of teaching. For, whilst teaching, he learns more about what he is conveying. In particular, he learns that God, rather than he, is the one who illuminates the intellect and transforms the human heart.

The two works that address these points most directly are *The Teacher* and *On Christian Doctrine*, whilst *Confessions* expresses how these principles impact Augustine's experience of being taught. To these works, discussion now turns.

9.2.1 Formation in "On the Teacher"

Augustine writes *On the Teacher* as a dialogue between him and his son Adeodatus (Augustine, 1995). Based on Plato's dialogue the *Meno*, which presents Plato's theory of *anamnesis*—the theory that knowledge is an act of memory—for our purposes here *On the Teacher* is more important for its demonstration of how learning takes place than for its arguments about what knowledge is. The reader sees Augustine at work bringing together his Christian belief with his appreciation of the importance of human reason and explanation. Significantly, *On the Teacher* demonstrates Augustine in action as the teacher who, as guide, works in cooperation with the divine illuminator: God. In fact, for Augustine the only real teacher is Christ. Robert D. Anderson describes how, when teaching this text, he and his students have identified the characteristics of Augustine the teacher. Most importantly, Anderson finds that *On the Teacher* presents an internal dialogue as a way of understanding, because "genuine education is an activity in which students are always the primary agents as they see things for themselves and make the truth their own" (Anderson, 2015). Seeing for oneself is, for Augustine, a response to divine light (Mathews, 2006). So, the teacher needs to become the one who prompts the student towards an openness to interior divine illumination. In other words, the task of the teacher is to prepare the mind for receptivity. In order to do this, he must first be receptive to that same light.

Essentially, *On the Teacher* presents how the educator does a great deal of work with the student, to open the student's mind towards reality. The dialogue demonstrates how teaching is the work of showing the student how to read the signs that surround him in the world. These signs will lead to comprehension of how God lovingly reaches out to each person through the beautiful world that he has made, and through his divine revelation—particularly in this case in Scripture. Topping discusses how the teacher in *On the Teacher* is like Plato's Socrates, who "present[s] the right questions and the right objects before the minds and senses of the students"

(Topping, 2010). Such presentation, though, cannot explain the comprehension that comprises deep intuition of truth—for this is where the learner meets Christ the teacher. Where Plato theorised that such understanding was *anamnesis*—remembering the forms—Augustine theorises that Christ illumines the mind. Learning, or knowledge, is in fact a response to grace.

Effectively, *On the Teacher* demonstrates that the Christian educator needs to be formed to be an occasion rather than an efficient cause, of learning for the student. For this to happen, the teacher must already have a relationship to Christ and also be adept at carrying out dialogical method. Only then can she present just enough of the right material for the student, in the right way, so that the student can then comprehend what is before him. The activity of dialogue, a key method in the liberal arts, is where teacher and student enter into a dialectical conversation. They see together that what at first seems to be an attractive option need not necessarily be the answer to what they seek. This is an energetic engagement in sorting out the true from the false, the beautiful from the merely attractive. In other words, they learn to differentiate true from false beauty. Such activity opens up a pathway, wherein Christ can shine his light, making evident the final answer to what student and teacher seek together. As *Teaching Christianity* further articulates, the teacher's activity is possible because she has studied how God speaks in Scripture. That training helps her to know and communicate how God's beauty shines throughout the created world. The teacher can find the hidden ways that God speaks to people and imitate these when working with the student.

9.2.2 Formation in "Teaching Christianity"

Teaching Christianity further develops Augustine's theory of signs, focussing on how God speaks to humans through Scripture as well as Creation. Much of the work is devoted to a systematic study of rhetoric, the science of presenting what one knows in such a way that the listener can understand. Rhetoric is important for Augustine because it offers the tools for the teacher both to learn from Scripture (which presents the ways that God speaks to his people) and then to teach the truths of Scripture. It depends on beautiful language to convey its meaning. *Teaching Christianity* also argues that at first we learn Scripture from a guide. Thus, a community of learning and teaching is essential. In his prologue to the work, Augustine states that:

> There are some rules for dealing with the scriptures, which I consider can be not inappropriately passed on to students, enabling them to make progress not only by reading others who have opened up the hidden secrets of the divine literature, but also by themselves opening them up to yet others again. I have undertaken to pass these rules on to those who are both willing and well qualified to learn, if our Lord and God does not deny me, as I write, the ideas he usually suggests to me in my reflections on the subject (Augustine, 1996).

This opening gives another key to Augustine's understanding of the formation of the Christian educator: that the teacher learns by engaging in reflective practice (Rushton & Suter, 2012). Such reflection, when undertaken within the context of prayer, is the teacher's way of actively engaging in learning. As Augustine studies Scripture and writes about it, God communicates to him. Augustine works, and God works through him as he works, by "suggesting" ideas that Augustine can then convey to others. If Augustine did not give himself up to study in this way, he could not claim to be worthy of being an educator, able to present ideas to others that might lead them further to God. Like *On the Teacher*, *Teaching Christianity* focusses how thought opens oneself to God. Two main themes in *Teaching Christianity* demonstrate how the teacher can forge that passage in the self, becoming more open to divine light.

The first of these is a key distinction in *Teaching Christianity*, between using and enjoying. Augustine argues that only God is to be enjoyed. Humans should use all else as a means to enjoy God. As Augustine develops this point, it becomes evident that the teacher knows the difference between what needs to be used and what should be enjoyed. The teacher can communicate this to others through the use of signs that, in turn, communicate the order of God's love. Augustine distinguishes: "Enjoyment is clinging to something lovingly for its own sake, whilst use consists in referring what has come your way to what your love aims at obtaining, provided, that is, it deserves to be loved" (Augustine, 1996). The well-formed person can appreciate that the created world is a gift, a beautiful pathway towards God. Everything in creation is, for the one turned towards the Creator, a communication of divine love. The one who loves properly finds God everywhere and in particular through the beauty of the world that he has made. A teacher can convey this to students, by helping them to understand how the world points to God and at the same time how to read the signs that indicate his divine presence.

The second theme is that this life is a pilgrimage. Like travellers in a foreign land, Augustine argues that we need to remember that the main purpose of our life on earth is to return home. This return is our conversion, or reformation, as discussed above. Quoting Paul's letter to the Romans, Augustine argues that to avoid "being perversely captivated" by pleasurable experiences: "we have to use this world, not enjoy it, so that we may behold *the invisible things of God, brought to our knowledge through the things that have been made* (Rom 1:20); that is, so that we may proceed from temporal and bodily things to grasp those that are eternal and spiritual" (Augustine, 1996). Evidently, human life is a journey during which we need to learn to love beautiful things appropriately. When they delight us, they should refer us to God. When they instead distract, they "block" our path, ensnaring us in what is inferior and ultimately dissatisfying. According to Augustine, the teacher is the one who knows this and so can find out what various signs are trying to tell us.

With these themes in the background, Augustine develops a science of signs intended to develop his main idea that "all treatment of the scriptures is aiming at a way to discover what needs to be understood, and a way to put across to others what has been understood" (Augustine, 1996). The Christian teacher must both discover and convey. He needs to learn how God speaks in order to understand what God says; and then, he must help others to understand the same. This means appreciating the relationship between signs and things, words and reality, physical and spiritual, exterior and interior, inferior and superior. This education towards truth is at the same time a formation in beauty. For, teacher and student alike need to learn how appropriately to delight in what is pleasing to the senses, thereby avoiding becoming ensnared. In his *Confessions*, Augustine illustrates this main point when he contrasts two of his teachers, Faustus and Ambrose.

9.2.3 Exemplars of Good and Bad Formation in "Confessions"

Faustus and Ambrose exemplify how Augustine understands the differences between those who comprehend and communicate truth and beauty, and those who do not. For nine years, Augustine was a follower of the Manichean heretical religion. In his quest for the truth, he often asked questions of other Manichees that none of them was able to answer, concerning the truth of reality and the meaning of human existence. During those years, the other Manichees would simply tell him to wait until he could meet Faustus, who would surely answer all of his questions. However, Augustine was entirely disappointed when this moment came. He describes Faustus as "a lethal trap set by the devil," going on to explain that "[m]any people were ensnared by the persuasive sweetness of his eloquence" (Augustine, 1997). Not only did Faustus not seem to know the truth. He did not care that he did not know it, and he willingly and lazily led others astray. Augustine's language here distinguishes between true and false beauty. The former always allies itself with truth and leads to joy and freedom; whereas the latter either denies or gives up on truth's existence and leads to confusion and misery. Distressing to Augustine, Faustus's eloquence ensnares those who do not see its falsity.

Furthermore, Augustine found that Faustus always resisted serious conversation and did not like exploring questions. Augustine finally discerned that the man gave the appearance of having knowledge but was in fact uneducated in all of the liberal arts except for grammar. Even there, says Augustine, Faustus was only average. Augustine the trained teacher of rhetoric is disappointed in Faustus on a professional level. On a moral level, he is distressed. Augustine escapes the devil's trap because he understands that eloquence leads the pilgrim astray when it does not express the truth.

The example of Faustus demonstrates what a disastrous effect a badly formed teacher can have on a student. Augustine is so disappointed in Faustus that he almost despairs of finding the truth himself. Then, though he discovers an authentic teacher in Saint Ambrose. Ambrose has a reputation for preaching beautifully, and so Augustine goes to hear him first out of professional interest. He is at this point uninterested in the subject matter of Ambrose's preaching. Augustine thinks that Scripture is illogical and replete with ill-turned phrases. Listening to Ambrose, however, he becomes aware that one should not read Scripture only literally. The spiritual senses are more important. Augustine learns even more from Ambrose because the older scholar is a powerful witness to good teacher formation. In fact, Ambrose reveals to Augustine that a Christian teacher is constantly in a process of formation.

In this respect, Augustine describes Ambrose's humility before others. This direct contrast to Faustus is compelling, but perhaps not as intriguing as another aspect of Ambrose's disposition. Augustine describes seeking out Ambrose. He finds the older scholar peacefully and silently reading Scripture. When Ambrose reads God's word, he is completely absorbed. This profound engagement intrigues Augustine, completely at odds as it is with the earlier example of Faustus, who was too busy seeking occasions to be flattered and admired to put in the work of study. It also contrasts with the way Augustine has been trained as a teacher, to attract a cult-like following in order to earn money as a tradesman in rhetoric. Augustine, at last, has found a model teacher, who studies, prays, constantly seeks the truth and unselfishly communicates it to others.

9.3 Findings for the Contemporary Christian Teacher

From this discussion of Augustine's understanding of the formation of the Christian educator, one can derive several factors important for teacher formation in the contemporary context. Each highlights that teaching is a virtuous communal activity that depends on formation in pursuit of truth and beauty, through study of Scripture and the liberal arts.

9.3.1 A Perpetual Student of Scripture

First, it is essential for the Christian educator to study Scripture. *Teaching Christianity* argues that the teacher must first learn how God teaches, before undertaking to do the same. God teaches most explicitly through Scripture and Creation, where he uses signs and things. Humans then learn from each other how to use the same to comprehend God. *Teaching Christianity* applies the liberal arts to Sacred Scripture. Grammar and logic help to analyse and understand Scripture. Together with rhetoric, they then help the teacher to learn how to communicate the meaning of Scripture to others. Augustine's discussions convey that this activity of learning from Scripture and from others should never end. As Williams describes, "learning from Scripture is a *process*—not a triumphant moment of penetration and mastery, but an extended play of invitation and exploration" (Williams, 2016). As process, this activity should last a lifetime. If ever it stops, the risk of becoming like Faustus, rather than Ambrose or Augustine, is real.

In the contemporary context, this means that forming the religious educator should focus on giving her the tools for lifelong study and communication of God's Word. This needs to include building up the capacity for reflecting, in prayerful silence as well as communal discussion, how God's language communicates itself throughout our lives. This should lead to an ever-deepening knowledge of how and why God acts as the loving communicator. Scripture, Augustine emphasises, speaks both literally and spiritually. Above all, the spiritual senses of Scripture tutor the believer in what to love, and with what kind of love. This makes study and life a realm of delight. Harrison observes that for Augustine this delight characterises the Scripture scholar who discovers truth (Harrison, 2000). Scriptural study leads to better discernment, fostering better relationships with others. All of this enriches classroom practice, by focussing on how education should foster a love of truth and beauty.

9.3.2 Making a Path for Divine Illumination

The teacher understands that God, not she, is the source of truth. Knowledge occurs when God illumines the intellect. To teach, then, is not to fill the minds of students with knowledge, but to engage them in "rational activity" that then helps them to become open to God's light (Kenyon, 2012). Augustine illustrates in *On the Teacher* that education involves dialogical more than didactic method. The religious educator's best beginning point for such communal inquiry will be Scripture, as *Teaching Christianity* makes clear. Augustine promotes the liberal arts as the training ground of a teacher. Clair explains the perennial importance of these arts for any healthy society (Clair, 2017). Augustine proposes the classical Roman model for education in Scripture, and certainly, any liberal arts methodology can be challenging for religious educators in the contemporary context (Kimball, 2010; Kohler-Ryan & Sharkey, 2019). Nonetheless, dialogue and rhetoric, which question and present the truth in as beautiful, open and logical a way as possible, are the best suited for seeking out knowledge of God. Furthermore, they require hard work, which Augustine thinks is important to prepare for divine illumination.

9.4 Fostering Reflective Practice

In fact, disciplined study and communication of ideas is essential for the Christian Teacher. The desire for truth and beauty drives this ordered inquiry. Only when truth and beauty operate together can the virtues of an educator properly develop. Faustus, the teacher who dissociated beauty and truth, became a tool of the devil. Vainly encouraging others to surround him with praise, Faustus was uninterested in fostering open dialogue and pursuing the truth for its own sake. This made him an ineffective teacher. Ambrose, on the other hand, astonishes Augustine by not cultivating the praise of others. Instead, Ambrose wants to know God and bring others to the divine Creator, and he is the more effective teacher.

Augustine particularly admires Ambrose when he hears the older saint preach and when he observes him engrossed in silent study. In *Teaching Christianity*, Augustine argues that in writing he comes to know his own thoughts better. Study of the divine word nurtures these thoughts. As he reflects, writes, and preaches, he comes to see the beauty of truth and the way that God constantly affects his life. Reflection here is key, because this is when God speaks to Augustine. Perhaps most explicitly in *Confessions*, in looking at his own life in the light of God's word, Augustine can communicate that Scripture is a call to divine love. The response to that call is in a life of virtue, where the human person strives to use all the tools available to comprehend divine Scripture. The educator consciously works with those means, to open up ways for others to contemplate God.

Constant reflective practice develops one's sense of life's meaning, by building upon Scripture and the revelation of divine beauty in creation and the human mind. Rushton and Suter argue that reflective practice can become a hackneyed concept if not embedded across a teaching career as a useful exercise in career management and professional development (Rushton & Suter, 2012). Augustine's point is even more pragmatic. Reflective practice brings the educator closer to God, making her better able to communicate the truth beautifully. Augustine thinks that teaching Christianity fosters communities of love that are permeated with a love of truth and beauty. The Christian teacher becomes increasingly aware of the ways that God speaks to humans through creation and Scripture, and so, an aesthetic sense becomes more active. This alertness to beauty is possible because of the teacher's love for truth. It enables the teacher to work with others towards the final end of all human life: the divine illumination of truth and beauty in human hearts and minds.

References

Anderson, R. D. (2015). Teaching Augustine's *On the Teacher*. Religions, 6, 404–408.
Augustine. (1995). The Teacher. In *Against the academicians and the teacher* (Peter King, Trans., pp. 94–146). Indianapolis: Hackett.
Augustine. (1996). *Teaching Christianity* (E. Hill, & O. P. Hyde Park, Trans.). New York: New City Press.
Augustine. (1997). *The confessions*. (Maria Boulding, O.S.B. Hyde Park, Trans.). New York: New City Press.
Clair, J. (2016). *Discerning the good in the letters and sermons of Augustine*. OUP.
Clair, J. (2017). *On education, formation, citizenship and the lost purpose of learning*. Bloomsbury.
Fiedrowicz, M. (2002). General introduction. In J. Rotelle (Ed.), *On Genesis*. New City.
Harrison, C. (2000). The rhetoric of scripture and preaching: Classical decadence or Christian aesthetic? In R. Dodaro & G. Lawless (Eds.), *Augustine and his critics: Essays in honour of Gerald Bonner* (pp. 214–230). Routledge.
Harrison, C. (2013). *The art of listening in the early Church*. OUP.
Kenyon, E. (2012). Augustine and the liberal arts. *Arts & Humanities in Higher Education, 12*, 105–113.
Kimball, B. A. (2010). *The liberal arts tradition: A documentary history*. Rowman & Littlefield.
Kohler-Ryan, R., & Sharkey, J. (2019). Studies in Catholic thought. A liberal arts approach to religious education in the classroom. In: R. Rymarz, & P. Sharkey (Eds.), *Moving from theory to practice: Religious educators in the classroom* (pp. 177–192). Vaughan.
Kohler-Ryan, R. (2020). Companions in the Between: Augustine, Desmond, and their Communities of Love. (Eugene: Pickwick, 2020)
Ladner, G. G. (1959). Saint Augustine and the difference between the reform ideas of the Christian East and West. *The idea of reform: Its impact on Christian thought and action in the age of the fathers* (pp. 153–283). Harvard.

Matthews, G. (2006). Knowledge and illumination. In N. Kretzmann & E. Stump (Eds.), *The Cambridge companion to Augustine* (pp. 171–185). CUP.
Rushton, I., & Suter, M. (2012). Why reflect on practice. *Reflective practice for teaching in lifelong learning* (pp. 1–11). McGraw-Hill.
Topping, R. (2010). *St. Augustine*. Continuum.
Topping, R. (2012). *Happiness and wisdom: Augustine's early theology of education*. Catholic University of America Press.
Williams, R. (2016). Language, reality and desire: The nature of Christian formation. In *On Augustine* (pp. 41–58). Bloomsbury.

Renée Köhler-Ryan is National Head of School of Philosophy and Theology at the University of Notre Dame Australia. Her Ph.D. from Katholieke Universiteit Leuven was on the Catholic Imagination of St. Augustine. She has been involved in education and teacher formation for teachers in New South Wales across several dioceses. Her book, *Companions in the Between: Augustine, Desmond and their Communities of Love*, was published in 2020. Other publications are in her research interests of teacher formation, the Catholic Intellectual Tradition and Catholic Imagination, including the thought of Augustine, Edith Stein and Karol Wojtyla and contemporary philosopher William Desmond. renee.kohler-ryan@nd.edu.au

Chapter 10
Teacher Formation in a Digital Age

Mary E. Hess

Abstract Catholic teaching suggests that we are created for relational communion. Yet how is this development to take place, how is this relational communion to grow, when societal shifts are producing ever more segmented, polarized, and sharply unequal communities? Context collapse requires that we rethink how we engage authority, what authenticity might mean, and how to nurture agency amidst digital media. The COVID-19 pandemic has rapidly accelerated both the challenges and the opportunities. An analogy to food offers a way forward, particularly for developing teachers who are capable of igniting curiosity and awe through reflection on God and God's creation. Trauma-informed pedagogies are particularly useful in the midst of discerning which digital technologies might be most helpful in this space.

Keywords Digital media · Context collapse · Trauma-informed pedagogies · Creative pedagogies · Faith formation

10.1 Digital Contexts and Pandemic Challenges: Practice Matters

This topic—teacher formation in a digital age—is both so large and so pressing that it is difficult to know how to engage it concisely, with practical effect. In what follows, I offer an analogy that can be helpful in the midst of this continual change, and I propose specific practices that teachers can employ, all the while keeping in mind that a "digital age" is an age of continual change and experimentation. We are all learning as we go.

Scholars and practitioners working in arena of teacher formation more broadly have long recognized the challenges posed by digital media (Boyd, 2014; Clark, 2003, 2013; Hess, 2015, 2017a, b; 2018a, b; Lytle 2013, etc.). The COVID-19 pandemic, global in nature, beginning in 2020 rapidly accelerated a shift into digital learning spaces, given the necessity of physical distancing for health reasons (Ong, 2021).

M. E. Hess (✉)
Luther Seminary, Saint Paul, MN, USA
e-mail: mhess@religioused.org

There remains enormous confusion and perplexity as teachers try to navigate these changing, dynamic, and often conflicted waters. Yet the need to prepare teachers to teach in Catholic settings with resilience, agility, and a deep sense of faith is more important than ever. Research into what formation looks like within digital media, and in spaces thoroughly shaped by digital media, has much to contribute to meeting these challenges (Hess, 2019, 2020).

It is clear that religious identity is formed and shaped primarily by one's most intimate relationships. Relationships with those who hold ultimate power over people when they are young—parents or other primary caregivers—are often the first and most stable metaphors and analogies for God (Rizzuto, 1979). But what are we learning about how the increasing presence of digital media affects these relationships (Boyd, 2014; Clark, 2013)?

We know, for instance, that daily practices fundamentally shape our faith. Growing up within a community that regularly shares table prayers, for instance, shapes a sense of God as a transcendent being worthy of gratitude, a being whose voice can be heard through community. The research of Martinson et al. (2010) into the elements that sustain faith in youth growing through adolescence has identified several faith factors that are embedded in practice. Historical and theological research confirms these insights. The *Practicing Our Faith Project*, for instance, has identified twelve practices of faith—practices which are neither creedal nor liturgical in character—which fundamentally shape Christian knowing (Bass, 2009; Hess, 2014).

Yet digital media—the hardware itself, the software which shapes its use, the networks which connect us—is constantly changing. So how are we to know which practices to use, and what might shape our discernment in using them? In the chapter that follows, I want to do two things: first, offer an analogy that can help us think about our practices no matter how the technologies themselves change, and second, lift up some of the practices that can have a constructive impact in teacher formation.

10.2 An Analogy: Practices with Food and Practices with Digital Media Have Much in Common

Consider this: We all require food to survive. Yet we are embedded in cultural contexts that offer us unhealthy choices (both in terms of what we eat, how much of it, and how often). There is also little if any social consensus about what healthy food practices might be. Further, the artful practices of preparing and eating food are stressed if not extinct. Prior to the COVID-19 pandemic, particularly in highly developed western settings, many children no longer had any direct experience of baking bread, making jam, or canning vegetables. The many enforced lockdowns, diminishing supply chains, and other factors brought about in response to the pandemic created a pressing need to retrieve some of these practices. There is increasing evidence that people are beginning to recognize how much it can be energizing and creative to do things "from scratch."

Now consider these same factors in relation to digital media. Digital media are primarily media of communication (Jenkins, 2006; Jenkins & Boyd, 2016). The reason cell phones are so ubiquitous, even given their expense, is that they help people to feel connected, and they help to maintain relationships. In a pandemic era, when physical distancing has become an important health practice, and children in many instances have been pushed into online learning, we rely more than ever on digital technologies.

Digital media provide pathways for communication, and like food, human beings require communication to survive. Yet patterns of communicative practice—and the etiquette necessary for thoughtful engagement—are still emerging. Two years ago, it could have been argued that there was a clear consensus of the inappropriateness of using a cell phone during shared worship. Yet today many parishes begin each service by asking people to use their phone to scan the QR code at the entrance of the sanctuary to download a worship bulletin, and hymnals may no longer be in use because of the work required to regularly disinfect them.

Similarly, in the past there was a clear consensus that digital screens should be avoided in the early years of childhood, and that children in primary schools should play together in close contact. Today that recommendation may not be possible in many settings, and the primary route by which many teachers interact with their students is synchronous video using tools like Zoom, Teams, Skype, and so on. There is still consensus that absent health risks, in-person learning is far better in general than online learning for young children. Yet the presence of COVID-19 and its many variants is changing that calculus.

So what are we to do? Particularly given that there is no clear path forward, and the vast uncertainties of a pandemic—not to mention the ever-changing capacities of digital tech—mean that teachers must learn to be agile and adaptive. Here I want to suggest that having an analogy by which to consider what to do, learning from the past as a way to explore possible futures, can be helpful. We can think about what we have learned about food as a way to think about how to shape our digital communication practices.

10.3 Engaging Media Together

Research suggests that children in families who eat a certain number of meals together every week are less vulnerable to problematic behaviors than children in families who rarely if ever eat together. Helping children grow and prepare food, and helping families find ways to eat family meals together are two very strong actions that faith communities can take to support families (Watts et al., 2018). Teachers in specifically Catholic schools also know something about how important it is to regularly participate in Eucharistic celebration together with their students. Part of what underlies this wisdom is the recognition that families and schools can socialize children into a variety of practices which have a major influence on children's lives.

Using this analogy, what are the practices for engaging digital media that we want to promote? And how does Catholic faith offer resources for that engagement? Let us start with where and how to engage digital media. How many "screens" (televisions, computer screens, video game controllers, etc.) does a family own, for instance, compared to how many members it has? If a family of four owns one computer, they are likely to have far more interaction around how to use it, then a family with six computers and four members. Arguing over who gets to use a computer and when they get to use, it might not be as pleasant as everyone doing their own thing by themselves, but it provides an important opportunity to struggle as a family over what values will guide your screen choices.

During this pandemic, the conflicts over access have had many more existential implications. If a family has one tablet, and people are working from home and going to school from home, who gets to use it, and when? What kinds of choices are they being forced to make? How are the assignments we craft for learning embodied in the various settings our students inhabit? We would never argue that children should go hungry while parents eat their fill, or vice versa. So how might we support managing the difficult challenge of accessing what might be a scarce resource in terms of digital access? Digital media scholars have offered much "food for thought" here by observing what they term "context collapse."

10.4 Context Collapse

Decades of research into the various intersections and entanglements of media and religions have led to the clear observation that we are living through a time of context collapse that has been hastened, if not catalyzed, by digital media (Davis, 2013; Wesch, 2009). Most people of faith recognize how important context is, and certainly most teachers understand that the context in which a student lives is crucial for their ability to learn. Yet we are living through a time in which context is collapsing all around us.

Digital media hold out the promise that we can erase geography, that we can conquer time, and that we have access to all the information ever created. Yet in reality, we live in specific places, time moves in a linear fashion for most of us, and the "World Wide Web" is full of more misinformation and lacunae than we allow ourselves to be aware of. As teachers have struggled to learn how to teach in the midst of a pandemic, many utilizing tools they had not previously picked up with students scattered widely away from them, we have been brought abruptly face to face with the reality that not everyone has access to digital tools, and even those with access may not have adequate access to high-speed broadband. For those with tools and adequate access, there are still obstacles that come from families all gathered in one place, often locked down or forced to distance physically, in ways that make learning not only very complicated but often nearly impossible.

Context collapse requires a thorough recognition of the need to build context with each other. When learning happened in physical places—school classrooms, parish buildings—the physical space was a default context, with people's senses drawing in information that was at least minimally shared. When we learn through synchronous video tools like Zoom, we no longer share the same physical space and may not even be in the same time zone. Now, even if a return to physical spaces is possible, we may be masking our faces—thus losing very important information—and be spaced further apart.

Here again, consider the analogy to food. Sharing food together shapes relationships. So how are digital media practices being shared? In what ways are teachers inviting students—and indeed, each other as teachers in faculty development spaces—to share with each other how to engage digital media?

The pandemic may have made it impossible to share food together in certain contexts. Can we share the practice of eating together even through synchronous screens? It may well be—only time and research will answer this question—that the time teachers take to talk about what food they enjoy, to lift it up to visibility on a screen, to offer a simple recipe that the children in their spaces can make at home—might have more transformative learning impact, than paper and pencil (or digital screen and form) worksheets might ever have, precisely because it creates a shared context for the learning. Similarly, working with food is a hands-on activity that requires physical touch and physical senses, even if—or perhaps especially if—the only way to convey that one has done the activity is to lift up something to be visible over a digital screen. Catholics are a Eucharistic people, and table fellowship is key to our beliefs.

The point is that while teachers may be using screens to sustain relationships, the screens are not the fundamental element of that relationship. The more that teachers can bring into explicit and intentional focus the embodied reality we share—the contexts we inhabit together—the more transformative the impact of learning and teaching is.

What are the elements of formation to which we must attend in the process of creating context in digital spaces? Scholars point to three shifts that are taking place amidst digital media: how we understand authority, the means by which authenticity becomes a key criterion for authority, and the implications of that argument for how we exercise agency (Hess, 2015).

10.5 Authority, Authenticity, and Agency

When people can no longer rely on shared context to inform what they view as credible and reliable information, they turn to their relationships with trusted peers (Cheong et al., 2011). They turn to whether the information and ideas they are drawing upon meet their definitions of authenticity. They ask to what extent the information and ideas, the narratives they inhabit, create opportunities for agency. These are elements that mark how we inhabit our identities (Hobbs, 2011; Hoover, 2013; Hoover & Emerich, 2011).

Let us take each of the three—authority, authenticity, and agency—in turn. First: authority. Catholic thought takes very seriously both vertical and horizontal descriptions of authority (Gaillardetz, 2003). Catholics also believe in the "sensus fidelium"—or a "sense of the faithful," which is a horizontal element of authority. If a teaching proffered by the vertical magisterium is not ultimately picked up and embodied by the faithful, it falls out of authority. Similarly, at least in theory and theology, if the faithful across the globe articulate shared concerns—think global climate change, for instance—that shared articulation must be acknowledged by the teaching magisterium. This is a dynamic process with both a vertical and a horizontal element.

A key challenge facing Catholic teachers, a key element of formation, requires the retrieval and embodiment of this nuanced framework for authority. In a world swirling in competing authorities, with vast amounts of confusing data being spewed like a firehose spews water, nuance is often lost, and this framework is often unfamiliar. Without the framework, without a complex way to engage authority, persons turn to each other, to the relationships we trust. We seek authentic connection within which to discern what is true, what is right, and what is holy. We seek context for our knowing, for anything which we choose to regard as authoritative.

Just as the foods prepared by our grandparents, the special dishes we share at holidays, hold deep meaning for us, so, too, does the information which comes to us through the relationships we hold most close. Yet just as some of that food—I think here of the rich cream and deep fried aebleskiver of my Danish forebears—is best eaten only occasionally, there are certain kinds of information that needs to be balanced by what we are learning. Think of masking requirements during a pandemic. Digital media offer a plethora of sharply contesting voices around whether or not wearing a face covering is a healthy and appropriate practice.

How can we help our students—indeed, each other!—navigate these conflicting currents? How are we to assess the information swirling around us? In what ways do we grant authority to voices, to digital media, that carry often sharply conflicting messages (Hobbs, 2020)? Here again our tradition has rich resources to offer. "For God so loved the world that he gave his only Son, so that everyone who believes in him might not perish but might have eternal life." (NAB, John 3:16). We are a tradition, a faith community, who perceives God through the lens of the incarnation, the embodied, experiential, encompassing love of God poured out into human form. We not only acknowledge, but also cherish and honor human experience.

Yet at the same time, we confess a deep commitment to community, to the personal always being part of the social. As Pope Francis writes in *Laudato 'Si*, a key conviction of our faith is that we have: "an awareness that each creature reflects something of God and has a message to convey to us, and the security that Christ has taken unto himself this material world and now, risen, is intimately present to each being, surrounding it with his affection and penetrating it with his light" (221). He continues with the assertion that "Social love is the key to authentic development" (231), and "the human person grows more, matures more and is sanctified more to the extent that he or she enters into relationships, going out from themselves to live in communion with God, with others and with all creatures" (241).

Such a belief demands the kind of nuanced approach to authority that both a vertical and a horizontal element to truth recognizes. Here is the challenge: Many people have become so locked into the horizontal, and the horizontal—the specific relationships they are embedded within—has become ever smaller and smaller, due to the press of algorithms which structure digital media spaces (Lim, 2020). Catholic assertions of faith can be a base from which to learn and to support each other in retrieving deeper and more complex understandings of both authority and authenticity. Catholic faith offers stories, it offers narratives that have stood the test of centuries, and from which we can acknowledge that a fundamental element of who we are rests in our interdependence and relationality. We truly "know as we are known by God" (Palmer, 1993).

This is a grounding, a base from which to develop all else. Yet it can only function that way if people learn those stories, if people grow to trust these understandings, and perceive them as authoritative and authentic. Here is where the third element named above becomes relevant that of agency. This is perhaps the most challenging of the shifts taking place. "Agency" has to do with making something happen, with the ability to take action, with making a difference. Far too much of the experience of human beings in parts of the world shaped by neoliberal forms of capitalism is that one has agency through the ability to purchase and thus consume. Young people are surrounded by stories of identity that are based in specific purchases, whether those purchases are of clothing or of music/video/gameplay. Even political participation, in far too many parts of the world, has been imagined as supporting candidates—largely through donations—who will in turn represent you (Jenkins & Boyd, 2016).

Further what does it mean, what can it mean, to honor and respect God's agency in these practices? There is little room in digital media for transcendence, for divine activity. Yet here is where formation within Catholic worlds offers so much hope and opportunity, because understanding that God is the first and primary agent, the one from whom and in whom and for whom human beings are created and have agency is a freeing and energizing catalyst for authentic, authoritative, and action in the world.

10.6 Trauma-Informed Learning and the Practices of Creation in Digital Media

There is a lot of recent evidence that supporting each other through the trauma incurred by various global calamities (COVID-19, climate catastrophes, etc.) necessitates (Imad, 2020):

- fostering safety
- nurturing trust and transparency
- inviting peer support and mutuality
- supporting collaboration by sharing agency
- empowering voice by identifying and building on strengths

- paying attention to cultural, gender, and historical issues, and
- supporting a sense of purpose.

There are many ways in which digital media can support such learning. Perhaps the first step is letting go of some of the fears about "not getting to content" and remembering how critical practices are. To go back to the analogy with food, the *practices* by which we engage food are essential to good health. So, too, the practices by which we engage digital media fundamentally shape the meaning we make with them. Each of these elements of trauma-informed learning is a practice. Notice the verbs: fostering, nurturing, inviting, supporting, and empowering. These are practices, and while we might long to engage these practices in person, in physically close spaces, we can and must learn to do so even when—perhaps especially when—we must be physically distant.

10.7 Learning to Create

Perhaps the single most effective way to build context, to attend to issues of authority, authenticity, and agency, involves helping people learn how to *create* in media. Helping children learn how to create their own webpages, for instance, helps them to gain a healthy critical stance toward all webpages. Once they discover how easy it is to put something "on the screen" of the web, they inevitably start to wonder how authoritative other pages are.

There are many ways in which communities of faith have already begun to do this, although they may not recognize it as a specific learning practice.[1] Think of mission trips, where youth come back with hundreds of pictures and turn them into musical slide shows that they share with the community through *TikTok* and *YouTube*. Doing a project such as this not only helps youth to integrate and reflect upon their experience on the trip, but it also helps them learn to share their faith beyond their immediate context.

The same can be said of engagement with social media. It is far better to help youth—and their parents, for that matter—learn to navigate social networks like Facebook, Instagram, and TikTok with the support and energy of a multi-generational faith community, than for them to have to teach themselves how to do so in isolation from that community.

Yet we must always remember the null curricula of dominant screen culture. Who has agency in these spaces? Is it individuals? Here is another place where the analogy is useful. Where is God in the midst of our food practices? We are learning to pay attention to where our food comes from, and the hands that plant and harvest it, the hands that prepare it, the hands—our hands!—joined together in prayer and thanksgiving for the bounty in front of us.

---

[1] For more on digital storytelling as a form of faith formation, see http://www.storyingfaith.org/.

We need to remember this on our screens as well. Where is God in the midst of our communication? Catholic teachers have to move from unacknowledged learning to intentional learning. We have to move from accepting our screen practices as "given" in our environment, to a place where we actively engage them and give thanks for our God who continues to reveal Godself even in the midst of our screens.

Consider these simple practices for doing so:

- make the password for logging into a computer a short prayer
- curate news sources in advance, and approach them as a catalyst for prayer
- take pictures on a phone in the midst of the day, and in the evening think about where God can be glimpsed through them
- ask questions which invite wonder about God, rather than only offering answers
- pick a popular song often heard, and think about it through a "God lens" (what is God inviting here? what if God is singing this song to you? what if you are singing it to God? what is life giving, and what is sorrowing, about this song?)
- seek beauty each day
- offer gratitude each day (the Ignatian examen is a wonderful resource for this, and the spiritual exercises have versions that can be done using films (Pungente & Williams, 2004).

Forming teachers is a context-specific practice, and yet—as noted—we are living through context collapse. The enforced physical distancing of a pandemic offers us a spur for learning ways in which digital media can both encourage—and also discourage—good practices. Remembering that we need to build context, and that we can do so through careful attention to authority, authenticity, and agency (particularly God's!), is both hope-filled and a forward-looking approach to teach formation.

10.8 Concluding Thoughts

Finally, using an analogy—in this case, that of practices of food preparation and sharing—offers a way into the challenging process of retrieving, or inventing where necessary, practices for engaging digital media that can ground us and support us. Each time we encounter a new tool, experience discomfort with a specific medium, observe our students doing something we find problematic, we can ask ourselves: What about our food practices that can help us with our practices of communication?

Just as with food, we want to know the ingredients, and with digital media, we want to know who has created and funded them. We know that safety in food has much to do with how it is gathered and prepared. There is much to be gleaned from the work in digital and information literacy about how to do this work, and it is ever more pressing (Boyd, 2014; Boyd and Hargittai, 2010; Clark, 2013; Hobbs, 2020; Ludvigsen and Steier, 2019).

Catholic thought, as Pope Francis notes, is centered on "an awareness that each creature reflects something of God and has a message to convey to us, and the security that Christ has taken unto himself this material world and now, risen, is intimately present to each being, surrounding it with his affection and penetrating it with his light (Laudato 'Si 221)." We need to find ways to continue to return to this central conviction and to experience it in embodied ways. Digital media offer many ways to do so, if we are canny about observing our *practices* along with whatever content is present.

References

Bass, D. (Ed.). (2009). *Practicing our faith*. Jossey-Bass.
Boyd, D. (2014). *It's complicated: The social lives of networked teens*. Yale University Press.
Boyd, D. and Hargittai E. (2010). Facebook privacy settings: who cares? *FirstMon, 15*(8). https://firstmonday.org/article/view/3086/2589
Cheong, P., Huang, S., & Poon, J. (2011). Religious communication and epistemic authority of leaders in wired faith organizations. *Journal of Communication, 61*(2011), 938–958.
Clark, L. (2003). *From angels to aliens*. Oxford University Press.
Clark, L. (2013). *The parent app*. Oxford University Press.
Davis, J, (2013). *Context collapse. Cyborgology*. https://thesocietypages.org/cyborgology/2013/01/10/context-collapse-a-literature-review/
Gaillardetz, R. (2003). *By what authority?* Liturgical Press.
Hess, M. (2014). A new culture of learning: Digital storytelling and faith formation. *A Journal of Theology: Dialog, 53*(1), 12–22.
Hess, M. (2015). Learning with digital technologies. *Moral Theology, 4*(1), 131–150.
Hess, M. (2017a). Exploring the epistemological challenges underlying civic engagement by religious communities. *Good Society, 26*(2–3), 305–322.
Hess, M. (2017b). White religious educators resisting white fragility. *Religious Education, 112*(1), 46–57.
Hess, M. (2018a). Adaptive action as a form of reflective practice in pastoral leadership. *Reflective Practice: Formation and Supervision in Ministry, 3*, 10–24.
Hess, M, (2018b), Using digital media In: S. Brookfield (Ed.), *Teaching race: How to help students unmask and challenge racism* (pp. 253–272). Jossey-Bass.
Hess, M. (2019). Why games and gaming might be the best way and place in which to consider the meaning and purposes of theological education. *Cross Currents*. https://doi.org/10.1111/cros.12361
Hess, M. (2020). Finding a way into empathy. *Religious Studies News*. http://rsn.aarweb.org/spotlight-on/teaching/empathy/story-exercises-religious-studies-classroom
Hobbs, R. (2011). *Digital and media literacy*. Corwin Press.
Hobbs, R. (2020). *Mind over media*. W. W. Norton.
Hoover, S. (2013). Evolving religion in the digital media. In K. Lundby (Ed.), *Religion across media*. Peter Lang Publishing.
Hoover, S., & Emerich, M. (Eds.) (2011). *Media, spiritualties, and social change*. Continuum Publishing Group.
Imad, M. (2020). *Leveraging the neuroscience of now*. Inside Higher Ed. https://www.insidehighered.com/advice/2020/06/03/seven-recommendations-helping-students-thrive-times-trauma
Jenkins, H. (2006). *Convergence culture*. NYU Press.
Jenkins, H., & Boyd, D. (2016). *Participatory culture in a networked era*. Polity Press.
Lim, M. (2020). Algorithmic enclaves. In: E. Davis (Ed.), *Affective politics of digital media*. Routledge.

Ludvigsen, S., & Steier, R. (2019). Reflections and looking ahead for CSCL: Digital infrastructures, digital tools, and collaborative learning. *International Journal of Computer-Supported Collaborative Learning, 14*, 415–423.

Lytle, J. (2013). *Faith formation 4.0*. Morehouse Publishing.

Martinson, R., Black, W., & Robert, J. (2010). *The spirit and culture of youth ministry*. EYM Publishing.

Ong, S. (2021). Remote everything. *MIT Technology Review, 124*(2), 46–49.

Palmer, P. (1993). *To know as we are known*. Harper Collins.

Pungente, J., & Williams, M. (2004). *Finding God in the dark*. Novalis.

Rizzuto, A. (1979). *Birth of a living god*. University of Chicago Press.

Watts, A., Berge, J., Loth, K., Larson, N., & Neumark-Sztainer, D. (2018). The transmission of family food and mealtime practices from adolescence to adulthood: Longitudinal findings from Project EAT-IV. *Journal of Nutrition Education and Behavior, 50*(2), 141–147.

Wesch, M. (2009). YouTube and you: Experiences of self-awareness in the context collapse of the recording webcam. *Explorations in Media Ecology, 8*(2), 19–34.

Mary E. Hess is a professor of Educational Leadership at Luther Seminary and the chair of the Leadership Division, where she has taught since 2000. Hess is a past president of the Religious Education Association, a consultant with the Wabash Center on Teaching and Learning in Theology and Religious Studies, and she serves on the editorial boards of several journals. Hess has created and maintains a number of websites (indexed here: meh.religioused.org). Her most recent book, co-written with Stephen S. Brookfield, is becoming a White Antiracist: A Practical Guide for Educators, Leaders and Activists, Stylus Publishers, 2021.

Chapter 11
Bridges into Mystical Wisdom: Using Carmelite Spirituality in Teacher Formation

Michelle Jones

Abstract This chapter proposes that the Carmelite spiritual tradition holds great potential as a resource for cultivating the interior lives of teachers in Catholic schools and thereby helping them to sustain the complex demands of their position. As an expression of the Church's mystical wisdom about the relationship of love between God and humanity, the insights of Carmelite spirituality are perennial and universal. The argument is made that the key to using the Carmelite spiritual tradition as a formative resource for teachers is to find bridges between the lived experience of teachers and the wisdom of Carmel. Such bridges are to be found in elements of contemporary culture that both already nourish the interior lives of teachers and are capable of functioning as pathways into the transformative wisdom of Carmelite spirituality. Secular self-development material is proposed, among others, as one such bridge. The ideas presented in the chapter are demonstrated through an imagined conversation between a contemporary Catholic primary school teacher, Brené Brown, St Teresa of Avila, St John of the Cross, St Thérèse of Lisieux, and Ruth Burrows.

Keywords Carmelite · Spirituality · Mysticism · Brené Brown · Educator · Formation

The interior lives of teachers in Catholic schools are required to sustain significant demand. In addition to being faced with complex situations arising both within and outside the classroom that take them beyond the role for which they were trained, educators are expected by ecclesial authorities to be "people whose lives give witness to Christian values and who are committed to engage in the Church's mission of evangelisation" (Bishops of NSW and the ACT, 2007, as cited in Gowdie, 2017, p. 20). In this chapter, I propose that the Carmelite spiritual tradition is a rich resource for cultivating the interior lives of Catholic school teachers. Central to this proposal is the assertion that the insights of Carmelite spirituality are most meaningful and valuable to educators when they are mediated by some element of contemporary

M. Jones (✉)
BBI—The Australian Institute of Theological Education, 423 Pennant Hills Road, Pennant Hills, NSW 2120, Australia
e-mail: michelle.jones1@bbi.catholic.edu.au

culture that is already meaningful and valuable to them. After discussing the particular suitability of Carmelite spirituality for the task of nurturing the interior life, I turn to explore the dynamic of establishing bridges between the lived experience of teachers and the transformative wisdom of the Carmelite tradition. The remainder of the chapter is taken up with a fictitious dialogue that demonstrates the principles I have set forth far more effectively than any other means could.

It perhaps seems audacious to claim that a spiritual tradition that has its origins in a small community of hermits who settled on Mount Carmel in Palestine at the end of the twelfth century is eminently suitable for nurturing the interior lives of teachers in Catholic schools today. Yet, as James McCaffrey (2004, p. 9) writes, "Carmelite spirituality answers to the deepest need for love in every human heart". As an expression of the Church's mystical tradition, Carmel (as it is known) is not hinged to a particular temporal work. Rather, it is focused on the timeless and universal work of cultivating the relationship of love between God and humanity. Thus, the contemporary Carmelite writer Ruth Burrows (2006, p. 186) can define the Carmelite charism "as an intense experience of human existence and its innate poverty, containing within it a summons of faith not to evade but to enter through it into a total trust, a leap of the self into divine love which is the essence of union with God". Clearly, the leading articulators of Carmelite spirituality—I particularly have in mind here the Carmelite Doctors of the Church, Saints Teresa of Avila, John of the Cross, and Thérèse of Lisieux—can be relied upon as experts in the interior life.

While asserting the particular value of the Carmelite spiritual tradition as a formative resource, it is necessary also to acknowledge a disjunction between the interior disposition of those for whom Teresa, John, and Thérèse wrote and that of today's teachers in Catholic schools. The great mystical texts of Carmel were addressed to people explicitly and fervently committed to growth in the spiritual life within the Catholic tradition. Catholic school teachers, however, can broadly be described as being content to be associated with the Catholic tradition yet not personally submersed within its spiritually transformative currents. This dual reality is well exemplified by Richard Rymarz's study of early career teachers working in Catholic schools in a regional Australian diocese. "By working in a Catholic school", Rymarz (2020, p. 115) notes, "the teachers are immersed in another world and one that they are pleased to be in. It is, however, not reflective of life". Moreover, "While 'saying prayers' and similar activities was seen as part of the life of the school and teachers were willing to take part in these, this same feeling did not extend to praying readily away from the school" (Rymarz, 2020, p. 116). It is likely, then, that if, convinced of their formative potential, a teacher-formation practitioner was to present insights from Carmelite spirituality "neat", so to speak, to teachers in Catholic schools, these insights would be graciously received and quickly forgotten.

It is because of this disjunction that it is necessary to establish bridges between the actual realities of teachers' lives and the spirit-nurturing wisdom of the Carmelite tradition. This approach to teacher formation embodies the insights of, for example, Jill Gowdie and Michael Paul Gallagher. In Gowdie's (2017, p. 173) words, "This is about respecting people where they are, and making that place the beginning place, and ensuring there is a line of sight between their personal meaning-making and their formative pathway". Such an approach proceeds by the conviction that, as Gallagher (2001, p. 2) puts it, "revelation also happens within seemingly 'non-religious' realities. God's Spirit is at work in all that is good. Like an artist, the Spirit shapes our entry into freedom on many levels". The task is to find wavelengths (to change the image) that both resonate with the lived experience of teachers and effectively convey Carmel's mystical knowing about becoming fully alive in love. It is a matter of both harnessing teachers' dispositions towards interior growth and meaningfulness—wherever they are to be found—and trusting that Carmelite wisdom can fulfil these inclinations to flourishing.

So, where are such bridges to be found? I suggest that they await discovery in elements of contemporary culture that both already nurture the interior lives of teachers to some degree and hold the potential to function as entrees into the transformative insights of Carmelite spirituality. One such bridge—and the one that will serve as our case study—is secular self-development material; this designation encompasses books, articles, podcasts, YouTube clips, and so on. Other cultural elements that could serve as bridges into Carmel's mystical wisdom include the visual arts, music, literature, models of behavioural psychology, movements for social justice, and environmental activism.

On the whole, self-development material appeals to one's inclinations towards depth and interior growth while remaining apart from any explicit institutional-religious commitment. As such, it perhaps forms a ready dialogue partner with teachers in Catholic schools: such non-institutional openness to transcendence seems a happy fit with people who, as we saw earlier, are generally content to be associated with, but not immersed in, the Catholic story. The challenge before the teacher-formation practitioner using self-development material to lead teachers into the formative wisdom of Carmel is, first, to identify trajectories towards transformation that are awoken but not entirely facilitated by this material, and then to show that these aspirations find a completion within the Carmelite expression of the Christian mystery.

Lest the ideas I am setting forth here remain merely theoretical, I will now present an imaginary dialogue to demonstrate them in action. The personal engagement and interior growth depicted here could unfold, for example, across a programme of faith formation for teachers in Catholic schools, in a retreat setting, or even within a course of academic study designed with personal transformation in view. The interlocutors are Nicole, a fictitious teacher in a Catholic primary school, Brené Brown, Teresa of Avila, John of the Cross, Thérèse of Lisieux, and Ruth Burrows. Brené Brown is a researcher who speaks and publishes on self-development topics including vulnerability, shame, courage, and connectedness. As an indication of her popularity, Brown has published six number one *New York Times* bestsellers, and her TED talks have received tens of millions of views. Brown's "Dare to Lead" training programme is used in leadership development within some Australian Catholic schools and school systems. The setting of the dialogue is "Formatorama"—an imagined annual formation convention for teachers in Catholic schools.

Nicole: *This is going to be the best Formatorama ever! Brené Brown is here! I just can't believe it! Usually it's only a bunch of saints and other holy old people. They seem really nice but I'm just too embarrassed to talk to them about what's really going on inside of me. Most of them are like monks and nuns, and their lives are so different from my life. But Brené Brown... Oh my goodness, that woman reads my soul. Everything she says and writes relates to my own life so closely, and her advice about wholehearted living is just so helpful. And I get to have a half-hour one-on-one session with her! I love my principal so much for paying for this opportunity for me! Sure, I'll have to pretend to be interested in the scary holy people for the rest of the convention—but it's worth it to have that precious time with Brené! Hopefully if I smile politely while they ramble on about their religious stuff, it won't be too painful. Well—it's 11am, time for my session with Brené!*

Brené: Hey! I'm Brené!

Nicole: I'm Nicole! I can't believe I'm meeting you—sorry, I'm *not* going to cry! It's just that I've read all of your books and watched your TED talks and Netflix special like a million times. I've never had anyone understand me so well; it's like you have an x-ray into my inner life!

Brené: Oh, you're so sweet. Thank you for being here. So, what's going on with you? What would you like to talk about during our session?

Nicole: I'm just going to jump right in. Even though I drink in everything you say and write about living and loving with our whole hearts like it's water—okay, merlot—it's another thing to translate what you say into my life. I kind of feel like I'm at square one.

Brené: Tell me more.

Nicole: I'm a mum of three and a full-time primary school teacher. And every day, in one way or another, I feel like I'm not enough. I'm not patient enough with the kids in my class who drive me crazy, I don't have the right words to say to certain parents who are really struggling at the moment, I don't do enough to mentor the new staff like I'm supposed to, I shout at my own kids way too much, I don't exercise enough and I've got the muffin top to prove it. Basically, I feel like I spend each day doing ten rounds with my "to do list" and waiting for my life actually to start.

Brené: You've got a lot going on there, Nicole. And you probably go to sleep exhausted and wake up exhausted?

Nicole: I sure do. I stay up late watching TV or playing Words with Friends on my phone just trying to relax and block out everything that I haven't done or shouldn't have done, and then I wake up so tired and feeling angry at myself because it's all my own fault that I didn't get enough sleep and the cycle of inadequacy begins again.

Brené: Oh I feel for you. You know that I know inside and out how you're feeling. Is there anything in particular in my books or talks that you find helpful?

Nicole: I love your definition of wholehearted living; I know it off by heart! "Wholehearted living is about engaging in our lives from a place of worthiness. It means cultivating the courage, compassion, and connection to wake up in the morning and think, *No matter what gets done and how much is left undone, I am enough.* It's going to bed at night thinking, *Yes, I am imperfect and vulnerable and sometimes afraid, but that doesn't change the truth that I am also brave and worthy of love and belonging*" (2020, p. 3).

The problem is that even though I have this quote stuck to my bathroom mirror, when I look in the mirror, all I can see are flaws and failure. I *want* to do everything you write and talk about. I *want* to be brave. I *want* to embrace my imperfections and live from that place of vulnerability. I *want* to be able to say "I am enough." But something is stopping me.

Brené: What's stopping you?

Nicole: Well, I don't believe it. I don't believe that I actually am enough. I don't believe that the real me is worthy of love and belonging. It's like I don't have any guarantor of my existence, so I need to sure myself up with all the externals—even if I can't keep up with them.

Maybe it comes down to how I was raised? I know that you say it's essential for me to love myself if I'm going to let myself be imperfect and enough at the same time. But it's been engrained in me that loving myself just isn't what good people do; to say that someone "loved themselves" was an insult when I was growing up. And, not to get too deep and meaningful—actually, that ship has already sailed, hasn't it—the only times that my parents told me that they were proud of me were when I performed well in some way. I know that they didn't intend to mess me up and that they did the very best that they could, but I internalised the message that "worthwhileness" and "doing" go together. It took my breath away when I read in your book *Daring Greatly* (2015, p. 220) that "worthiness… doesn't have prerequisites."

It's not all bleak! My husband often tells me that he loves me just as I am; well, he used to—we tend to talk more about the kids and work these days! But even when he said it, it just bounced right off me. It's like my internal program has already been set and it's not budging!

Brené: Thank you so much for sharing your story with me, Nicole. I'm really moved by your self-awareness.

So, what I hear you saying is that you need to cultivate within yourself a belief in your worthiness. When you believe in the fibre of your being that you're loved and accepted just as you are, without prerequisites, you can finally drop the mask of "doing" and start living from that place of "enough."

Nicole: And that's exactly what I want! A wholehearted, vulnerable, messy, real life is so much more attractive than this relentless cycle of self-doubt and never-enough.

Brené: Nicole, you teach in a Catholic school. Is faith important to you?

Nicole: Oh well because I'm Catholic, there aren't really any points of connection between my faith and this inner work that we're talking about. It would be nice if there were. But Catholicism is more about the things you have to do to be a good person. And to be completely honest, I'm pretty against some of the things the Church teaches—like being anti-gay marriage and IVF and divorce. There are plenty of divorced and gay people in my life and people who have used IVF, and they're all good people. There's some good stuff about the environment and social justice though.

I love teaching at St Joseph's and I do believe in God; actually, I'm involved in preparing the kids in my class for First Holy Communion. But going to church on Sunday isn't my thing personally; it doesn't do anything for me, and anyway, the weekends are really our family time.

Brené: Well, there sure are a lot of Catholic stalls here at Formatorama! Unfortunately, our time together has come to an end—but perhaps you'll find something out there that will help you as you do your inner work and develop your belief that you're worthy of love and belonging.

Nicole: Hahaha, I doubt it, but you never know! It's been *such* a privilege to speak with you, Brené. Thank you! Good bye!

Wow, that was amazing. I just love Brené, and she just so totally gets me. Now I've got about 45 minutes to kill before lunch. Is there a corner somewhere where I can tuck myself away and catch up on some work emails? Oh no. That nun is smiling at me. Oh no—now there are three nuns smiling at me, and they've got some kind of monk with them too. I can't just give them the slip; I'll have to go over to them. This sucks—just when I was on such a high from seeing Brené...

Hello there! Do you offer counselling for people with Obsessive Compulsive Disorder?

Teresa: Hola! No, OCD stands for our religious Order! We are Discalced Carmelites! I'm St Teresa of Avila, and this is St Thérèse of Lisieux, Ruth Burrows, and St John of the Cross. Ruth's real name is Sister Rachel—but people know her as Ruth Burrows; she writes books about the three of us.

Nicole: It's nice to meet you all. I'm Nicole.

Thérèse: Hi Nicole! We saw that you've just come from speaking with Brené Brown. We're trying not to feel jealous of the long queue to her stall!

Nicole: Oh yes, she's absolutely wonderful. But I'm sure that the four of you are great too. Actually, I think I've seen a statue of you in the church next to my school, Thérèse.

Ruth: Would you mind sharing with us, Nicole, some of the themes that Brené explores?

Nicole: Oh, well, they're not very religious. It's more to do with working on your inner self and living a wholehearted life.

John: Try us!

Nicole: Well, Brené's main thing is vulnerability. She (2015, p. 2) defines it as "the uncertainty, risk and emotional exposure we face every day." Brené says that this vulnerability is inevitable, so it comes down to being a matter of how we choose to engage with it. Do we try to protect ourselves from vulnerability by things like perfectionism, practices that numb our fear and fragility, rehearsing tragedy during moments of joy, making anxiety a lifestyle, operating out of self-doubt, and trying to be always in control? Or do we embrace vulnerability by cultivating self-compassion, resilience, gratitude and joy, calm and stillness, meaningfulness, and laughter, song and dance. Like I said, it's not very religious so it's probably a bit boring to you.

Teresa: On the contrary! In fact, you had me at that definition of vulnerability! Brené is pointing to the very essence of what it means to be human. This is something all four of us have written about in one way or another.

Nicole: Really? I didn't know that you saints were into the messy business of being human!

Ruth: Oh that's our area of specialisation! Our great insight is that the vulnerability Brené talks about is the other side of the glory and beauty of our humanity. You see, as much as we all try to deny it, we aren't the authors of our own existence, nor can we orchestrate our fulfilment all by ourselves. No, we have been loved into existence by God and we find our meaning in relationship with God. Our vulnerability, this trembling we feel before life's uncontrollability and unpredictability, is a reminder of the glorious truth that we are an emptiness only God can fill.

Tell Nicole about your image of the interior castle, Teresa!

Teresa: I'd love to! The image of the interior castle is one of the ways in which I tried to convey this idea Ruth has been talking about—we are so vulnerable deep down because we are created for a splendour that is beyond our capacity to fulfil: we are ultimately a home for God to dwell in.

I describe our interior self to be like an exquisite castle made out of diamond that has many rooms within it, with Jesus himself dwelling in the very heart of that magnificent castle. We can't get our minds around how beautiful our inner reality is and the wonder that we are created to be a paradise for the Lord to live in; it's an exquisite mystery shining through our often painful experience of vulnerability.

Nicole: That's just so beautiful. I'd never connected the vulnerability Brené talks about with anything like God or spirituality before. And I've certainly never thought of my interior self as being a castle for God to dwell in. Everything you're saying adds such depth and hope to Brené's insights.

Ruth: Oh yes, with our assent, vulnerability is the sacred ground where God is at work within us. And it has everything to do with Jesus. After all, Jesus is the one who leaned absolutely into his human vulnerability, embracing it completely as capacity for God's love. This is what it means to say that Jesus is fully human and fully divine.

Nicole: No way! Jesus! Vulnerable! I teach the children in my class about Jesus being a great healer and miracle-worker. I always end up feeling guilty because while I'm assuring the kids that the stories are true, deep down I'm wondering if it's all fairy-tales. But a Jesus who knows about vulnerability—well, that's a Jesus I can relate to! What did you mean when you said that "with our assent" vulnerability is where God is at work within us?

Ruth: Ah, this is where John's dark night and Thérèse's little way come in!

John: Yes, you were sharing before, Nicole, about how Brené says that it all comes down to how we engage with our vulnerability—whether we try to numb our fear and fragility or cultivate a resilient spirit, whether we live in anxiety or practice calm and stillness, and so on. Well, when she says that, Brené is pointing to the insights that I convey with my image of the dark night. The dark night is a growth process by which the ego, or the armoury with which we shield our vulnerability, is progressively dismantled so that we become who we truly are—a quivering, beautiful receptivity to the outpoured love of God. This journey includes letting go of God being a reality that we try to comprehend or control and allowing ourselves to be comprehended, or embraced, by the mystery of God—a mystery that is so bright and glorious that it is darkness to our limited human sight.

Nicole: Okay—and so how does it actually happen? I'm sorry for all the questions, but I've just never heard this stuff before!

John: Ah, you've stumbled onto *the* great question here, Nicole! Ultimately, it's a mysterious interplay between our decision and God's grace. And it all comes back to what Ruth was saying before about Jesus being the one and only one who has embraced human vulnerability and held it out as capacity for the life of God. All of our moving away from shielding ourselves from vulnerability to embracing it is done through, with, and in Jesus. In the beginning, Jesus is the model that we try to imitate. And as we progress down the track a bit, Jesus gently breaks into our depths and lives out his openness to God's love within the reality of our lives.

Nicole: My head is starting to spin a bit! But that bit you said about "through, with, and in Jesus" —that's from the Mass, isn't it? I prepare kids for First Holy Communion.

John: Yes it is! And the Eucharist is a powerful way in which we can join with Jesus in shedding the vulnerability armour and instead leaning into the gift of our vulnerability.

Nicole: I'm totally mind-blown! I didn't see this coming at all! When I think of the Mass, I'm basically thinking of corralling kids and hiding my imperfections so that I look good in front of God (and the principal). I never would have connected it with living out Brené's insights.

So, how does the little way fit in? I think there's a poster about the little way in our staff room at school, something about doing little things with great love? To be honest, I've always seen it as a kind of passive-aggressive way to make us clean up after ourselves.

Thérèse: Ah yes, those diluted presentations of my teaching are everywhere! The little way is essentially my way of saying what John says with his image of the dark night; it's gladly accepting rather than fleeing from the poverty, the vulnerability, of being human. I experienced wave after wave of "not-enoughness" when I became a nun: I couldn't love others enough, I couldn't concentrate in prayer enough, I couldn't do domestic tasks well enough and so on. Instead of becoming discouraged, I decided to embrace this littleness, all this "not-enoughness," as space for God's love. Of course, I didn't give up trying to love, to pray well and so on. But I came to do everything from a place of contented childlike imperfection, rather than from a place of trying to prove myself.

Nicole: I hope that this doesn't come out wrong, but I truly had no idea that people like you could speak my language—like Brené does. My heart feels like it's on fire! I'm conscious that it's nearly time for lunch. Before I go, can you help me figure out where to from here? I don't want all of this just to fall away after I leave Formatorama and go back to my daily life.

Ruth: Nicole, the foundation to everything we have been talking about is belief in your own worthiness, belief that you are loved and lovable.

Nicole: Oh my goodness, that's what Brené says too. But I'm stuck on exactly that point. Even though I know it's the first step to shedding my vulnerability armour and accepting that I am enough, even with all my imperfections, I find it really hard to believe that I am worthy of love and belonging. As I said to Brené earlier, it's like I don't have a guarantor of my existence, I don't have a secure source of love in which to ground myself, so I try to secure my identity with the things that I do—and when I don't do them well (which is always), my sense of self comes crashing down.

Ruth: Ah, but you do have an utterly secure source of love in which you can ground yourself: God's love for you.

Nicole: But I don't *feel* that love—even though I tell my students that God loves them and I guess I believe in theory that God loves me.

Ruth: You must take me at my word when I say I know exactly how you feel. Nicole, it's a matter of shifting our focus away from our feelings of unlovability and choosing to trust in the God of tender, personal love that Jesus has revealed. And for this, it's essential to immerse ourselves in the Gospels and truly make them our own. Be the woman at the well receiving Jesus' gift of God's love, be the woman who touched the fringes of Jesus' cloak and who Jesus gazed upon face to face, be the rich young man who Jesus looked at and loved. Slowly, slowly, or maybe all at once, you'll come to be convinced that you are utterly and intimately loved.

Nicole: That was exactly what I needed to hear today, and I didn't even know it. Thank you. This truly has been the best Formatorama ever—and not entirely for the reason I expected.

Thomas Merton (1981, p. ix) once stated, "There is no member of the Church who does not owe something to Carmel". Over these pages, I have extended that claim and proposed that Carmelite spirituality is a rich resource for cultivating the interior lives of teachers in Catholic schools when it is conveyed by a means that is both meaningful to the teachers and authentic to the tradition. Centred on how men and women can become truly themselves by becoming more and more receptive to the outpoured love of God, Carmel's mystical wisdom is evergreen in its relevance. There is much scope for further development of these ideas. The imaginary dialogue offered a taste of how self-development material could function as a bridge between the lived experience of teachers and the transformative insights of the Carmelite tradition. What about the other possible bridges that I mentioned earlier; how might they function in this regard? Furthermore, it would be worthwhile to explore ways in which the wisdom of other expressions of the Catholic mystical tradition could be mediated to teachers for the nourishment of their interior lives. As we saw in Nicole's experience, the interior transformation we most need is ultimately Christological. The ancient Carmelite tradition has the potential to inflame teachers' lives with the fire of Christ's love so that they are able to face ever more effectively the complex and unremitting demands of their vocation.

References

Brown, B. (2015). *Daring greatly*. Penguin Life.
Brown, B. (2020). *The gifts of imperfection*. Vermilion.
Burrows, R. (2006). *The essence of prayer*. Burns and Oates.
Gallagher, M. P. (2001). *Dive deeper: The human poetry of faith*. Darton, Longman and Todd.
Gowdie, J. (2017). *Stirring the soul of Catholic education: Formation for mission*. Vaughan Publishing.
McCaffrey, J. (2004). *The Carmelite charism: Exploring the biblical roots*. Veritas Publications.
Merton, T. (1981). *The ascent to truth*. Harvest (Originally published 1951)
Rymarz, R. (2020). I like the practical side. Early career teachers in Catholic schools, interpretative autonomy and negotiating secular and religious boundaries. A preliminary study. *Paedagogia Christiana, 46*(2), 107–119.

Michelle Jones is a consecrated woman affiliated with the Quidenham Carmelite Monastery (UK). She lives a life of prayer in rural Western Australia and is an online lecturer with BBI—The Australian Institute of Theological Education and the Teresianum (Rome). Michelle is the author of *The Gospel Mysticism of Ruth Burrows: Going to God with Empty Hands* (Institute of Carmelite Studies Publications) and the editor of *Ruth Burrows: Essential Writings* (Orbis Books) and *Extravagant Love* (Paulist Press) and has also published numerous journal articles. michelle.jones1@bbi.catholic.edu.au

Chapter 12
Valuing and Cultivating Dialogue Amongst Learner–Educators: Ongoing Challenges for Post-Primary Religious Education Teachers in Catholic Schools

Bernadette Sweetman

Abstract Over recent years, due to changing cultural, political and economic factors, many education systems the world over have been facing the challenge of adapting to continuous 'new eras', while striving to maintain their identity as the bulwark of society. Amidst all the developments and policy changes in education, the context within which the school community exists is also in a constant state of flux. The chapter initially draws on the work of philosophical anthropologist, Martin Buber. His theoretical framework of education as dialogical relationship is used. In this context, this chapter supports and promotes the central role of the religious education teacher in the Catholic school as one who can navigate the ongoing changes faced in the educational sphere. More than just an educator, the nature of the RE teacher in particular as a lifelong learner will be highlighted. Reflecting on Buber's philosophies of education, dialogue and relationship, it is proposed here that by forming in the RE teacher the ability to see him/herself as learner-educator, a further extension of Buber's theory could be explored—that of the RE teacher as professional dialogian. While the arguments and proposals in this chapter will be illustrated using the current Irish context, they aim to inspire meaningful conversation in educational contexts around the world.

Keywords Professional dialogue · Religious education · Catholic · Dialogical mindset

12.1 The Importance of Dialogue

To value any set of ideals and to cultivate it into an effective process requires deep reflection on the nature and purpose of such ideals and the intentional investment into their manifestation. This chapter proposes the importance of dialogue for religious

---

B. Sweetman (✉)
Mater Dei Centre for Catholic Education, Dublin City University, St. Patrick's Campus, Drumcondra, Dublin 9 D09 DY00, Ireland
e-mail: bernadette.sweetman@dcu.ie

educators in Catholic schools. In doing so, it is firstly necessary to clarify both the author's understanding of dialogue and her perspective on the religious educator.

Dialogue has become a buzzword in many circles especially in the last number of decades, most notably in politics and Church. To take the Irish context as an example, centenary commemorations have been taking place in recent times marking significant historic events relating to the country's complex political, cultural and religious identity. The Good Friday Agreement, now twenty-five years old, is seen as a pivotal moment in which dialogue between political parties and religious bodies was focussed upon as a way to heal the severe wounds caused by dissonance, misunderstanding and fear. Such examples of dialogue like that relating to Northern Ireland often conjure images of attempts at reconciliation in recognition of differing, though not always opposing stances, with the overall aim at improving cohesion, mutual understanding and collegiality. From this viewpoint, dialogue may be seen as a solution to a problem.

In the sphere of education, in Ireland and elsewhere, dialogue has also been proposed as desirable amongst the solutions to combat the problems seen to emerge from changing cultural and social contexts. In Ireland, during curriculum review processes, stakeholders such as governing authorities, patron bodies, parents, teachers and of course students are amongst those invited by the National Council for Curriculum and Assessment (NCCA) to participate in the consultations and make their submissions as to what changes in curriculum content or methodology is advocated. This process, no doubt replicated in many other countries, acknowledges that there is a multitude of perspectives, belief systems and values that can contribute to how education is shaped over time. The stakeholders having their voices heard and their stances recognised is all part of the inclusive process of dialogue. The danger, however, is that only a superficial understanding of the nature and purpose of dialogue could result in only short-term gain, if any. To illustrate, educational systems are largely reactive—identifying needs and creating desired outcomes through appropriate content and methodologies, and incorporating these innovations in teacher education. Readers the world over will easily recall instances where new programmes, new resources or new training was introduced, hopefully with some success. However, when responding to such needs, for example, the impact of changing social and cultural contexts on Catholic education as is the setting for this volume, there can be dangers. As Wessels (2015) notes, a pitfall can be to

> mostly resort to replacing these actions, habits, modes of operation or rules with a different set of rules, without first reflecting on the intentionality or the 'why' behind the scenes…alternating between various initiatives in the 'landscape of action' provides only temporary respite to the problem, if any. (Wessels, 2015, p. 1)

Effective dialogue is more than just another strategy for solving problems. In the particular context of Catholic education, seeing dialogue as a 'discourse between spheres' (Cullen, 2017, p. 38) is a helpful analogy as it allows for the dynamism and openness to change that affirms the vision of Catholic schools. Byrne (2017) describes it as that which develop[s] as part of a living tradition, evolving all the time, responding to changing needs, and seeking to continually renew their creative engagement with the world and its peoples. (Byrne, 2017, p. 114)

Cullen (2017) proposes that it is in the space between these spheres that religious education 'finds its proper identity [as both] hermeneutical and communicative' (p. 38). This places an onus on the religious educator to have a professional competence in dialogue in order to negotiate these spheres, both protecting and nurturing religious education. Far from being a burdensome task, it will be proposed that the religious educator in a Catholic school is in fact well positioned to fulfil this role, and in doing so, act as a model of professional dialogue for all educators, not just those involved directly in the subject of religious education.

Briefly returning to the terminology, etymologically 'dialogue' suggests a two-way conversation. Dialogue understood as conversation honours the two widely recognised interconnected skills of listening and speaking that are essential for effective teachers (Madden, 2020). Though Buber (1947) signalled against seeing dialogue as 'merely the interchange of words—genuine dialogue can take place in silence, whereas much of conversation is really monologue' (Buber, 1947, p. xvi). In its Catholic education resource, *Voices and Vision*, the La Salle Academy (2018) advocates a very important aspect of conversation which is pertinent to this author's argument for religious educators as professional dialogians. That is the openness to being changed, to discovery and the concept of being on a journey. One of the descriptions of conversation given in the resource is 'an interpersonal journey, undertaken by friends, who are prepared to be changed by what they may subsequently discover' (Introduction, p. 6). This proactive approach to dialogue, one that welcomes the possibility of positive challenge and subsequent growth affirms the need for intentionally attending to the process of dialogue and its potential, rather than letting it diminish into, as Buber said 'merely the interchange of words'. Castelli (2012) rightly cautions against neglecting the importance of discipline and purpose in dialogue. Without this intentionality or teleological perspective (Wessels, 2015), dialogue is reduced into another form of rhetoric.

12.2 From Dialogue to Dialogical Mindset

Alongside intentionality and purpose, dialogue in the educational sphere also requires an understanding of relationship as a core principle in all education. In this regard, Boschki (2005) provides a useful elaboration on the seminal work of Buber as he incorporates the related theories of Janusz Korczak. In the first half of the twentieth century, Buber arguably held centre stage in the philosophy around dialogue and its relationship to education. In his writings, he often used the terms dialogue and relationship interchangeably, sometimes under the broader concept of mutuality. This idea of mutuality is a key stepping-stone in this author's argument of moving from dialogue to dialogical mindset and its pertinence to the religious educator in Catholic schools in the current changing contexts.

The relationship between master and student, between I and Thou, that permeates Buber's theory of education as personal relationship and as dialogical, has its basis in his Hasidic background. As Boschki (2005) explains, this relationship though special and close is still unequal as long as one sees the educator or teacher as master. Despite the clear dialogical thinking, and the fluidity between the parties of the educational relationship, Buber still retains a sense, albeit subtle, of inequality in the educational setting. While not necessarily a defect in Buber's theory of education as relational and dialogical, it is nonetheless improved upon when the work of Janusz Korczak is also incorporated. The Polish paediatrician and educator (1875–1942), applied his lifelong dedication to disadvantaged children, to his proclamations on the positionality of the child to the teacher in the educational relationship. He passionately advocated for a pedagogy of equality where teachers and children must be recognised on the same level. The teacher has no superiority over the child. His educational creed was "Children don't turn into people, they are people already" (Korczak, 1996, 475, cited in Boschki, 2005). He further affirmed the ability of children to act as educators for the educators. This level of mutuality and openness to growth is at the heart of the dialogical mindset.

12.3 The Religious Educator as Learner-Educator with a Dialogical Mindset

We are always learning. It is a lifelong endeavour. We are not perfect and we do not know it all. Regularly being challenged within ourselves, we move to and fro between what we understand and what puzzles us, what we accept and what tests us. This mutual movement is both internal in the *self* as we are learners, but also connects us with *others* in our encounters that make up the educational relationship. Internally, regarding the self as learner, if we take Cullen's (2017) interpretation of this 'discourse between spheres', pointed out earlier as a means to explore our understanding of dialogue, we see it is supported by her reference to Gadamer's (1989) thesis on understanding. Looking at the constant flow between learning and educating within this conceptual learner-educator, then we can grasp Gadamer's description of the

> 'revelation of meaning [being] the encounter with truth... when we enter 'the fusion of horizons'. Such fusion occurs when the learner's horizon, the limit of their vision and understanding, fuses with the horizon of the tradition.' (Cullen, 2017, p. 41)

The dialogue is happening within the religious learner-educator throughout his/her lifelong educational journey. Aware of this, they have the potential to model for the entire educational community how to negotiate between these 'spheres of discourse' and 'fusions of horizons' through the valuing and cultivation of a dialogical mindset.

Initial teacher educators should encourage student teachers to not see themselves as having reached their peak of learning on completion of their teaching qualification lest they close themselves off to the all the insights, challenges and growth that follows throughout their teaching career and beyond. For the qualified teacher, rather than seeing continuing professional development or lifelong career development as merely a way of upskilling, it is more important that the educator continues to see him/herself on a journey of discovery. Lifelong learning, an ongoing journey of discovery sustains the learner within (self) and inspires the learner beyond (student).

> To be human means to learn. To be fully human entails a lifelong effort in acquiring knowledge, attitudes, skills and behaviours. The complexity of life and the constant changes that persons face, increasingly demand that adults continue to learn through their lives. (Elias, 1993, p. 93)

12.4 Lifelong Learning for All in the Catholic School Community

In a Catholic school setting, it is important to remember that the students are not the only ones being educated, or the only ones learning. So too are the staff and wider school community. Of course, this is hopefully true in all educational establishments, but the articulation of the vision and mission of the Catholic school is special. In Ireland, the Catholic Schools Partnership (2014) described it as follows:

> The primary aims of all schools are educational, including in the area of Religious Education, but Catholic schools should also provide opportunities for catechesis, for formation in faith in the living God revealed in the person of Jesus Christ (pp. 25–26).

These opportunities apply to all of the Catholic school community, not just the students. For the purposes of this paper, the focus is on the religious educator as a particular person in the school community. The Catholic school 'invites everyone in the school community into dialogue with the vision and mission of the school…it encourages all the partners in the Catholic school to reflect, to listen, to discuss and to be open to deepening their spiritual lives' (Mullally, 2021, p. 257). The whole school community must deal with the various challenges and opportunities that arise as a result of changing contexts. The students will not magically develop these skills by chance. They will learn from the wider school community, especially, of course, their religious educators, who themselves as adults on faith journeys will also 'recontextualise' their beliefs and values in a changing culture (Boeve, 2007). Adults have the right and the need to flourish too. As an individual, each and every educator in a Catholic school is invited to engage with the person of Jesus, whose living presence 'is the foundation of the whole enterprise in a Catholic school' (Congregation for Catholic Education, 1977, para 34). This recognises the dignity of each person. No matter what role he/she assumes, be that as educator, student, citizen, neighbour, friend, parent and so on, each person as a child of God is invited to grow fully, to 'have life in abundance' through a relationship with God in Jesus Christ. The

Adult Religious Education and Faith Development project (AREFD), ongoing at the Mater Dei Catholic for Catholic Education in Dublin City University has, since 2018, placed a spotlight on the desire amongst adults in Ireland for appropriate opportunities to engage with their faith and spiritual lives. The research has affirmed the need to consult with adults as to their needs for AREFD rather than continue with the existing culture of provision that has dominated, certainly in Ireland, up to now. Similarly, the research findings suggested that those already involved in adult religious education and faith development, wherever they are, review their practices and purposefully strategise as to how they could accommodate for the changing contexts faced by adults in their setting (Byrne & Sweetman, 2021). Catholic anthropology both supports the person's individuality but also encourages him/her to 'contribute to our community's growth and development, rather than being focused simply on self' (Irish Episcopal Conference, 2010, para 28). The benefit to the adults in their own journey can inform their educational encounters with their students.

> The message of faith that once spoke in a different era, now needs to be recontextualised if it is to speak meaningfully to adults in a contemporary situation of many faith options and life choices…adult formation is essential for the articulation of Christian beliefs, mission, identity and practice, especially to make sense for those who think in a different frame of reference or who need to deal with secular and professional elements of Christian life in complex circumstances. (Stuart-Buttle, 2021, p. 40)

The religious educator in the Catholic school has the ability to model for his/her students how to engage in lifelong learning imbued by Gospel values. It is no coincidence that most people involved in education become involved in it out of a deep love of learning. It is quite likely that it is this love of learning that could be identified as one of the key attributes of those teachers who students remember years later as having had a profound effect on them. Palmer (1997) refers to how we 'teach who we are' (p. 15), that the integrity of our identity is key and that this authenticity fuels our education encounters to optimum levels. This author promotes the nurturing of lifelong learning and the understanding of the educator as both learner and educator. These are fundamental to both the personal and professional identities of the educator, and subsequently to the students and wider community.

12.5 Valuing and Cultivating a Dialogical Mindset in Post-Primary Religious Educators in Catholic Schools: An Example from the Irish Context

It is accepted that cultural, political and economic and factors influence policies across societies no matter where they are in the world. Following in-depth and careful consultation between many stakeholders, the Framework for Junior Cycle in Ireland was launched in 2015. It primarily focuses on the educational provision for Irish junior cycle post-primary students (12- to 15-year-olds) but the principles underpinning it and its development are applicable to other age groups and educational settings. The development of the Framework came about directly from calls to revitalise and recontextualise educational provision at this level in the light of the growing pluralist and multi-faith nature of Irish society. All subjects and examinations were revised. Fundamental to all changes was the commitment to 'valuing, acknowledging and affirming all the students' learning opportunities and experiences' (Department of Education & Skills, 2015, p. 8). Of significance was a clear shift from emphasis on subject knowledge to the development of skills, attitudes and critical thinking abilities to enable learners.

> 'to use and analyse information in new and creative ways, to investigate issues, to explore, to think for themselves, to be creative in solving problems and to apply their learning to new challenges and situations'. (Department of Education & Skills, 2015, p. 7)

One can already see parallels here with the presentation of the dialogical mindset that negotiates between 'spheres of discourse' and 'fusions of horizons'. It is even clearer, however, when one looks in particular at the Junior Cycle Religious Education Specification finally launched in Ireland in 2019. This was arguably the most contentious subject area under review with even the question of whether Religious Education should remain a subject at post-primary level being raised. Byrne (2021), however, highlights how it has in fact 'an irreplaceable role to play in the school curriculum for all young people whether they belong to a faith tradition or not' (pp. 71–72).

> Religious education provides a particular space for students to encounter and engage with the deepest and most fundamental questions relating to life, meaning and relationships. It encourages students to reflect, question, critique, interpret, imagine and find insight for their lives. (NCCA, 2019, p. 6)

This 'encountering and engaging' is characteristic of an operant dialogical mindset—one that sees challenge and takes it on with an openness to discovery and change from the encounter.

12.6 Recommendations

The self-awareness of the religious educator as both learner and educator needs to be explicated and intentionally addressed. If being a model of how to continue to learn throughout changing contexts is an identity attribute valued in religious educators, then specific attention must be given to it in the formation of Catholic educators, and in their own work subsequently with students in Catholic schools. Castelli's (2012) understanding of a religious education faith dialogue pedagogy 'proposes the development of skills and attitudes that teach pupils how to respond to beliefs different from their own while developing an articulation of their own' (p. 207). This pedagogy echoes the methodological underpinnings of the Irish Junior Cycle Religious Education Specification (2019) namely 'enquiry, 'exploration' and 'reflection and action'. This dialogical methodology should be intentionally used in Catholic teacher education so that those educators can not only benefit themselves but give greater depth and meaning to the development of the dialogical mindset for their students. If in his/her own formation, the religious educator is immersed in the same methodology as their students, then the valuing and cultivating of the dialogical mindset becomes more than just the 'development of sympathetic knowledge and understanding of another's beliefs' (Castelli, 2012, p. 207). According to Castelli (2012), dialogue could 'entail the recognition of *self* facing *the other* eliciting a willingness to be drawn out of the protective defence of *the same* into what de Certeau calls 'the never-ending, yet life-giving journey which makes faith credible' (Castelli, 2012, p. 207). This author proposes that such an endeavour would make the educational encounter more credible too.

Cultivating a dialogical mindset requires skills in reflective practice. Research on student teachers' emerging personal and professional identities by Leijen et al. (2018) affirmed the need for guidance for student teachers in reflective practice. Their studies in the application of dialogical perspectives to assist in professional identity development found such reflective practice does not happen by accident. Rather, students need to be guided in the process of negotiating between their personal identity and their professional identity. This research dealt with how the participants could cope with and work through tensions experienced between their personal and professional identity development. In their study, values and convictions were identified as amongst the most prevalent areas of tension felt by participants. Values, convictions, beliefs and worldviews are the bedrock of religious education discourse and negotiating between these tensions (or 'spheres' or 'fusions') is inevitable for Catholic religious educators and their students.

The biggest challenge for religious educators in Catholic schools, however, will not be the various factors of social, cultural and economic change. Instead, it will be the intentional allocation of time and space for dialogue. This applies for both educators in their initial and ongoing formation and students in their formal educational curriculum. As evident in research from the Australian context (Madden, 2017, 2020), when time is intentionally given to educators to professionally dialogue, it benefits the entire educational community and should be seen as a 'strategic investment in…teachers as both people and professionals' (Madden, 2017, p. 139). The valuing and cultivation of a dialogical mindset will enable learner–educators to be proactive and creative no matter whats challenges arise, for their benefit and the benefit of their students.

12.7 Conclusion

The necessary self-awareness and reflective practice amongst learner–educators to embody and facilitate dialogue through a dialogical mindset has been evidenced in this chapter. It should be noted that these attributes are also necessary for Catholic schools as organisations. Catholic schools continue to inhabit a significant space in Irish, and indeed, the global educational landscape despite the emergence of institutions under different patron bodies in response to parental demand for diversity.

A consequence of this shift in governance has been the need for Catholic schools to reflect upon their ethos and mission so as to distinguish themselves amongst the different models of school available. By becoming more self-aware and clarifying what makes their school a Catholic school, boards of management can provide their staff and school communities with a comprehensive understanding of their mission statement, the values and the principles in which their daily work and overall ethos is rooted. The Catholic school identity becomes clearer. Prospective teachers to Catholic schools are increasingly expected to have a solid grasp of the identity and ethos of the schools to which they apply for employment, and a willingness to uphold the Catholic values that are espoused. This transparency and clarity would suggest the possibility of greater collegiality and joint sense of mission. The cultural shift in the patronage of schools should therefore be seen as a positive development for the Catholic sector. It demands an ongoing self-awareness and clarity of purpose from Catholic school management that in the preceding period of perceived homogeneity of patronage was perhaps not considered necessary.

Catholic schools have and always will encounter challenge. In Ireland, they are increasingly seen as countercultural with the tension between Church and State, particularly in the area of religious bodies providing education increasingly evident in Irish society. Continuing to adhere to, uphold and foster Gospel values is part of the life of the Catholic school and part of the mission of the religious educator within the Catholic school. Being challenged is to be welcomed because it fuels lifelong education and the full development of the human person. That is not to claim it is easy to endure. It is recognised that Catholic educators can at times feel overwhelmed by the seemingly incessant call to justify their mission and proceed. The words of Francis (2020) bring comfort in his recent volume *Let Us Dream* when he reminds us that 'fear of the mission can, in fact, be a sign of the Holy Spirit. We feel, at once, both inadequate to the task and called to it' (p. 21). In operationalising the dialogicial mindset, the religious educator must resist both such fear as well as indifference. 'The indifferent person is closed to the new things that God is offering us' (Francis, 2020, p. 20). This is the final piece in the jigsaw of the dialogical mindset that makes the religious educator so well placed to thrive with such a mindset in their educational endeavours. More than 'mere interchange of words', more than conversation, the religious educator when embracing the dialogical mindset is opening him/herself to the Holy Spirit who is mutually present and at work in these 'discourses of spheres' and 'fusions of horizons'. Supported by the Holy Spirit, the discerning religious educator negotiates between all the tensions that arise in the development of the human person, and openly encounters and engages with these challenges in the special space that is good Religious Education. Welcoming challenges as opportunities to clarify and grow, the learner–educator furthers his/her own lifelong development. They also model that for the wider Catholic school community and facilitate their students to flourish no matter what challenges may arise.

Dialogue is a complex phenomenon (Di Sipio, 2019). Valuing dialogue and cultivating a dialogical mindset is, however, of enormous benefit. As Francis (2020) says:

To enter into discernment is to resist the urge to seek the apparent relief of an immediate decision, and instead be willing to hold different options before the Lord, waiting on that overflow. You consider reasons for and against, knowing Jesus is with you and for you. You feel inside yourself the gentle pull of the Spirit, and its opposite. And over time, in prayer and patience, in dialogue with others, you reach a solution, which is not a compromise but something else altogether. (Francis, 2020, p. 21).

References

Boeve, L. (2007). *God interrupts history: Theology in a time of upheaval*. Continuum.
Boschki, R. (2005). Re-reading Martin Buber and Janusz Korczak: Fresh impulses toward a relational approach to religious education. *Religious Education, 100*(2), 114–126.
Buber, M. (1947). *Between man and man* (English edition). Buber, M. (2002). (R. Gregor-Smith, Trans.) Routledge.
Byrne, G. (2017). Religious education in Catholic second-level schools in Ireland today: An invitation to love, understanding, commitment, hospitality and dialogue. In M. Shanahan (Ed.), *Does religious education matter?* (pp. 114–129). Routledge.
Byrne, G. (2021). Catholic education: Breathing in an out the spirit of God's love. In G. Byrne, & S. Whittle (Eds.), *Catholic education: A lifelong journey* (pp. 63–82). Veritas.
Byrne, G., & Sweetman. B. (2021). Opening up religious education and faith development: The AREFD project. *British Journal of Religious Education*, April (online)
Castelli, M. (2012). Faith dialogue as a pedagogy for a post secular religious education. *Journal of Beliefs & Values, 33*(2), 207–216.
Catholic Schools Partnership. (2014). *Catholic education at second-level in the Republic of Ireland: Looking to the future*. Veritas.
Congregation for Catholic Education. (1977). *The Catholic school*. Vatican Polyglot Press. Available at www.vatican.va
Cullen, S. (2017). Interpreting "between privacies": Religious education as a conversational activity. In M. Shanahan (Ed.), *Does religious education matter?* (pp. 37–47). Routledge.
Department of Education and Skills. (2015). *Framework for junior cycle, 2015*. Available at www.education.ie/en/Publications/Policy-Reports/Framework-for-Junior-Cycle-2015.pdf
Di Sipio, L. (2019). Teacher readiness: A pedagogy of encounter. In M. T. Buchanan & A.-M. Gellel (Eds.), *Global perspectives on Catholic religious education in schools, Volume II Learning and leading in a pluralist world II* (pp. 191–202). Springer.
Elias, J. (1993). *The foundations and practice of adult religious education*. Krieger Publishing Company.
Francis, P. (2020). *Let us dream: The path to a better future*. Simon & Schuster.
Gadamer, H. G. (1989). *Truth and method* (J. C. Weinsheimer & D. Marshall, Trans.) Sheed & Ward.
Irish Episcopal Conference. (2010). *Share the good news: National directory for catechesis in Ireland*. Veritas.
Korczak, J. (1996). *Sämtliche Werke* (16 vols.). Gütersloher Verlagshaus.
La Salle Academy. (2018). *Voices and visions: Catholic schools in conversation*. Australian Catholic University.
Leijen, A., Kullasepp, K. & Toompalu, A. (2018). Dialogue for bridging student teachers' personal and professional identity. In H. Hermans & F. Meijers (Eds.), *The dialogical self theory in education: A multicultural perspective* (pp. 97–110). Springer (Imprint)
Madden, R. (2017). The practice room: A space for teachers to engage in dialogue about learning in religious education. In K. Smith & J. Loughran (Eds.), *Quality learning: Teachings changing their practice* (pp. 127–140). Sense Publications.

Madden, R. (2020). Dialogue in community: Conditions and enablers for teacher professional development in Catholics schools. *Journal of Religious Education, 68*, 125–139.

Mullally, A. (2021). Why are Catholic schools afraid to be Catholic schools? In G. Byrne and & S. Whittle (Ed.), *Catholic education: A lifelong journey* (pp. 247–260). Veritas.

National Council for Curriculum and Assessment. (2019). Junior Cycle Religious Education Specification. Available at: https://ncca.ie/media/3785/junior-cycle-religious-education-specification.pdf

Palmer, P. J. (1997). The heart of a teacher identity and integrity in teaching. *Change: The Magazine of Higher Learning, 29*(6), 14–21.

Stuart-Buttle, R. (2021). Adult learning, theology and faith formation. In G. Byrne & S. Whittle (Ed.), *Catholic education: A lifelong journey* (pp. 31–48). Veritas.

Wessels, F. (2015). Getting to why? Contemplative practice as reflection on intentionality. *Hevormde Teologiese Studies, 71*(1), 1–7.

Bernadette Sweetman is a post-doctoral researcher investigating Adult Religious Education and Faith Development at the Mater Dei Centre for Catholic Education, Dublin City University. Formerly a primary school teacher, Dr. Sweetman completed her doctoral studies in religious education in 2016. She is the author of the *Our Family Mass* series and was part of the writing team for the *Credo* series of high school Catholic education textbooks in the USA (both published by Veritas). She has been a lecturer and researcher at third level since 2013 and is building an international publication portfolio. bernadette.sweetman@dcu.ie

Epilogue: Teacher Training and Policies in the Global South: Approaches and Tools from the World Bank

Quentin Wodon

Abstract Much of the work in Western countries on teacher formation in Catholic schools has focused on ways to strengthen the schools' identity. In the Global South too, even if the challenge from secularization may be less salient, there is a need to train teachers so that they can be faithful to the mission of the schools. However, apart from paying attention to the Catholic identity of schools, there is another pressing issue: ensuring that children learn while in school. The Global South is facing an acute learning crisis. Most schools, including Catholic schools, fail to ensure that students learn foundational skills. This creates a different set of challenges, which requires a different response. As an epilogue to the contributions in this volume and a call for more research by Catholic education scholars on the pressing issues faced by Catholic schools in the Global South, this chapter introduces readers to recent thinking on how to improve teacher policies in low and middle income countries. The analysis focuses on analytical work and tools developed at the World Bank, including the SABER initiative to assess policies and the TEACH and COACH tools to help improve teacher pedagogy in the classroom.

Keywords
Catholic schools • Teacher policies • Teacher training • Global south • Learning crisis

Introduction

The chapters included in this volume discuss for the most part approaches to teacher formation in Western countries. The focus is on improving the ability of teachers to promote and strengthen the Catholic identity and mission of Catholic schools

---

Q. Wodon (✉)
1569 Dominion Hill Ct, McLean, VA, Mexico
e-mail: rotarianeconomist@gmail.com

© The Editor(s) (if applicable) and The Author(s), under exclusive license to Springer Nature Singapore Pte Ltd. 2022
L. Franchi and R. Rymarz (eds.), *Formation of Teachers for Catholic Schools*, Catholic Education Globally: Challenges and Opportunities 1,
https://doi.org/10.1007/978-981-19-4727-8

that typically have substantial autonomy from the state. The context in high income countries is one of secularization, however it may be defined. This may lead many teachers to not be sufficiently familiar with Catholic doctrine, social thought, or approaches.

There is no universal agreement on what Catholic identity should entail for schools and universities, but several benchmarking approaches have been suggested. In the USA for example, the Center for Catholic School Effectiveness at the School of Education of Loyola University Chicago published the *National Standards and Benchmarks for Effective Catholic Elementary and Secondary Schools* in partnership with the Roche Center for Catholic Education at the School of Education of Boston College. The objective was to serve as both a guide and assessment tool for Catholic school effectiveness and sustainability. The standards contain three components: (1) nine defining characteristics related to the identity of Catholic schools; (2) thirteen standards for policies, programmes, structures, and processes that should be present in Catholic schools in four domains: Mission and Catholic Identity, Governance and Leadership, Academic Excellence, and Operational Vitality; and (3) 70 benchmarks with observable, measurable descriptors for each standard.

Another useful resource is the *Catholic Identity Curriculum Integration* (CICI) developed by the National Catholic Education Association, universities, and other partners. CICI was developed to help teachers and school leaders develop curriculum that is both Catholic and rigorous. This is accomplished through focused integration of Catholic identity into locally developed standards-based curriculum in PK-12 Catholic schools and dioceses. CICI provides frameworks, guidelines, and resources to assist teachers and school leaders as they develop their curriculum. Still another useful resource is NCEA's Information for Growth (IFG) which offers tools designed to assess the effectiveness of school and parish religious education programmes over time. Offering both a student and an adult survey, IFG allows for data-driven decisions regarding student catechesis and adult faith formation. In particular, Assessment of Child/Youth Religious Education (ACRE) assists in the evaluation of catechetical/religious education programmes in Catholic schools and parishes (for grade 5, grades 8 or 9, and grades 11 or 12).

For universities, the Association of Catholic College and Universities (ACCU) has developed surveys to assess how Catholic identity and the charism of the founding group for a university are expressed on campus and assimilated by students. The *Catholic Identity and Mission Assessment* (CIMA) project helps ACCU member institutions understand how Catholic higher education adds distinct value to the student experience through surveys for four target groups: (1) entering new undergraduate students; (2) graduating students; (3) alumni (normally 5 and 10 years out); and (4) graduate and professional students. Assessment topics include Catholic Intellectual Tradition; Moral and Ethical Development; Climate for Non-Catholics; Interreligious Dialogue; Leadership, Service, and Vocation; Religious Beliefs and Values; and Religious Practices. ACCU recognizes that there are many ways through which Catholic colleges and universities may express, enhance, and convey their Catholic identity. ACCU's website provides a simple tool to search for promising practices by keyword and/or institution.

At the international level, the International Federation of Catholic Universities has developed the *Newman Benchmark: An Evaluation Framework for Catholic universities*. Most rankings schemes for universities are based on a small number of criteria that overlook the importance of values in higher education. To promote social responsibility among universities, the Newman Benchmarking Framework, the result of a three-year collaborative endeavour, is based on 160 indicators and 20 criteria in four main areas: (1) institutional governance; (2) environmental protection; (3) practices as an employer and in the implementation of universities' missions; and (4) consistency with regard to institutional identity.

To my knowledge, no similar frameworks exist for assessing the Catholic identity of schools and universities in the developing world. Or rather, when frameworks exist, they tend to be specific to each country. This makes sense given that the context and issues faced by Catholic schools and universities differ between countries. For example, in South Africa, the Catholic Institute of Education (2008) published *Signs of God's Presence: Appraising the religious character of the Catholic school*. The guide assesses schools in terms of the religious dimension of school life, religious education, harmony with the values of the Church, and the level of understanding with each member of the school community. School characteristics are appraised by considering three statements, each of which is accompanied by a set of indicators: (1) the Catholic school ensures that its policies and procedures are in line with, and give effect to, its distinctive religious character; (2) the Catholic school offers a substantial and coherent Religious Education Programme, across the whole school; and (3) the Catholic school works to uphold, develop, and celebrate its distinctive religious character in all aspects of school life.

There is clear value in such guides for strengthening the Catholic identity of schools or universities. In the Global South as well as in Western countries, there is a need to train teachers so that they can be faithful to the Catholic identity and mission of the schools even if the challenge from secularization may be less salient than in Western countries. However, the point that I would like to make in this chapter is that apart from paying attention to the Catholic identity of the schools, there is another pressing issue: that of assessing the ability of Catholic schools and more broadly Catholic education systems in fulfilling another core mission: ensuring that children learn while in school. The Global South is facing an acute learning crisis. Responding to this crisis should be a top priority. Most schools, including Catholic schools, are simply failing to ensure that students learn foundational skills while in school. This creates a different set of challenges, which requires a different set of response.

The importance of the Global South for the future of Catholic education cannot be overstated. Globally, the Catholic Church is by far the largest non-governmental provider of education. According to the latest annual statistical yearbook published by the Secretariat of State (2021) of the Vatican, 62.1 million children enrolled in its schools in 2019 (7.5 million in pre-primary schools, 35.2 million in primary schools, and 19.4 million in secondary schools). Enrolment is stagnant or declining in many upper-middle and high income countries. But it is rapidly rising in low and lower-middle income countries. In 2019, some 27.0 million children were enrolled in

Catholic schools in the Africa continent (2.3 million children in pre-primary schools, 19.2 million in primary schools, and 5.4 million in secondary schools). In other words, Catholic schools in Africa accounted for 43% of all children enrolled in Catholic schools in the world. At the primary level, the proportion was 55%. Given population growth and rising educational attainment, these proportions are expected to increase over time (Wodon, 2019, 2021), even though there may be a pause for a few years due to the COVID-19 crisis.

The challenges faced by Catholic schools in the Global South are daunting. In sub-Saharan Africa, which is where Catholic schools have the largest enrolment after India, nine in ten children were "learning poor" before the COVID-19 crisis, which means that they could not read and understand a simple age-appropriate text by age 10. For low and middle income countries as a whole, the proportion of the learning poor in the children's population was at 53% (World Bank, 2019). The COVID-19 crisis is likely to have made the situation worse. Simulations suggest that learning poverty may have increased in low and middle income countries by 10 percentage points under a pessimistic scenario (Azevedo, 2020; Azevedo et al., 2020; UNICEF, 2020). While strengthening the Catholic identity and mission of Catholic schools is important, improving the quality of the education provided to children is at least as important, especially today given the impact of COVID-19 crisis on learning poverty (on the impact of the COVID-19 crisis on Catholic schools specifically, see Wodon, 2020a, 2020b).

Teachers are the most important resources that schools have to improve learning. In their synthesis of systematic literature reviews on factors that improve learning in low income contexts,[1] Evans and Popova (2016) suggest—not surprisingly, that improving pedagogy in the classroom comes first. If teacher training is to improve pedagogy, it must be tailored to the teachers benefitting from the training, repeated over time, and focused on specific tasks. Efforts to increase accountability for teachers and principals may also be beneficial. But broader policies towards teachers are also needed.

How can we assess teacher policies? The tools mentioned above to assess the Catholic identity of schools rely on a benchmarking approach. Similar approaches can be used for broader teacher policies. Benchmarking typically involves (1) defining standards or factors leading to success based on a review of the literature; (2) designing tools to measure how well an education systems or individual schools are performing along those standards; and (3) providing assessments and, even more importantly, practical suggestions for improvement. This is also the approach that has been taken at the World Bank to assess teacher policies in developing countries, including teacher training policies.

Given the importance of teacher policies to end the learning crisis, as an epilogue to the contributions in this volume and a call for more research by Catholic education scholars on the pressing issues faced by Catholic schools in the Global South, the objective of this chapter is to introduce readers to recent thinking on how to improve

---

[1] See Conn (2017), Glewwe et al. (2014), Kremer et al. (2013), Krishnaratne et al. (2013), McEwan (2015), and Murnane and Ganimian (2014).

teacher policies in low and middle income countries. The focus is therefore not on issues pertaining to Catholic identity or mission, but rather on broader policies and programmes that should apply to Catholic schools as well as other types of schools. The analysis focuses on analytical work and tools developed at the World Bank as the largest provider of development financing for education. The hope is that some of those analyses and related tools may also be beneficial to Catholic school networks. If just one Catholic school network (including perhaps in high income countries) was to use those tools after reading this chapter, writing the chapter will have been worth it.

The structure of the chapter is as follows. The first part of the chapter introduces the initial phase of the SABER initiative used at the World Bank for about a half dozen years to assess country policies related to teachers that are essential for student learning. Again, while the initiative targeted government policy and was thus intended for public schools, it can also be used by Catholic school networks. The second part of the chapter discusses more recent analytical work and tools developed over the last three years, again with a view to share them with those interested in Catholic schools. The focus of the most recent work has been on improving pedagogy in the classroom. A conclusion follows.

SABER 1.0: Assessing Teacher Policies

Systems approach for better education results (SABER) is an initiative that was launched by the World Bank in 2011 to help countries assess their education policies. The initiative had essentially two goals when it was launched: (1) providing advice to countries on what works to improve educational outcomes in various domains through a review of the available international evidence and (2) assessing county policies against good practice benchmarks based on the same international evidence on what works. The approach looked at education systems as a whole, thereby recognizing that beyond financial and other resources or inputs, what was needed to improve learning was a detailed look at education system's policies and institutions. The analysis of education systems was based on country policies "on the books", and thereby on policy intent, as opposed to the actual implementation of existing policies. In more than a dozen "domains", data on laws and regulations were collected and analysed in a systematic way, which made cross-country comparisons feasible. In each domain of analysis, the foundation for data collection and policy advice was a "What Matters" framework paper. This section describes the conceptual framework for SABER 1.0 and provides the average estimates on the quality of teacher policies in developing countries based on data collected for 36 countries and their implications.

The context for SABER 1.0 was the World Bank's education strategy whose structure is visualized in Fig. 1. The strategy had three pillars, of which "investing for all" was the first with the other two pillars being "investing early" (through early childhood development) and "investing smartly" (through a systems approach, as

Fig. 1 Pillars of the World Bank education strategy. *Source* World Bank (2011)

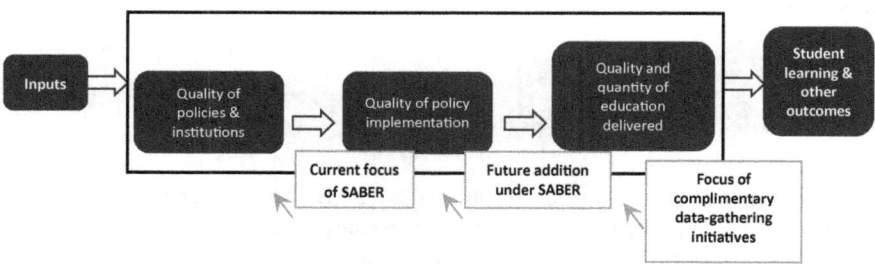

Fig. 2 SABER 1.0 and the results chain for learning. *Source* World Bank (2013a)

represented among others by the SABER initiative). These three pillars would help ensure learning for all, which was the theme and the title of the strategy. In turn, learning for all would help achieve the World Bank's twin goals of ending extreme poverty and promoting shared prosperity.

SABER was designed to help governments examine and strengthen the performance of their education systems so that all children and youth could be equipped with knowledge and skills for life. The premise was that while improving the quality of education systems required actionable information, acknowledging that synthetized knowledge about education policies and institutions is often not available to policymakers (World Bank, 2013). The aim was for SABER to fill the gap in the availability of policy data, information, and knowledge about factors that influence educational quality and about ways to improve learning (see Fig. 2 on how SABER conceptualized education systems).

SABER 1.0 relied on diagnostic tools and policy data to evaluate country policies through the lens of global evidence-based standards, helping countries determine which changes in policies could be implemented to improve learning. The initiative

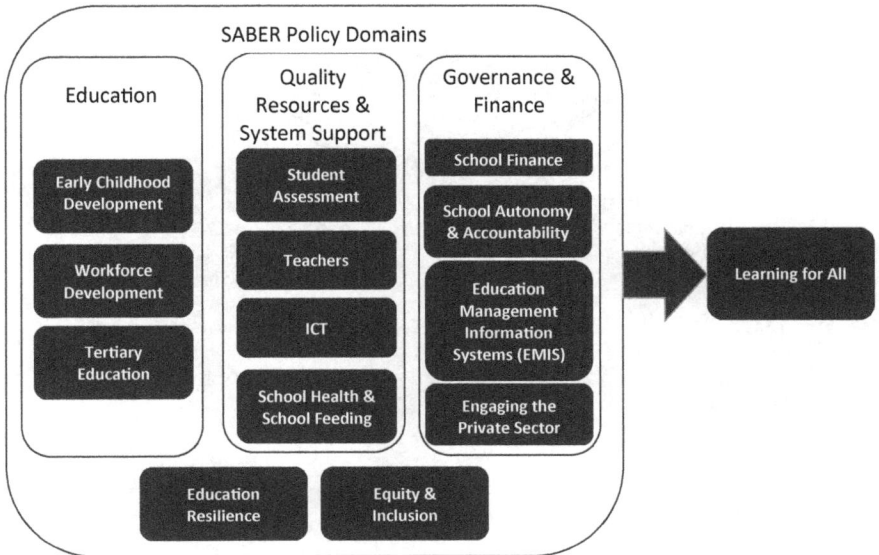

Fig. 3 SABER 1.0 policy domains. *Source* World Bank (2013a). *Note* ICT means information and communication technology

was organized around 13 domains of analysis (Fig. 3). Three domains are related to levels of instruction: pre-primary education and early childhood development, primary and secondary education, and tertiary education. Four domains are related to resources and "inputs" required for education systems, including student assessment, teachers, information and communication technology (ICT), and school health and school feeding. A third set of domains is related to governance and financing, with domains related to school finance, school autonomy and accountability, education management information systems (EMIS), and engaging the private sector (with that last domain especially important for relationships between the state and Catholic schools). Finally, two additional domains look at the system as a whole for matters of resilience and equity and inclusion.

In particular, the SABER-Teachers domain analysed the information collected to assess the extent to which teacher policies in an education system were aligned with the policies that international evidence suggested had a positive effect on learning (World Bank, 2013b). SABER-Teachers suggested that education system should aim to achieve eight policy goals: (1) setting clear expectations for teachers; (2) attracting the best into teaching; (3) preparing teachers with useful training and experience; (4) matching teachers' skills with students' needs; (5) leading teachers with strong principals; (6) monitoring teaching and learning; (7) supporting teachers to improve instruction; and (8) motivating teachers to perform (see Fig. 4). The choice of those eight goals was based on three criteria, namely the fact that they were associated with better student performance, a priority for resource allocation, and actionable. For each policy goal, policy levers were identified. These were actions that governments

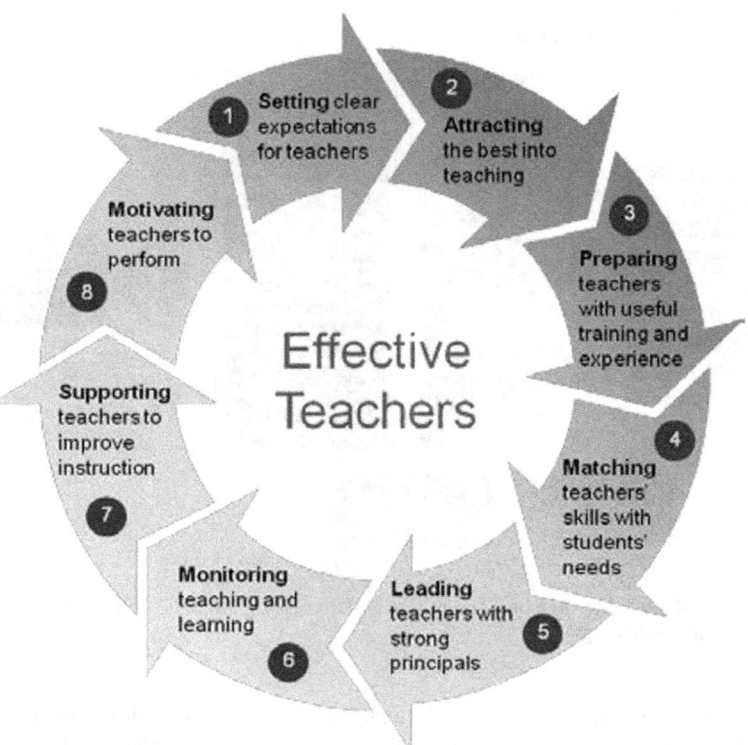

Fig. 4 Policy goals for SABER-Teachers. *Source* World Bank (2013b)

could take to reach the goals. In order to assess whether governments were making effective use of these policy levers, indicators were defined. The performance of education systems on the policy levers and thereby on the policy goals was assessed on a four-point scale with latent, emerging, established, and advanced ratings. The assessment essentially provided a set of options for potential reforms.

How did countries perform on the SABER-Teachers assessment? Table 1 provides the average ratings for the eight goals and their policy levels for the 36 countries for which the SABER-Teachers analysis was completed.[2] The average rating for the eight policy goals was 2.26 across the 36 countries (just above the emerging rating). The two goals that are most closely related to teacher formation are (1) preparing teachers with useful training and experience (essentially pre-service training with average rating of 2.50) and (2) supporting teachers to improve instruction (essentially in-service training with an average rating of 1.94). These ratings are all pretty low,

---

[2] These countries were Benin, Bulgaria, Cambodia, Cote d'Ivoire, Croatia, Djibouti, Egypt, Georgia, Guinea-Bissau, Guyana, Jamaica, Jordan, Kazakhstan, Kenya, Kyrgyz Republic, Lebanon, Macedonia, Mali, Moldova, Morocco, Mozambique, Nigeria, Norway, Papua New Guinea, Paraguay, Romania, Russian Federation, Samoa, Serbia, Singapore, Slovenia, Solomon Islands, Tunisia, Uganda, West Bank and Gaza, and Yemen.

Table 1 SABER-Teachers average ratings (36 countries)

	Average rating (36 countries)
Setting clear expectations for teachers	2.81
Lever 1: Are there clear expectations for teachers?	2.81
Lever 2: Is there useful guidance on the use of teachers' working time?	2.69
Attracting the best into teaching	2.22
Lever 1: Are entry requirements set up to attract talented candidates?	2.31
Lever 2: Is teacher pay appealing for talented candidates?	1.91
Lever 3: Are working conditions appealing for talented applicants?	2.03
Lever 4: Are there attractive career opportunities?	3.06
Preparing teachers with useful training and experience	2.50
Lever 1: Are there minimum standards for pre-service teaching education programmes?	1.94
Lever 2: To what extent are teacher-entrants required to be familiar with classroom practice?	2.75
Matching teachers' skills with students' needs	1.83
Lever 1: Are there incentives for teachers to work at hard-to-staff schools?	2.56
Lever 2: Are there incentives for teachers to teach critical shortage subjects?	1.52
Leading teachers with strong principals	1.86
Lever 1: Does the education system invest in developing qualified school leaders?	1.58
Lever 2: Are principals expected to support and improve instructional practice?	2.39
Monitoring teaching and learning	2.80
Lever 1: Are there systems in place to assess student learning to inform teaching and policy?	2.25
Lever 2: Are there systems in place to monitor teacher performance?	2.42
Lever 3: Are there multiple mechanisms to evaluate teacher performance?	3.22
Supporting teachers to improve instruction	1.94
Lever 1: Are there opportunities for professional development?	1.81
Lever 2: Is teacher professional development collaborative and focused on instructional improvement?	2.40
Lever 3: Is teacher professional development assigned based on perceived needs?	2.00

(continued)

Table 1 (continued)

	Average rating (36 countries)
Motivating teachers to perform	2.08
Lever 1: Are career opportunities linked to performance?	2.06
Lever 2: Are there mechanisms to hold teachers accountable?	2.50
Lever 3: Is teacher compensation linked to performance?	1.47
Average rating for the eight policy goals	2.26

Source Author's estimation based on World Bank SABER data

and the average values would be even lower if only countries from sub-Saharan Africa were included. The basic message is that most countries are not doing well in terms of policy intent on most policies that were related to improving learning. If the actual implementation of the policies had been assessed, performance would probably be even lower.

Could the SABER assessment tool be used by Catholic school networks to assess their own policies? It could indeed. All of the documentation for assessing policies is freely available on the website of the World Bank. Catholic school networks could use the tool in its entirety, or they could focus on particular sections of interest. For example, the first lever for supporting teachers in improving instruction is whether there are opportunities for professional development. Three indicators are used: (1) Are primary school teachers are required to participate in professional development?; (2) Are secondary school teachers required to participate in professional development?, and (3) Are individual teachers responsible for paying for their professional development? For the second lever, namely whether teacher professional development is collaborative and focused on instructional improvement, two indicators are again used: (1) Does professional development include activities that may promote best-practice sharing? and (2) Does professional development provide opportunities for the analysis of instructional practice? For the third policy lever, namely whether teacher professional development assigned based on perceived needs, two indicators are used: (1) If a teacher obtains an unsatisfactory result in an evaluation, is he or she assigned to a supervisor? and (2) Are teacher performance evaluations used to assign professional development? Documentation is available on how to assess all those indicators and how to use rubrics for aggregating the detailed information into ratings for policy levers and policy goals.

SABER 2.0 and the Future of Learning

While the initial phase of SABER focused on assessing country policies according to benchmarks informed by the international evidence on what works to improve learning, tools related more closely to the implementation of policies as opposed to policy intent were also progressively developed, in particular for measuring and analysing service delivery at the school level. But in the last few years, following the publication of the World Development Report on the learning crisis (World Bank, 2018) and the adoption of the World Bank's Human Capital Project (World Bank, 2019), the focus of the SABER initiative shifted. Under SABER 2.0, the emphasis was placed on measuring learning across counties and identifying binding constraints to improving learning. As a result, the SABER programme introduced new initiatives, including the Global Comparability of Learning Outcomes (GCLO), a policy dashboard, and Education Policy Design Labs. In addition, a number of new tools were introduced.

There is no silver bullet to end the learning crisis, but a new blueprint from the World Bank (2020) offers suggestions as well as a new conceptual framework that takes into account the latest evidence, including new developments since the SABER initiative was launched together with the World Bank education strategy of ten years ago. The blueprint is organized around five pillars: (1) Learners are prepared and motivated to learn—with a stronger emphasis on whole-child development and support to learning continuity beyond the school; (2) teachers are effective and valued—and ready to take on an increasingly complex role of facilitators of learning at and beyond the school with use of education technology; (3) learning resources, including curricula, are diverse and of high quality—to support good pedagogical practices and personalized learning; (4) schools are safe and inclusive spaces—with a whole-and-beyond-the-school approach to prevent and address violence and leave no child behind; and (5) education systems are well managed—with school leaders who spur more effective pedagogy and a competent educational bureaucracy adept at using technology, data, and evidence.

As shown in Table 2, for each pillar, specific policy actions are recommended based on an in-depth review of the literature. For example, to keep learners engaged, four key actions are suggested: (1) increase the provision of early childhood development services; (2) remove demand-side barriers; (3) put conditions in place for learning to occur with joy, rigour, and purpose; and (4) bolster the role of the family and communities. Similar actions are outlined for the other four pillars in the framework. Or to support teachers, education systems should focus on four actions: (1) establish the teaching profession as a meritocratic, socially valued career; (2) expand engagement in pre-service training; (3) invest in at-scale in-service professional development; and (4) give teachers tools and techniques for effective teaching. In addition, five principles to guide policy reforms are suggested: (1) pursue systemic reform supported by political commitment to learning for all children; (2) focus on equity and inclusion through a progressive path towards universalism; (3) focus on results and use evidence to keep improving; (4) ensure financial commitment commensurate with what is needed to provide basic services to all; and finally (5) invest wisely in technology.

To avoid a long document, the discussion of the policies pertaining to each of the five pillars is limited in the blueprint, but more details are available in background documents. In the case of teacher policies, the guidance provided in the blueprint is based in part on a policy deep dive by Beteille and Evans (2018) who suggest principles to recruit and support teachers which have been slightly adapted in the

Table 2 New World Bank framework for realizing the future of learning

Learners are engaged	Teachers facilitate learning	Learning resources are adequate and diverse	Schools are safe and inclusive	Systems are well managed
Five pillars in the framework for realizing the future of learning				
All learners engage in learning that is personalized, inclusive, holistic, and relevant to their realities	Teachers play the role of facilitating learning of all students rather than delivering content and are provided with the training and holistic support they need to play this role	Learning resources are adequate and of rich variety so that each child can access quality learning experiences anywhere	School environments have the necessary infrastructure, human resources, policies, and norms to enable all children to learn in a welcoming environment, free from discrimination, violence, and bullying	At the school level, school leaders are pedagogical leaders and engage with technology to enable more elective and efficient school management
Parents, Caregivers, and the Home Learning Environment Supported Technology Promoting Learning Objectives				
Key policy actions for each of the five pillars				
• Increase provision of early childhood development services • Remove demand-side barriers • Put conditions in place for learning to occur with joy, rigour, and purpose • Bolster role of family and communities	• Establish teaching profession as a meritocratic, socially valued career • Expand engagement in pre-service training • Invest in at-scale in-service professional development • Give teachers tools and techniques for effective teaching	• Ensure the curriculum is effective • Provide pedagogical tools to teach to the level of each student • Use assessments judiciously • Ensure access to high-quality, age-appropriate books • Effectively harness technology	• Ensure minimum infrastructure • Prevent bullying and any form of discrimination and violence • Increase inclusiveness so that all learners feel welcome and thrive • Teach students first in a language they speak and understand	• Strengthen human resource function of education systems to professionalize school leadership • Provide school leaders with the tools to manage with autonomy • Invest in system leadership and management capacity to support schools

Source World Bank (2020)

blueprint. The five principles suggested by Beteille and Evans were (1) making teaching an attractive profession by improving its status, compensation policies, and career progression structures; (2) promoting meritocratic selection of teachers, followed by a probationary period, to improve the quality of the teaching force; (3) ensuring pre-service education includes a strong practicum component to ensure teachers are well equipped to transition and perform effectively in the classroom; (4) providing continuous support and motivation, in the form of high-quality in-service training and strong school leadership, to allow teachers to continually improve; and (5) using technology wisely to enhance the ability of teachers to reach every student, factoring their areas of strength and development.

I mentioned earlier that under SABER 2.0, a number of new tools were introduced. Two tools in particular are worth mentioning here: TEACH and COACH. TEACH is a classroom observation tool that can be used for system diagnostic as well as for professional development. As a system diagnostic tool, TEACH allows school networks to monitor the effectiveness of their policies to improve teacher practices. As a professional development tool, TEACH can be used to help teachers improve how they teach. The initial version of the TEACH was intended for use in primary schools (grades 1–6), but other versions are under preparation for early childhood education and for secondary schools.

What does TEACH measure? The tool differs from other classroom observation tools in that it captures (i) the time teachers spend on learning and the extent to which students are on task and (ii) the quality of teaching practices that help develop students' socioemotional and cognitive skills. As part of the time on task component, three snapshots of 1–10 s are used to record both the teacher's actions and the number of students who are on task throughout the observation. The quality of teaching practices component, on the other hand, is organized into three primary areas as shown below: classroom culture, instruction, and socioemotional skills. These areas have nine corresponding elements that point to 28 behaviours. The behaviours are characterized as low, medium, or high, based on the evidence collected during the observation. These behaviour scores are translated into a five-point scale that quantifies teaching practices as captured in a series of two, 15-min lesson observations.

COACH aims to help countries improve in-service teacher professional development (TPD) programmes and systems to accelerate learning. The types of TPD considered include one-to-one coaching, group training sessions and workshops, as well as other approaches. This can include in-person and remote or hybrid modalities. While TEACH helps in identifying teachers' professional development needs, COACH leverages these insights to tailor the support teachers receive to improve their teaching.

Could the TEACH and COACH tools be used by Catholic school networks to provide professional development opportunities to their teachers? Again, they could indeed. Information on both tools is available from the World Bank, and both tools are provided at no cost. In fact, one of the rationales for developing the tools was that they would be freely available, but there may be a cost in providing training on how to use the tools (this is typically done through training of trainers in the methodology).

Conclusion

Much of the research on Catholic education focuses on issues related to the Catholic identity of the schools or universities, and the chapters in this volume are no exception. This is an important area of research, but especially in the Global South where most schools, including Catholic schools, are confronted with a severe learning crisis, this cannot be the sole focus of research. Basic literacy and numeracy are foundational skills needed for children to progress through school. When children cannot read, it is unlikely that they will be able to learn in other areas, including in matters related to values and faith. More than half of all children in low and middle income countries are not learning enough to achieve basic literacy by age 10, and learning poverty is likely to have increased substantially due to the COVID-19 crisis. In order to improve learning, adequate teacher training and other policies are needed.

As an epilogue to this book, and an implicit call for more research among Catholic education scholars in this area, the objective of this chapter was to introduce readers to recent thinking on how to improve teacher policies in the Global South. The focus was on assessment tools developed at the World Bank, with the hope that those tools may be beneficial to Catholic school networks, as they have been for public school networks. If just one Catholic school network (including perhaps in high income countries) was to use those tools after reading this chapter, writing the chapter will have been worth it.

In closing, perhaps one last comment is in order. The principles on which the World Bank's analysis of teacher policies is based make sense, but while World Bank documents recognize the importance of school culture and intrinsic teacher motivation, they do not emphasize those issues very much in the guidance being provided, in part because of a limited body of evidence on what works to improve school culture and boost intrinsic motivation. There are many areas where Catholic schools could learn from the expertise of international organizations such as the World Bank, but this could be an area where international organizations could learn from the experience of Catholic educators.

References

Azevedo, J. P. (2020). *Learning poverty: Measures and simulations. Policy research working paper No. 9446.* The World Bank.

Azevedo, J. P., Hasan, A., Goldemberg, D., Iqbal, S. A., & Geven, M. K. (2020). *Simulating the potential impacts of COVID-19 school closures on schooling and learning outcomes: A set of global estimates.* World Bank Policy Research Paper 9284. The World Bank.

Beteille, T., & Evans, D. (2018). *Successful teachers, Successful students: Recruiting and supporting society's most crucial profession.* The World Bank.

Catholic Institute of Education. (2008). *Signs of God's presence: Appraising the religious character of the Catholic school.* Catholic Institute of Education.

Conn, K. (2017). Identifying effective education interventions in Sub-Saharan Africa: A meta-analysis of rigorous impact evaluations. *Review of Educational Research, 87*(5).

D'Agostino, T. J. (2017). Precarious values in publicly funded religious schools: The effects of government-aid on the institutional character of Ugandan Catholic schools. *International Journal of Educational Development, 57*, 30–43.

Evans, D. K., & Popova, A. (2016). What really works to improve learning in developing countries? An analysis of divergent findings in systematic reviews. *The World Bank Research Observer, 31*(2), 242–270.

Glewwe, P. W., Hanushek, E. A., Humpage, S. D., & Ravina, R. (2014). School resources and educational outcomes in developing countries: A review of the literature from 1990 to 2010. In P. W. Glewwe (Ed.), *Education policy in developing countries*. University of Chicago Press.

Kremer, M., Brannen, C., & Glennerster, R. (2013). The challenge of education and learning in the rise of catholic schools in the developing world. *Science, 340*(6130), 297–300.

Krishnaratne, S., White, H., Carpenter, E. (2013). Quality education for all children? What works in education in developing countries. *International Initiative for Impact Evaluation* (3ie).

McEwan, P. J. (2015). Improving learning in primary schools of developing countries. *Review of Educational Research, 85*(3), 353–394.

Murnane, R. J., & Ganimian, A. J. (2014). *Improving educational outcomes in developing countries: Lessons from rigorous evaluations. Working Paper 20284*. National Bureau of Economic Research.

Secretariat of State [of the Vatican]. (2021). *Annuarium statisticum Ecclesiae 2019/Statistical yearbook of the Church 2019/Annuaire statistique de l'Eglise 2019*. Libreria Editrice Vaticana.

UNICEF. (2020). *Averting a lost COVID generation: A six-point plan to respond, recover and reimagine a post-pandemic world for every child*. UNICEF.

Wodon, Q. (2019). Implications of demographic, religious, and enrollment trends for the footprint of faith-based schools globally, *Review of Faith & International Affairs, 17*(4), 52–62.

Wodon, Q. (2020a). Covid-19 crisis, impacts on Catholic schools, and potential responses, Part I: Developed countries with focus on the United States. *Journal of Catholic Education, 23*(2), 13–50.

Wodon, Q. (2020b). Covid-19 crisis, impacts on Catholic schools, and potential responses, Part II: Developing countries with focus on sub-Saharan Africa. *Journal of Catholic Education, 23*(2), 51–86.

Wodon, Q. (2021). *Global Catholic Education Report 2021: Education pluralism, learning poverty, and the right to education*. Global Catholic Education, OIEC, IFCU, OMAEC, & UMEC.

World Bank. (2011). *Learning for all: Investing in people's knowledge and skills to promote development*. The World Bank.

World Bank. (2013a). *The what, why, and how of the systems approach for better education results (SABER)*. SABER Overview. The World Bank.

World Bank. (2013b). *What matters most for teacher policies: A framework paper.* SABER Working Paper Series No. 4. The World Bank.
World Bank. (2018). *World Development Report 2018: Learning to realize education's promise.* The World Bank.
World Bank. (2019). *Ending learning poverty: What will it take?* The World Bank.
World Bank. (2020). *Realizing the future of learning: From learning poverty to learning for everyone, everywhere.* Washington, DC: The World Bank.

Quentin Wodon is Lead Economist at the World Bank. Previously, he managed the Bank's unit on values, faith, and development and served as Lead Poverty Specialist for Africa and Economist/Senior Economist for Latin America. Before that, he taught with tenure at the University of Namur. He also taught at American University and Georgetown University and currently serves as Distinguished Research Affiliate with the College of Business at Loyola University New Orleans. Trained in business engineering, he first worked in brand management for Procter and Gamble before shifting career and joining a non-profit working with the extreme poor. He has tried to remain faithful to the cause of serving the less fortunate ever since. He holds four PhDs, served as President of two economics associations, and has 500+ publications. His research on education, global health, poverty/inequality, and sustainability has been covered by leading news media globally. As part of his volunteer work, he has held multiple positions of leadership with non-profits. globalcatholiceducation@gmail.com

End Matter: Catholic Teacher Formation: Why It Matters

Leonardo Franchi and Richard Rymarz

This book has offered many ideas and questions about how we approach the formation of future and indeed serving teachers. There is enough material for a succession of CPD events!

In beginning with a study of some local contexts, it was our intention to bring the wisdom and practice of national education systems to bear upon wider issues. There is no universal template for the organization and structure of Catholic teacher formation, and the local studies here presented afford us glimpses of the practical ways teacher formation is addressed but also gave insights into some local challenges.

Michael Buchanan's study of Catholic teacher formation "down under" brings to the table the question of lay teachers. The history of Catholic education since the rise of mass schooling in the late nineteenth century has been dominated to a greater or lesser extent by the teaching orders and congregations. Their influence continues to be felt today even if the number of professed teaching brother and sisters is in ongoing decline. It would be wrong simply to bemoan this sociological reality and it is necessary, Michael reminds us, to redouble our efforts to improve the formation offered to lay teachers. Additionally, Michael has recalled for us the importance of the Catholic school as the principal site of formation for teachers, a timely reminder that parish structures are struggling to find their role vis-à-vis the advance of secularization. It is a call for school leaders (principals) to take seriously their role as leaders of formation.

L. Franchi (✉)
School of Education, University of Glasgow, Glasgow, UK
e-mail: leonardo.franchi@glasgow.ac.uk

R. Rymarz
Broken Bay Institute-TAITE, Sydney, NSW, Australia
e-mail: richard.rymarz@bbi.catholic.edu.au

© The Editor(s) (if applicable) and The Author(s), under exclusive license to Springer Nature Singapore Pte Ltd. 2022
L. Franchi and R. Rymarz (eds.), *Formation of Teachers for Catholic Schools*, Catholic Education Globally: Challenges and Opportunities 1,
https://doi.org/10.1007/978-981-19-4727-8

Niall Coll reminds us of the strong connections between the life of Catholic schools and the political situation in which the schools operate. The history of Catholic schools in Northern Ireland is wrapped up in the cultural issues which are part of life in Northern Ireland. In common with Catholic school systems elsewhere, there are significant challenges with recruitment to the profession and commitment to religious practice. Niall highlights in particular the issues around what are called "Generation Z" and other concerns which emerge from the marketization of education. Such issues require careful and strategic responses if Catholic schools are to be successful.

Roisín Coll and Stephen Reilly discuss the status of Catholic schools as not just state-funded but part of the state system of education in Scotland. They highlight the importance of building a critical mass of young people interested in becoming teachers: the prospect of Masters level study at one of the world top universities is among the "carrots" offered to potential students. They also recognize the importance of developing the theological literacy of the teaching force as a way to boost their professional identity. It is the growing awareness of the rich theological traditions we have inherited that will equip teachers to respond better to the challenges of secularization.

Max Engel highlights the lack of standardized formation processes in the United States of America as a factor to be considered in determining the best ways ahead for Catholic schools. America, like much of the West, is dealing with the sociocultural challenges of secularism, and this requires schools to be careful in the selection of teaching staff. The wider picture of religious disaffiliation, powered by cultural forces, leads Max to conclude that Catholic teacher formation needs a more structured template if it is to prepare young people for mission in Catholic schools. With two broad headings of "What Catholic school teachers need to know" and "What Catholic school teachers need to experience", Max offers a five-part template for Catholic school formation standards. This should go some way towards offering clear standards for all in the years to come.

John Paul Sheridan explores how the Church in the Republic of Ireland has dealt with its changing status in the life of the country and what this means for how it understands, lives and communicates its message. From being at the heart of Irish life, it is now in a much shakier position in society. John Paul identifies three challenges: *Changing Society and Cultural Landscape*, *The Changing Landscape of the Catholic School*, and *Religious Identity*. While such challenges exist in many other jurisdictions, they are perhaps magnified in Ireland given its history of culturally embedded Catholicism and the influence of missionary Irish priests, brothers, and sisters across the globe. For John Paul, a way ahead lies in a greater appreciation of a multicultural and multi-religious society alongside a renewed commitment to deeper and richer formation for prospective teachers.

Sean Whittle explores the challenge of formation and Catholic teacher identity in England and Wales. There are considerable questions around not just what we "do" as an educational community to promote the initial and ongoing formation of teachers, but there are many challenges which arise from different definitions of the term "formation". There are issues across the Church around religious practice, and these have different resonances according to context. Sean suggests that a greater awareness of and commitment to collegial formation, including higher studies in education, will be a boon to the life of the Catholic school.

In summary, Part I offers an interesting panorama of formation processes for teachers in a number of jurisdictions. It will leave the reader in little doubt about the energy currently expended in developing models and processes of Catholic teacher formation but with the related awareness that much still needs to be done.

In Part II, the contributors raised a number of questions relating to some current topics of interest. While there is not claim that this list is exhaustive—far from it—there is sufficient material here for ongoing and deeper study of how best to manage and support the formation of Catholic teachers.

Ken Avenell draws on his many years of experience in educational leadership in Australia to offer some important pointers with more global potential. At the heart of such debates is the relationship between professional and spiritual formation as this is where the energy for articulating a meaningful Catholic "identity" can be found. To be successful, formation for leadership in Catholic schools needs an integrated and collegial approach but also requires embedded review processes so that those who have graduated from such programmes are able to demonstrate their ability to lead successfully.

Kathleen Kerrigan and Julie Harvie offer a rich understanding of the vocation of the Catholic teacher in a secularized context. They bring forward the suggestion that the professional exercise of teaching duties is an expression of the vocation of the teacher. They lay before the reader an ecological model of agency as a possible template for the work of the Catholic teacher. They also propose the idea of pilgrimage (or journey) as a way to deepen belief and a sense of vocation in the teaching force.

Renée Köhler-Ryan offers a set of historical lenses on the work of the teacher. She presents three important texts of St Augustine of Hippo—*On the Teacher*, *De doctrina Christiana*, and *Confessions*—as sources for contemporary teacher formation. The emphasis on the need to appreciate truth and beauty is a necessary corrective to overly utilitarian processes of teacher formation. The requires a commitment to reflective practice, not just on professional practices as such but on Scripture itself as it in the *sacra pagina* that the teacher will find meaning and, ultimately, truth.

Mary E. Hess explores the contemporary imperative of digital awareness. The pandemic has brought online and blended learning models to greater prominence, yet we need to be much more aware of how to use digital technology well and to teach young people how to get the best from the array of devices and platforms which lie before them. This can range from simple yet effective critical practices like using short prayers as passwords to any number of wider initiatives which seek to make the digital space one of creativity and meaningful context. There is much to ponder here.

Michelle Jones brings her deep experiential knowledge of the Carmelite mystical tradition to bear on contemporary teacher formation. Central to her thought is the need to align interior life with contemporary culture and thus bring together the rich traditions of Carmelite mysticism with the here and now. An imaginary dialogue (or "Formatorama") reveals how the importance of loving and being loved cannot be placed outside the circles of teacher formation but lies at its heart. The resulting Christological transformation of the teacher is an asset to their developing vocation.

Bernadette Sweetman picks up on the crucial topic of dialogue and the Catholic school. She locates this in the life of the teacher of religion who has the potential to be a living example of a way of being which is core to the life of all educators. Lifelong learning, itself a valuable tool for all educators, is even more crucial for the Catholic teacher. As Catholic schools develop and grow in different parts of world, it is vital to appreciate the ways and means of dialogue as a core function of their unique mission to education. In so doing, the fear of change is lessened, and mindsets are liberated.

Part II, to be sure, is a cluster of insights into specific aspects of the life of the Catholic teacher. The importance of formation is woven through each chapter, reminding us of the multifaceted nature of the enterprise. While much of the contemporary practices of Catholic teacher formation can be rooted in the witness of the teaching congregations, the demands of the New Era require fresh thinking.

In a data-rich epilogue, Quentin Woden reminds us that issues of identity and mission, while of importance, cannot be fully explored in a context of what he describes as "learning poverty". Drawing on tools developed by the World Bank, he argues that the Catholic educational community must keep its focus on the many sociopolitical issues which affect education in the Global South, in particular the need to improve levels of attainment.

Catholic Teacher Formation: A Tentative Roadmap

A tentative roadmap will now be proposed as a framework for further discussion on teacher formation in Catholic schools. The exact contours of the roadmap are complex and difficult to delineate in brief concluding comments such as these. The chapters in the volume all point, in a generalized way, to aspects of a more comprehensive approach to teacher formation, but three more specific features of the roadmap will be mentioned. We argue that formation programmes for teachers should be diverse, integrated, and high quality.

The first feature of the roadmap highlights the need for a diversity of programmes. This feature arises from the human diversity that makes up the community of Catholic schools. This is certainly true in a generic sense, but here we are focused on teachers and leaders, a critical part of this human community. In many parts of the world, especially those with viable and vigorous Catholic school systems, there has been some emphasis on ongoing formation programmes for teachers. This is highlighted in several chapters in the first half of this volume such as the chapters by Buchanan and Sheridan. As part of a general roadmap for teacher formation, a worthy consideration at the outset is to ponder how well such initiatives acknowledge and cater for the range of human experiences that teachers bring to Catholic schools. This is not a pious aspiration detached from the practical realities of managing ongoing teacher formation. There does, however, need to be a starting point, but beyond this we must ask how well existing programmes recognize the diversity of the teacher population. The most obvious distinction is between those teachers who nominate a religious affiliation and those who are part of the increasing number in the general population who identify as having no religious affiliation. Is there a recognition of this diversity and how well is this reflected in the formation offered to teachers in Catholic schools? A number of the chapters in this volume point to this type of nuanced thinking around teacher formation, and this is a trend that is to be greatly encouraged. A second distinction, not as obvious but perhaps even more important, is to recognize the elastic nature of a self-declared Catholic religious affiliation. This encompasses a wide range of beliefs, practices, and experiences among Catholics. Some teachers identify strongly with the religious tradition and see their lives in terms of striving for a closer communion with the Trinitarian God. For many others though, their sense of identifying as a Catholic is more diffuse and is often closely aligned to working in a Catholic school. For these teachers, the school and not the parish is the locus of their sense of religious belonging. There are, of course, other distinctions, but the general question being raised is how well formation programmes cater for the diversity evident among those who work in Catholic schools. This is not a call to a diminution of the specific religious character of Catholic teacher formation programmes but to recognize the multiple starting points of prospective teachers.

The second feature of the roadmap highlights the need for integrating contemporary sensibilities with the fullness of the Catholic tradition. Formation programmes must recognize both the unique insights from the Catholic tradition and evolving cultural dynamics. Integrated formation programmes should place a strong emphasis on encouraging new and responsive praxis models. These formation models must also be thoroughly grounded in a strong theological context and have deep and obvious referents in the Catholic tradition. In the recent past, teacher formation in Catholic schools was largely based around the charism of teaching religious orders which for many years had provided the personnel needed to maintain Catholic schools. This era is now well past in most parts of the world. Formation within religious teaching orders had a clear theological and transcendent referent. An open question is, in the new era, how can formation be provided that reflects the best thinking in Catholic theology and pastoral care and is also aware of the changes in how people live and interact with each other? To take just one example, as discussed in the chapter in the volume by Hess, how is formation seen in an era when a predominant means of personal interaction is via social media. To extend the point, how do we see formation in an era when learning in general is increasingly taking place on various online platforms? This is a complex question, and there cannot be a single answer. In this volume, the chapter by Jones gives an indication of one such approach. This makes links with contemporary lifestyle and the enduring Carmelite tradition. More of this type of connection and development needs to be cultivated.

The final feature of the formation roadmap highlights the need for high-quality and well-resourced programmes of study. This is a particular consequence of a renewed cultural sensitivity, and as a response to this, there must be an acute emphasis on quality of content. This is an extension on the previous stated features. Catholic education must be cognizant of the significant social changes that have altered the way in which religion and religious institutions are perceived in many parts of the world. A feature of a volume such as this is that it approaches teacher formation from a variety of national vantage points. Before drawing universal conclusions, it is prudent to consider whether these can be framed in a way that covers the numerous contexts in which Catholic schools operate. It is fair to conclude, however, that for many of these contexts, the place of religion in society is now more contested. This has implications for Catholic schools which are often the sole site of religious formation for young people. This is particularly so in contexts where formal religious affiliation as expressed by involvement in active worshipping communities is greatly diminished. And it seems this trend is likely to become more pronounced.

There are a range of important questions that face the leadership of Catholic education in this emerging social reality. The focus of this volume though is on one aspect of Catholic education, namely teacher formation as an integral part of the general Catholic educational enterprise. Catholic schools need to be able to provide an ongoing justification and rationale for their role, and an important part of this is the formation of teachers to support and animate the stated goals of Catholic education. An awareness of the fragility of religious institutions should bring with it a resolute determination to make sure that Catholic schools exemplify the highest standards, and that the aims of Catholic schools are actualized in the priority that schools themselves place on ongoing teacher formation.

To illuminate the link between the more contested nature of Catholic education in a changed cultural context and the importance of strong teacher formation, two questions and responses will be given.

1. To begin, why do we have Catholic schools? A short answer is that we have Catholic schools because in their stated aims, they contribute to the educational offerings available in society.
2. How do we know that Catholic schools do this? In response, because they are well managed and seek to meet their aspirations by a range of well-funded and supported programmes, including initiatives for the ongoing training and formation of teachers who work in schools. Without this type of clear, transparent response, attempts to satisfy the demands of regulatory bodies may be imperilled.

In conclusion, it is appropriate to return to the human face of Catholic education, the young people we educate, and also those who educate them. Some of the importance of the vocation of the teacher is given in the chapter by Harvey and Kerrigan. As mentioned in the introduction to this volume, Pope Francis refers to education as an act of love and as a gift. The role of the teacher is to act as a human vessel of this love. Their unique position in education enables them to touch the hearts of students, and it is to this capacity that formation can look to as an ultimate goal.

CPSIA information can be obtained
at www.ICGtesting.com
Printed in the USA
LVHW010505181022
730943LV00006B/181